Canada in NORAD, 1957–2007: A History

16010l

Canada in NORAD, 1957–2007: A History

Joseph T. Jockel

Queen's Centre for International Relations and
The Queen's Defence Management Program
McGill-Queen's University Press
Montreal & Kingston • London • Ithaca

Library and Archives Canada Cataloguing in Publication

Jockel, Joseph T., 1952-
    Canada in NORAD, 1957-2007 : a history / Joseph T. Jockel.

Includes index.
Includes bibliographical references.
ISBN 978-1-55339-135-7 (bound).—ISBN 978-1-55339-134-0 (pbk.)

    1. Canada—Defenses—History—20th century. 2. Canada—Politics and government—20th century. 3. North American Aerospace Defense Command—History. 4. Cold War. I. Queen's University (Kingston, Ont.). Centre for International Relations. II. Title.

UA600.J623 2007   355'.033071   C2007-904927-3

The Cover

NORAD's first commander-in-chief, General Earle E. Partridge, USAF, and its first deputy commander-in-chief, Air Marshal C. Roy Slemon, RCAF, shortly after the command's creation in 1957.

Source Cover Images: NORAD

CONTENTS

ACKNOWLEDGEMENTS

During the 2005–2006 academic year I was fortunate to be Distinguished Visiting Professor at the Canadian Forces College, Toronto, where I wrote the manuscript for this book. It was a special academic pleasure to be at the college while enhancements to its faculty, staff, curriculum, requirements, and facilities were all visibly taking hold. I am particularly grateful to the friendly members of college's Directorate of Academics/Department of Defence Studies who, led by Professor Peter Foot, counted me that year among their number; to the staff of the college's Information Resource Centre who helped me use its great collection of materials on Canadian and international security; and to the officers on course and staff who, in both the residence and mess, warmly welcomed me in their midst. I cannot imagine a better place to spend a sabbatical year.

A research grant from the Canadian Studies program of the Canadian Embassy in Washington allowed me to travel to Ottawa and Colorado Springs. My travel to Washington was supported by the Dean's research fund at St. Lawrence University. Publication of this book was supported in part by a subvention from the Canadian Institute of International Affairs, Toronto.

My special thanks go to Professor Jane Boulden of the Royal Military College of Canada for giving me the NORAD-related research materials of her late husband, Professor David Cox. The Department of Foreign Affairs and International Trade allowed me, through its Access program, to look at files that were key to my trying to understand events 1981–1991. Dr. Thomas Fuller and his colleagues at the NORAD/USNORTHCOM History Office were most hospitable during the two weeks I spent looking at their collection. Andrea Schlecht, the declassification officer at the DND Directorate of History and Heritage in Ottawa, opened troves for me. I appreciate the Canadian and US officials who brought me up to date on recent developments.

Professor James Fergusson of the University of Manitoba, Dr. George Lindsey, Major-General Fraser Holman (CF, Ret) Philippe Lagassé, and Lieutenant-General George Macdonald (CF, Ret) all made helpful suggestions upon reading the draft manuscript. Thanks go as well to Professor Douglas L. Bland, Chair of Defence Management Studies at Queen's University and Professor Charles Pentland, Director of the Queen's Centre for International Relations, for incorporating this book in their publication programs.

LIST OF RECURRING ABBREVIATIONS

ABM	Anti-ballistic missile
ADCOM	Aerospace Defense Command
ADI	Air Defense Initiative
ALCM	Air-launched cruise missile
ASAT	Anti-satellite system
AWACS	Airborne warning and control system
BMD	Ballistic missile defence
BMEWS	Ballistic Missile Early Warning System
Bomarc	Boeing-Michigan Aeronautical Research Center surface-to-air missile
CADIN	Continental air defence integration-north
Canada COM	Canada Command
CANR	Canadian NORAD Region
CDS	Chief of the defence staff
CONR	Continental US NORAD Region
CINC	Commander-in-chief
CONAD	Continental Air Defense Command
C3I	Command, control, communications and intelligence
DCINC	Deputy commander-in-chief
DEFCON	Defence condition
DEFSMAC	Defense Space and Missile Activity Center
DEW Line	Distant Early Warning Line
DOB	Dispersed operating base
FAA	Federal Aviation Administration
FOL	Forward operating location

GPALS	Global Protection Against Limited Strikes
GMD	Ground-based Midcourse Missile Defense
ICBM	Intercontinental ballistic missile
ITW/AA	Integrated tactical warning and attack assessment
JSS	Joint Surveillance System radars
JUSCADS	Joint US–Canada Air Defence Study
MOT	Ministry of Transport
NATO	North Atlantic Treaty Organization
NEADS	Northeast Air Defense Sector
NMD	National Missile Defense
NORAD	North American Air Defence Command, later North American Aerospace Defence Command
NSDM	National security decision memorandum
NWS	North Warning System
ONE	Operation Noble Eagle
OTH-B	Over-the-horizon backscatter radar
RCAF	Royal Canadian Air Force
SAC	Strategic Air Command
SAGE	Semi-automatic Ground Environment
SPADATS	Space Detection and Tracking System
SDI	Strategic Defense Initiative
TAC	Tactical Air Command
USAF	United States Air Force
USELEMNORAD	US Element NORAD
USNORTHCOM	United States Northern Command
USSPACECOM	United States Space Command
USSTRATCOM	United States Strategic Command

INTRODUCTION

NORAD'S TWO FOUNDING DATES

Early in September 1957, various military headquarters in Canada and the United States, including those of the Royal Canadian Air Force, received official word that "operational control over the Canadian Air Defence Command and the air defense forces assigned, attached or otherwise made available to that command will be assumed by the Commander-in-Chief, North American Air Defense Command, with headquarters at Ent AFB, Colorado, USA effective 0001 Zulu 12 September 1957."[1] When NORAD stood up on the 12th, its operational control extended to all of the vast continental air defence forces in Canada, the 48 US states, and Alaska. NORAD's first commander-in-chief (CINCNORAD), General Earle E. Partridge, also remained head of the US interservice air defence command that had been created three years before. His deputy commander, (DCINCNORAD) Air Marshal C. Roy Slemon, who had most recently been the chief of the air staff in Canada, was empowered to exercise in Partridge's absence his NORAD authority over both US and Canadian air defence forces. Partridge and Slemon were supported by a headquarters staff of Americans and Canadians, largely drawn from the two air forces, who were located at the air base just outside of downtown Colorado Springs. NORAD was to watch for, warn of, and, using fighter interceptors and surface-to-air missiles, actively defend against an attack on North America by Soviet bombers carrying nuclear weapons. "This mighty task of air defence," Slemon called it a year after he had arrived.[2]

While Partridge had at his disposal nuclear air defence weapons capable of destroying Soviet bombers in or near North American airspace, the strategic nuclear weaponry with which the US could strike the Soviet Union itself was entirely outside his hands. That was the task of the bombers of the US Strategic Air Command (SAC). However, NORAD would warn SAC and offer it a measure of protection, lest it be destroyed on the ground. This was a relationship that was at times misunderstood in Canada during NORAD's earliest years. Some Canadian politicians seemed to think that NORAD could launch the deterrent.

There was a place for Canada in Colorado Springs precisely because the US kept air defence and warning of attack apart from both SAC and the Central Intelligence Agency. It might have been otherwise. Paul Bracken observed in *The Command and Control of Nuclear Forces* (1983), that it was "important to note that for warning of nuclear attack the United States was not to depend on a civilian staff group such as the CIA, but instead on a military organization which was more tightly coupled to the direct control of atomic weapons." But not too tightly: SAC was not given the warning responsibility, either. This "… reduces the possible biases in the warning decision that stem from putting too much decision-making responsibility in the hands of one organization."[3] Linking Canadian air defence efforts directly to either the CIA or SAC would have been bureaucratically awkward and all but politically impossible in both countries. Canada had neither spies nor nuclear bombers.

During the 50 years after its creation, NORAD, which was renamed in 1981 the North American *Aerospace* Defence Command, remained the most important institution of Canada–US defence cooperation. It became fairly well known in both countries for its famous combat operations centre, hollowed out deep in Cheyenne Mountain just to the west of Colorado Springs, that opened in 1966 and whose impending placement in warm storage was announced in 2006. NORAD evolved from an air defence command into one whose chief task, while it forever waited to be equipped with a robust capability to intercept ballistic missiles, was not to defend actively, but rather to provide immediate (tactical) warning and assessment of nuclear attacks on this continent. This role, or ITW/AA (integrated tactical warning and attack assessment) in NORAD parlance, was developed as the US sought, in the face of its complete vulnerability to Soviet ballistic missile attacks, to bolster the credibility of its deterrent through a nuclear strategy based on limited strikes and protracted war. At the Cold War's end, NORAD reduced its alert posture. After the shock of 9/11, during which forces under its authority were unable to protect New York and Washington from the air attacks that had arisen not from without, as had so long been expected, but from within the continent, NORAD acquired new responsibilities for what had come to be called homeland defence. These included reconfigured air defences and maritime warning, which gave NORAD a role for the first time beyond aerospace defence. They did not, however, in the wake of a 2005 decision of the Liberal government of Paul Martin, include operation of the missile defences the US had begun to deploy.

All along, an American was in command of NORAD and a Canadian was his deputy. Their titles were also changed when in October 2002 US Secretary of Defense Donald Rumsfeld, having concluded that there should be only one commander-in-chief in the US military, namely the president, downgraded the titles of the heads of the various US commands. The Canadian government quietly went along with CINCNORAD being renamed commander, NORAD (CDR NORAD).

In the years before the command's 50th anniversary in September 2007, it was increasingly forgotten by both Canadian and US officials that NORAD had become operational in 1957. To give but one example, the Martin government's 2005 defence policy statement observed that "NORAD is a bi-national military organization established in 1958 to monitor and defend North American airspace."[4] Even NORAD itself, in both its internal and external communications, especially in briefings (except sometimes the ones the command's own historians had first been able to get their hands on), had taken to dating its existence not back to that day in 1957 when Partridge and Slemon had stood it up and taken operational control over all continental air defence forces, but rather to 12 May 1958, the day Ottawa and Washington exchanged diplomatic notes setting the terms for NORAD. That exchange of notes, often called "the NORAD agreement," was followed by renewals in 1968, 1973, 1975, 1980, 1981, 1986, 1991, 1991, 1996, and 2001; there was an amendment in 2004 and then again a renewal in 2006.

As will be discussed in Chaper One, a political furor erupted in Canada over the rushed and impromptu manner by which the newly elected Diefenbaker government had authorized the command's creation, under heavy pressure from the military. NORAD's international status seemed to rest on little more than a brief press release issued by Diefenbaker's minister of national defence and Eisenhower's secretary of defense. Diefenbaker was obliged, contrary to original intentions, to turn to the negotiation with Washington of the notes, which were submitted to the House of Commons for its approval.

It is tempting to conclude that in the late 20th and early 21st centuries, historically aware officials in Ottawa, Washington, and Colorado Springs, embarrassed by the memory of the illegitimate creation of 1957, preferred to put the focus on the NORAD rebirth in diplomatic and Canadian constitutional wedlock six months later. But that would be a stretch. Rather, because NORAD has long operated under a diplomatic charter that has so constantly been renewed, it was logical for officials to just look for the date that the charter first came into existence and simply assume that that was when the command began. It would be pedantic to chide them here for a lack of historical awareness. After all, NORAD officials, as well as those in Ottawa and Washington, have more pressing things to do.

Nonetheless, 12 September 1957 is worth underlining, not just for prickly professorial reasons of historical accuracy or because it was a revealing moment in Canadian military history, but rather because on that date NORAD became what its prime creators in the United States Air Force (USAF) and Royal Canadian Air Force (RCAF) originally wanted it to be: namely, just a practical and useful continental air defence headquarters, and little more. As such, they thought, NORAD should be no big deal politically. This point of view was effectively summarized in 1968 by General Charles Foulkes who, as chairman of the Canadian Chiefs of Staff Committee in 1957, had been one of the prime movers behind NORAD. His take on the command was purely functional; as he put it, "NORAD is very efficient for processing of intelligence information regarding the aerospace threat from all sources, and operational control of the forces for anti-bomber defence and has proven a most useful channel for technical information and planning between Canada and the United States."[5]

The Department of External Affairs immediately contested the military's approach to NORAD as a purely functional and exclusively military matter. A couple of weeks after the command was stood up, officials of the department pointed out that "[t]he establishment of NORAD is a decision for which there is no precedent in Canadian history in that it grants in peace-time to a foreign representative operational control of an element of Canadian forces *in Canada*"[6] (original emphasis). Under that department's lead, NORAD became, starting in 1958, not just a command and a diplomatic agreement but also the linchpin to what the diplomats hoped would be a consultative arrangement between the United States and Canada in the event of a severe international crisis.

Thereafter, NORAD has often been regarded as being still more. The first conclusion out of a 1998 study exercise that the command itself undertook to think about its future was that each of the participants "defined the term NORAD differently. To some it was a binational military relationship, to some a HQ building or tasked mission and to others a political agreement."[7] NORAD has also carried broad and heavy symbolic value, especially in Canada, but also in the US. A group of Canadian and American officials gathered in 1994 to ponder NORAD's post-Cold War future pointed out that "NORAD stands as a convenient symbol for the expenses associated with air sovereignty, alert, peacetime air surveillance, warning and characterization of attack and preparation for air defence as needed."[8] A head of the defence and arms control bureau at the Department of External Affairs once went even farther. "The NORAD agreement," he wrote, "is only one of a number of bilateral arrangements with the United States. But it has become symbolic of our alliance with the US in continental defence. That we might abandon the NORAD agreement would be to argue for an abandonment of that alliance which would not, in my view, carry the judgment of most Canadians."[9]

In other words, "NORAD" can be taken so broadly that it can mean Canada–US defence cooperation itself. This historical study of NORAD's fifty years will try to keep things concentrated. It will focus on three things. The first is the course of Canadian involvement in the missions that have made up North American strategic defence over a half century as the threat to the continent shifted from bombers to ballistic missiles to terrorists while the US – which called most of the shots for continental defence – adjusted accordingly.

NORAD's enduring mission – the one that precipitated the command's creation and one with which it would remain involved over the fifty-year course of its history – was air defence. Air defence operations on Canadian territory and in Canadian airspace were essential to the security of both the US and Canada. Since the early 1950s, Ottawa was faced with having to decide how much air defence it wanted to provide on its own. This decision became all the more difficult almost at the time NORAD was created, inasmuch as the technology for air defence had improved greatly but the threat to the continent was expected to shift from bombers to ballistic missiles. The Diefenbaker government had to decide whether to equip the RCAF with the expensive, made-in-Canada AVRO Arrow interceptor. That government later collapsed spectacularly in 1963 amidst its failure to reach a decision over equipping the Canadian military with nuclear weapons, including nuclear warheads for Canadian Bomarc surface-to-air missiles and the US-made Voodoo interceptors that it had deployed instead of the Arrow.

Beginning in the 1950s, a lot of continental air defence in Canada was undertaken by US interceptors and US-manned radar stations. In the early 1960s much of Canadian airspace was placed, for air defence purposes, under the operational control of NORAD regional headquarters located in the US and, mirroring the situation in Colorado Springs, commanded by USAF officers with Canadian deputies. When both the US and Canadian governments had concluded that the need for continental air defence had shrunk, Ottawa was afforded the opportunity to repatriate most of the air defence of Canada. The Trudeau government publicly emphasized sovereignty as a role for the military and the Mulroney government was able to claim the credit for completing the Canadianization of day-to-day air defences when it announced an air defence modernization agreement with the US in 1985. For all that, the US devoted more effort and funding than Canada did to integrating its remaining air defences with its control of civil aviation. But it was still not enough on 9/11.

The US did not need Canadian participation in any other aspect of strategic defence except in the early years for communications purposes, until satellites replaced the ground-based links across Canadian territory. This point tended to be little understood by Canadians who walked around with the geographic model of air defence in their heads. A good deal of the story in the following pages will be about how, when, and why Canada became involved in some strategic defence missions but not others. In addition to air defence, Canada opted into space surveillance, warning of aerospace attack, and maritime warning, all of which accordingly became NORAD missions. Canada never participated in the little-known anti-satellite system the US deployed in the 1960s. Far more well-known were the decisions of the Pearson government in 1968 and the Martin government in 2005 not to participate in ballistic missile defence – at least not directly. Because of these two Canadian decisions, NORAD was never given operational control over the missile defences that were deployed. In between, during the 1980s, many Canadians focused for the first time on what US nuclear strategy really was, fretted about Ronald Reagan's Strategic Defense Initiative or "Star Wars" program and worried that it would lead to a vast missile defence system that NORAD somehow might drag their country into.

The second concentration will be on NORAD as a US–Canadian command. NORAD's authority over Canadian and US air defence forces was not absolute. As that September 1957 message pointed out, CINCNORAD had "operational control" over the forces assigned to him. Command remained in national hands. How was such divided authority expected to work and how did it work in practice? There was no doubt that if the Soviet Union suddenly attacked, CINCNORAD had full authority to do what he could. But what about putting the air defence forces on alert in the event of a more slowly developing major international crisis? What would happen, in particular, if Ottawa and Washington had not reached agreement? Two such major crises in fact occurred, namely the Cuban missile crisis of 1962 and one during the Yom Kippur War of 1973. In both cases Washington put US forces on alert. These crises will be examined in Chapters Two and Three respectively, with a view towards looking at how NORAD conducted itself and what Washington's failure to consult Ottawa meant. Two additional issues related to CINCNORAD's authority will also be considered. One is NORAD's role, and hence the role of Canadians, in the command and operational control of the nuclear air defence weapons that were deployed until the early 1980s. The other relates to air defence in the age of terror. After the 9/11 attacks, Ottawa was obliged to decide whether CINCNORAD's operational command over Canadian air defence forces should include the authority to order the destruction of highjacked civilian aircraft.

There was another form of divided authority: NORAD always shared its commander, its headquarters, and its operations centre with a purely US command. From 1957 to 1975 this was the Continental Air Defense Command (CONAD), from 1975 to 1985 the Aerospace Defense Command (ADCOM), from 1985 to 2002 US Space Command (USSPACECOM), and since 2002 US Northern Command (USNORTHCOM). DCINCNORAD was not the deputy commander of these commands, their staffs were at times exclusively and at other times overwhelmingly US, and unlike NORAD they reported only to Washington. At the start, when NORAD was an air defence command, the idea was that the US "twin" would play a decidedly secondary role to it. With the decline of air defence, and as Colorado Springs expanded into areas in which Canada was not directly involved, the "twins" loomed larger. The Canadian military fretted about their being shut out, and about NORAD being overwhelmed or rendered irrelevant. With the establishment of USSPACECOM, other Canadians worried about what this particular twin might involve Canada in. Its replacement in 2002 by USNORTHCOM, which had a broad mandate for homeland defence, created an existential crisis for NORAD that was made only more acute by the Canadian military's creation in 2006 of Canada Command, which had a roughly similar mandate.

The third focus will be on the evolution of the NORAD accord, starting with the original exchange notes in 1958 and continuing through the renewals. There should be no false drama here. Except arguably in 1968 when Prime Minister Lester B. Pearson seems to have seriously pondered ending the command, there never was any good chance that NORAD would not be renewed at any of the eleven times time the agreement expired. It was all about the terms. Negotiating the diplomatic notes provided civilian officials, including the cabinet in Canada, with the opportunity to assess recent changes in the threat and in US plans for the defence, to consider the military's wishes, and then to set public conditions for NORAD's continuing existence.

The 1958 agreement and several of the renewals provide useful, if admittedly somewhat artificial endpoints to the chapters in this study. Chapter One ends with a discussion of the original accord, especially its emphasis on consultation. Each of the following five chapters ends with a discussion of the events surrounding a renewal. The concluding chapter looks at the state of NORAD on the eve of its fiftieth anniversary, in the light of its history.

NOTES

[1] Quoted in "Seventeen Years of Air Defense," Historical Reference Paper no. 9, Directorate of Command History, Headquarters NORAD, 1 June 1963, 66.

[2] "North American Air Defence," address by A/M C.R. Slemon, RCAF, DCINCNORAD to the Canadian Industrial Preparedness Association, Montreal, 22 October 1958. Department of National Defence, Directorate of History and Heritage, Raymont fonds, 30/522.

[3] Paul Bracken, *The Command and Control of Nuclear Forces* (New Haven: Yale University Press, 1983), 7–8, 21. Bracken seems unaware, it should be added, of the establishment of CONAD three years prior to NORAD.

[4] Minister of National Defence. *Canada's International Policy Statement: A Role of Pride. Defence.* Ottawa, 2005, 23.

[5] General Charles Foulkes, notes for Canadian–American Committee meeting, October 1969, "Some of the Problems of Continental Defence." Department of National Defence, Directorate of History and Heritage, Foulkes fonds, 119/3022.

[6] Meeting of Consultation September 30, 1957, DEA briefing book (copy for Foulkes). Department of National Defence, Directorate of History and Heritage, Raymont fonds, 73/1223 file 2509.

[7] "NORAD Pathway Event," 1998. Copy in NORAD/USNORTHCOM History Office.

[8] "Options for Canada–US Cooperation in Aerospace Defence: A Report Directed by the NORAD Renewal Steering Group," October 1994. Copy in NORAD/USNORTHCOM History Office.

[9] J.J. McCardle (DG Bureau of Defence and Arms Control Affairs), "NORAD linkage with other controversial issues in Canada/US relations," 26 May 1980. Library and Archives Canada, RG 25, Department of External Affairs records, 2-14-NORAD.

CHAPTER ONE

AIR DEFENCE, THE 1957 COMMAND, AND THE 1958 AGREEMENT

INTERTWINED AIR DEFENCES

In 1957 and 1958, vast North American air defences were still growing in capability. The Canadian and US efforts were increasingly intertwined, both geographically and operationally. A Canada–US air defence command thus made good military sense, the next logical step in the continuing expansion of Canada–US air defence cooperation.

The geographic intertwining of the air defences is evident by looking at Map 1, which shows the base location and range at the time of RCAF air defence fighter aircraft in Canada and Map 2, showing the location and range of counterpart USAF aircraft in the northern states and Newfoundland. RCAF Air Defence Command, headquartered at St. Hubert, Quebec, commanded nine squadrons of all-weather CF-100 "Canuck" aircraft. One had been located in Comox, BC; the eight other squadrons were all in southern Ontario and Quebec.

There were sixty-four regular USAF squadrons committed to continental air defence under the USAF Air Defense Command, headquartered at Colorado Springs. Others could back these up in an emergency and the establishment of still more squadrons had been authorized by the Eisenhower administration. The US, like Canada, had located much of its air defence in the national industrial heartland in the east and secondarily on the west coast. But it also had aircraft deployed across the northeast approaches to the continent in Newfoundland (at bases it had obtained as a result of the 1941 bases-for-destroyers agreement with the UK), the northwest approaches in Alaska, and along the border with Canada in the heart of the continent to prevent Soviet bombers from entering freely. To fill a fighter gap there it had to build new bases in North Dakota and Montana. Asked why not put the aircraft to the north instead, a USAF spokesman told a Congressional committee in 1954: "I think there is an unquestioned advantage to having them to the north, but of course that is the territory of another sovereign nation and we don't have the arrangement now."[1] A different kind of gap to the north remained though, namely in Canadian radar coverage across the Prairies, and it was somewhat of a worry for the US air defence, mitigated by coverage provided by radars located in the US just south of Alberta and Saskatchewan.

While US forces to the northeast and northwest first might engage in attacking Soviet bombers, the main continental air defence battle was expected largely to begin in southern Canada using Canadian interceptors and US interceptors which would fly into Canadian skies or which, in anticipation of impending attack, would be temporarily located to Canadian airfields. To fly towards and attack enemy bombers, modern air defence fighters needed ground control radar coverage. "Gone were the days of the 'head-up' fighter pilot with his few instruments to follow and the seat of his pants to fall back on when something went wrong. The jet all-weather pilot flew by the radar scope and the beam given him by his co-partner, the radar director on the ground. ... Perhaps never before in the history of combat aviation was the success of a mission so dependent on ground-air teamwork as it was in air defense operations."[2] Such ground radar coverage was in place in much of Canada as a result of a 1951 Canada–US agreement whereby the US paid much of the construction cost and operated some of the radar stations. The stations in Canada, which were fully operational in 1955, were often called the "Pinetree Line," and Map 3 shows them as such a line. But the Pinetree radars were in reality an extension northward of the vast "Permanent" radar system which the US had been putting in place on much of its own territory and so provided, in addition to some early warning, an extensive, largely contiguous ground control environment for Canadian and US fighter aircraft, flying across the border when necessary, to be guided towards attacking Soviet bombers.

There was good reason for US fighters to fly into Canada or to be based there in an emergency. By first engaging to the north, the continental air defenders could establish defence in depth, subjecting the Soviet bombers to repeated attacks before they reached their targets. This meant that the US got more protection, a fact that certainly had not gone unnoticed in Canada. George Lindsey, a scientist and analyst with the Department of National Defence who throughout his career remained deeply involved in the development of the Canadian air defence system, had written in 1952: "if defence in depth is necessary and is successful, then the place to live is down deep in the system."[3] The Canadian army later echoed Lindsey's point in a 1958 critique, pointing out that the air defence battle would occur over southern Canada. "Either by accident or by design, Canadian air defences contribute to the perimeter defence of the USA while using Canada as the killing area," it observed.[4] On the other hand, assuming that most of the ultimate targets of Soviet bombers were in the US, it needed more protection. Moreover, it is

hard to imagine the governments of either the US or Canada footing
relocate to the high Canadian north the heavy radar stations, scores
aircraft, and support facilities that were required to make up that killing area.

The early warning zone could, however, be more readily moved northward,
especially as a result of new technologies. For most of the 1950s, the Pinetree/
Permanent radars would also provide the first tactical warning that a Soviet
attack had begun. The USAF had been counting on receiving from them an
alert of at best only an hour or two, upon which it would be able to get only
about forty percent of its fighters into the air. The RCAF was able to get a still
lower percentage of its fighters up because of their location closer to the radars'
edge. That changed, however, with the building of two more northerly early
warning lines in the mid-1950s. The first was the Mid-Canada Line, or "McGill
Fence," along the 55th parallel that the Canadian government constructed using a technology developed in Canada. It depended on the Doppler effect,
which changed the frequency of radiation directed along a beam transmitted
from one station to the next in the line if something in the beam were moving.
This could be used to sound an automatic alarm, indicating that something
was crossing between the two stations. While this equipment was much sim-
pler to construct and maintain than orthodox radar, and did not require a staff
to provide continuous observation, it could only signal that a rapidly moving
object had come across the line somewhere between the two stations. The line
was declared operational in 1958.

A more dramatic improvement was thereafter provided by the Distant Early
Warning (DEW) Line built and operated by the US across the high Canadian
and Alaskan Arctic. While the main equipment resembled that of the radars of
the Pinetree Line, able to detect and track aircraft out to a considerable range,
the construction and operation costs were kept down by the recently developed technology of "aural presentation" of radars. As it was at the Mid-Canada
Line, this meant that an alarm would go off when an aircraft was detected,
making it unnecessary for staff to remain at their posts continuously watching
radar screens. When it came on line in 1957 it provided well over four hours'
warning, allowing more fighters to be readied, more to get into the air (including roughly seventy percent of the US fighters) and more to engage over
southern Canada. Cooperation between the RCAF and USAF became, accordingly, all the more useful.[5]

By the mid-1950s such cooperation was already far advanced, as the two
air forces came to see the air defence of North America more and more as a
problem to be tackled jointly with resources which were becoming increasingly intertwined. A political and legal framework had been put into place to
permit and facilitate cross border air defence operations. In 1951 Ottawa had
agreed that US fighter aircraft could enter Canadian airspace to identify and
follow suspicious aircraft that were heading towards the border. There could

be no shooting by such Americans in Canada though; that would have to wait until the target and interceptor were in US airspace. That same year, the RCAF and USAF air defence commanders also received standing authority, in the event of an emergency, to order air defence reinforcements to cross the border, meaning that US aircraft could be deployed temporarily to Canadian bases. Plans were worked out to do so. In 1953 Ottawa removed most of the limitations it had imposed in 1951 on cross-border operations. Henceforth, if an unknown and potentially hostile aircraft appeared in North American skies, the air defence commanders could send the nearest available interceptor across the border to identify and, if need be, destroy it. Here, too the USAF and RCAF air defence commands worked out with each other how this would be done.[6]

To accommodate their increasing interoperability, direct and more permanent ties were forged between the commands, bypassing the slower, more formal channels running through Washington and Ottawa. In 1951 RCAF liaison officers took up duties at USAF air defence command headquarters. Three years later the two national air defence commanders created a joint planning group which set itself up, on a permanent basis, at the Colorado headquarters and was given the task of drawing up one common plan for the air defence of the entire continent.

Beginning in 1957, the cross-border arrangements were expanded to provide for the use of US nuclear air defence weapons in Canada. Early that year the first nuclear air defence weapon, the MB-1 or "Genie," a rocket carried by a fighter interceptor, began to enter the US inventory. It was expected to improve the air defence significantly. Its warhead had an explosive yield of 1.5 to 2 kilotons, which would generate a lethal envelope upon explosion of about a mile across and a mile and a half deep. The fighter pilot would fly towards an aim point being approached by the bomber, launch the unguided Genie and then manoeuvre in time to escape a lethal concentration of radiation from the explosion. A more powerful yield would probably have killed the fighter crew as well as destroying the Soviet bomber. In a February exchange of diplomatic notes with Washington, Ottawa agreed that if a red or yellow air defence emergency were declared, meaning that an attack by Soviet aircraft was either probable, imminent, or actually taking place, US fighter aircraft carrying Genies could fly from their US bases into southern Canadian airspace.

In light of the enormous controversy that developed both within Canada and between Ottawa and Washington a few years later over the equipping of Canadian forces in Canada and Europe with nuclear weapons, it is striking that the government of Prime Minister Louis St. Laurent so readily agreed in early 1957 to the US MB-1 request. Perhaps it just believed that such weapons strengthened defence and deterrence and so Canada should be prepared to do its part by allowing them. It no doubt had been assured by the Americans that because the Genies would be fired at fairly high altitudes, little ground damage and fallout was expected from them. Because the weapons were to remain based in the US and the arrangements for their being flown into and used in Canada were being kept secret – at Ottawa's behest – perhaps the government decided that Canada's vaunted status as a country without nuclear weapons would not be challenged. As a junior partner of the US and Britain during the Second World War in the development of the atomic bomb, and a country with a sizable supply of uranium, it could have relatively easily, after the war, put together at least a modest arsenal of its own. While Canadians sometimes talk about having been first to "renounce" the acquisition of nuclear weapons, there apparently never was a clear-cut decision by Ottawa not to acquire them. Rather, it never really seriously occurred to the Canadian government that an alternative to reliance on the American nuclear arsenal was ever necessary.

The St. Laurent government may simply have concluded that the USAF would go ahead anyway in an emergency and just fly the Genies into Canada to be used whether or not Ottawa agreed. It would have been unrealistic for Canadians to have believed that should Soviet bombers carrying death for millions of Americans ever appear in North American skies, the US air defence would not send nuclear weapons into Canadian airspace to destroy them because written advance permission from Ottawa had never been received. If Canadian officials did have any hesitations, under the circumstances there probably was no alternative to going along while including in the exchange of notes various assertions of Canadian sovereignty. The agreement set an initial geographical limitation on where in Canada US aircraft with such weapons could operate (which was later expanded), a time limit to the initial agreement (which was renewed and still later incorporated into standing NORAD arrangements) and an insistence that within Canada, RCAF rules for interception and destruction of hostile aircraft be observed (which was fine with the USAF).[7]

Negotiations between the RCAF and USAF were also underway between 1956 and 1958 over how to improve Canadian air defences further and link them more tightly with US efforts. With the encouragement of the Diefenbaker government, a service-to-service agreement was reached in 1958. The US National Security Council staff summarized the problem the two air forces had been addressing:

> The present air defense system in Canada does not provide sufficient radar coverage in depth for adequate protection of heavy industrial areas in Northeast Canada and the US, and lack of radar coverage across the prairie Provinces leaves a large gap in the defense of the center of the continent. We are therefore planning to integrate the Canadian and US air defense systems by increasing Canadian radar

coverage and by adding BOMARC missiles to the Canadian system. This CADIN (Continental Air Defense Integration-North) program is intended to increase defense in depth against attack from the North and to provide semi-automatic control of interceptor aircraft and BOMARC missiles.[8]

The agreement provided for improving the Pinetree radars (which were later renamed the CADIN/Pinetree Line) by building stations to fill the gap in Manitoba, Saskatchewan and Alberta, giving extra warning and allowing US fighter interceptors just to the south to move their operations into Canadian skies, and by improving coverage in the Ottawa area.

Just as important, though, was the planned extension into Canada of the Semi-automatic Ground Environment (SAGE). This was a computerized system, highly advanced for its day, and expensive. It was semi-automatic in that intricate plotting and telling functions were run electronically, while tactical decisions, such as which fighter aircraft would fly where and which hostile aircraft they would attack, were left in human hands. Also gone were the days when ground controllers would record aircraft tracks with crayon on plexiglass, writing backwards so that those on the other side of the panes could read the notations. The first of the SAGE centres in the US became operational in 1958. While the air defence radars in all of southern Canada were to be brought under SAGE control, Canada was prepared to fund just one SAGE centre on Canadian soil, to control the priority air defence operations in the eastern part of the country. It was eventually built at North Bay. With but one SAGE control centre in Canada, most of Canadian airspace would have to be ground-controlled from centres located in the US and commanded by USAF officers.

The USAF's longer-range Bomarcs were one of three types of surface-to-air missiles with which the US air defence could strike at Soviet bombers, the other two being the US Army's shorter range Nike-Hercules and Hawk missiles. Map 4, showing where the USAF was planning in 1958 to deploy Bomarcs, also gives a quick indication of why deploying some of them instead in Ontario and Quebec could make sense. The defence minister in the Diefenbaker government, George Pearkes, encouraged this option. By filling the gap along the 49th parallel, they would provide additional protection for the Quebec City–Windsor axis, and more coverage of the approaches to the US northeast. US officials were, of course, particularly interested in the latter, as a further strengthening of air defence in depth. According to US plans, fighter interceptors "would strike first at incoming aircraft, then land on northern bases (rather than returning to their initial bases) in order to clear the way for missiles. BOMARC, with its longer range, was expected to come into action first, then Nike-Hercules, with Hawk filling in as needed against low-flying aircraft."[9]

Starting in 1956 with the F-102, the USAF had begun to bring into service for air defence supersonic "century-series" aircraft. Canada had under development a supersonic improvement of its own, the CF-105 AVRO Arrow interceptor, to replace the CF-100, which was the mainstay of RCAF air defence operations. Although the CF-100 had only entered service in 1953, it was aging swiftly, having but a very limited capability, including a lack of speed, against the newer types of Soviet bombers. It was also not compatible with the SAGE system. The CF-100 had been built almost entirely in Canada. Ottawa and the Canadian aircraft industry had high hopes that it could be done again with the Arrow. As will be discussed in the next chapter, the fates of the Arrow and Bomarc were to be closely linked politically by the Diefenbaker government towards the end of 1958, making them the two most controversial and famous weapons systems in Canadian history.

Both the US and Canada had originally started out to build air defences primarily to protect cities, in the hope of saving lives and preserving as much of the economy as possible. But how much protection could this vast continental system of radars, Doppler detectors, sub- and supersonic fighter interceptors, long- and short-range surface-to-air missiles, conventional and nuclear weapons, computers, and ground control centres really provide, especially as the Soviets brought into service the high-performance bombers they had introduced in May 1954 and upgraded their nuclear inventory from atomic weapons in the twenty-kiloton range to hydrogen bombs with megaton yields, each one capable of completely destroying a small city? Nobody really knew. In the early 1950s there had been talk in the US, especially among some prominent scientists, of a crash program for an all but perfect, leakproof air defence, which had helped expedite construction of the DEW Line as the cornerstone of such a high-attrition defence. Such talk had soon died. While both countries had increased funding for air defences in the face of the growing Soviet threat, neither was prepared to even try to fund a perfect defence. If war came, Soviet bombers with nuclear weapons would get through, it had to be recognized, and the Soviets had hundreds. How many of them would the defence destroy, especially if Russia struck first? Air defence officials shied away from giving a percentage. Kenneth Schaffel, the official USAF historian of early continental air defence efforts, concluded that "it is difficult to determine in retrospect."[10] Senior officials in the Eisenhower administration reached the same conclusion in the mid 1950s. Continental air defence was so new, it was "impossible to tell whether we were getting our money's worth," Secretary of Defense Charles Wilson told a meeting of the National Security Council in 1956. Admiral Arthur W. Radford, chairman of the Joint Chiefs of Staff, added that until the system was used in combat, its value would never be known.[11] In realistic exercises, in which SAC provided "Red Force" bombers and the air defence commands flew real interceptor fights, although no weapons were launched it was concluded that most of the bombers would always have gotten through to their targets.

Any way you looked at it, if the Soviets struck, especially if they struck first, in full force, millions of Americans would die. It was easy to be pessimistic, if not despairing, about the possibility of defence. But the American air defenders strongly resisted the notion that an active air defence system was not worth the money and the effort. It was unthinkable to them that in the event of a nuclear war, Soviets bombers could be allowed to attack their targets in the US freely. While millions of lives would be lost, millions of lives could also still be saved by an air defence effort. While the US would undergo a calamity beyond anything in its history, it might still be possible to disrupt the attack enough to allow for long-term survival of the US as a society. Schaffel also pointed out that, despite the "gloomy prognosis, the Air Force believed it was responsible for doing everything it could to limit damage to American soil ... while destroying as many enemy bombers as possible."[12]

The air defenders at Colorado Springs would remain, over the next several decades, tenaciously committed to the retention of "damage limitation," as it was later called, as a prime mission. The Soviets "have the aircraft right now and they have the weapons to destroy all the important targets in the United States and Canada," General Partridge said in 1957. "Now, we can't just sit quietly by and let them do this without doing our best to oppose them, and we play for extremely high stakes. If you shoot down a bomber coming in – one that was going to hit a big city like Washington – you save billions of dollars and maybe a million lives by just shooting down one bomber."[13]

Nonetheless, Partridge had also emphasized, a few years earlier that "[a]s a matter of doctrine, we believe that the best defense is a good offense and we believe that our primary mission in the Air Defense Command is to defend the bases from which the Strategic Air Command is going to operate."[14] SAC itself seemed throughout most of the 1950s strangely nonchalant, if not oblivious to the danger of its being attacked on the ground, prompting a series of warnings from the outside. The RAND Corporation, a think tank sponsored by the USAF, led the way with a 1955 Report, R-266, *Selection and Use of Strategic Air Bases*. Its author, Albert J. Wohlstetter began a veritable campaign to spread its message. A special presidential committee to study civil defence – appointed in 1957 under the chairmanship of H. Rowan Gaither of the Ford Foundation and Robert C. Sprague, a Massachusetts industrialist – was drawn into the issue with its astonishing discovery that not a single SAC bomber would be able to get off the ground in fewer than six hours, well outside the margin of safety provided by early warning. In a private conservation with General Curtis E. LeMay, commander-in-chief of SAC, Sprague discovered why the command had remained so untroubled about its vulnerability. The US, LeMay told him, had ways of knowing what the Soviets were up to, including secret spy planes flying over the country picking up various kinds of information, especially from Russian military radio transmissions. These could provide advance *strategic* warning, as opposed to the *tactical* kind coming later that the air defenders would provide. LeMay went on to say that once he got early wind from these sources of any Soviet preparations for an attack, he would order SAC on his own to strike and completely destroy Soviet bombers on the ground. To Sprague's objection that LeMay's intention to launch all-out nuclear war all by himself if necessary was completely counter to US policy, LeMay replied, "I don't care. It's my policy. That's what I am going to do."[15] While the Eisenhower administration initially found the Gaither Committee's warnings of SAC vulnerability alarmist, it later required the command to put into place a serious program of dispersal and alerts for its bombers, allowing it thereby to make good use of the warning time the air defence system would provide.

If SAC was demonstrably secure, the Soviets might be deterred from striking. That was the point. Of course, if you had unshakeable confidence in such deterrence of the Soviets, then any active North American air defences were unnecessary. Just the warning lines and a few interceptors to provide visual confirmation of the attack were all that would be necessary to get SAC on its way.

There was still another way of looking at the issue of defence vs. deterrence, though. Active air defence would not only limit the damage in case deterrence failed, but would thereby also strengthen deterrence. SAC bases could be protected, and if the Soviets could be persuaded that an attack on American society and economy might not be successful because of North American air defence, they might be further dissuaded from such an attempt. The US Joint Chiefs of Staff subscribed to this view. In a definitive *Statement of Policy on Continental Defense* they concluded in 1957 that "[t]o the extent the Soviets believe the North American continental defense system is effective, this belief will constitute one of the key deterrents to an attack on North America." Their statement went on to set several goals for continental defence, to be pursued "in collaboration with Canada and other free world nations," of which the first four were:

a. Contributing to deterring Soviet aggression;

b. Providing sufficient warning to alert the nation to the maximum state of readiness possible and to permit the launching of alert nuclear forces;

c. Preventing the carrying-through of an attack of such effectiveness that US national survival would be threatened;

d. So minimizing the effect of any Soviet attack as to permit an immediate and effective counter-offensive and the successful prosecution and completion of a general war;[16]

...

Looming over all continental defence calculations when the JCS adopted its policy statement was the prospect that the Soviets soon would acquire intercontinental ballistic missiles (ICBMs) with which it could strike at North America. What good would extensive air defences do if the Soviets could soon use ballistic missiles to strike unhindered? Partridge told a US Congressional committee in 1956: "If the aggressor's weapon is the ICBM the continent stands almost as naked today as it did in 1946, for I have no radar to detect missiles and no defense against them."[17] While the 1957 launch of Sputnik, the world's first satellite, underscored the danger, US defence planning had begun seriously to address the possibility several years earlier. The second problem, destruction of incoming missiles, was more difficult. Still, the US had a number of programs underway to develop missile defences. The one that seemed at the time the most promising was based on the US Army's interceptor, dubbed Nike-Zeus. The general in charge of the program went so far in 1956 as to make the flat assertion that Nike "was capable of killing any known guided missile and will be effective against the intercontinental missile when it materializes."[18] Many defence scientists were not so sure and the Eisenhower administration remained quite unwilling to spend millions to deploy a system based on still-unproved technology.

The Diefenbaker government was not willing to get heavily involved in missile defence either. In November 1957, General Charles Foulkes, Chairman of the Chiefs of Staff Committee, contacted the prime minister on behalf of the Chiefs, urging him to write Eisenhower proposing that missile defence be made a "joint research and development project" between the two countries and helpfully enclosing a draft letter to the president.[19] Although Diefenbaker made vague but strongly positive noises in public about missile defence, apparently he did not act on the Canadian Chiefs' suggestion. Nonetheless, and perhaps unbeknownst to the prime minister, the Department of National Defence already was cooperating in aspects of missile defence research with its British and US counterparts.

The first problem Partridge mentioned in his 1956 testimony, that of detecting Soviet missile launches, could be fairly speedily addressed. In early 1958 the US began construction at Thule, Greenland, of the first station of the Ballistic Missile Early Warning System (BMEWS). The others were to be located in Fylingdales Moor, England and Clear, Alaska.

To Canadians who, when it came to continental defence, had been growing used to thinking of their country as being located between the US and the Soviet Union, the "ham in the sandwich" or "Belgium of the Cold War" as it was sometimes called, the siting of BMEWS stations elsewhere must at first have been puzzling. But unlike aircraft, Soviet ballistic missiles traveling first beyond the atmosphere and then sharply downward to targets in the US would cross above the altitude of the Canadian air space. A look at a map, or still better, a globe, shows how the three sites could provide good radar coverage looking over the top of the globe towards Russia. The Fylingdales Moor site had the additional advantage of being able to provide warning of missile attack on Britain. (Map 6, showing 1981 capabilities, includes the three BMEWS stations.)

Ground communication links from BMEWS to the US would have to pass through Canada; arrangements for such were soon negotiated between Ottawa and Washington. (In later years they would be replaced by communication satellite links.) Nonetheless, as the BMEWS site selection indicated, the impending shift in the threat to North America from bombers toward missiles heralded the decline in the importance of Canadian territory and airspace to the US continental defence. It indicated to Foulkes that the era of heavy investment in continental air defence was approaching an end. He told a military planning committee in early 1958 that "the concept of air defence of North America had been developing since 1947 and we are now at the point of rounding out the air defence against the manned bomber. The next improvement should render it adequate until the threat of the manned bomber disappears."[20]

For some time, Foulkes had been quite pessimistic about limiting the losses Soviet bombers would inflict, putting more of his bets on deterrence through nuclear retaliation. As he wrote privately in 1955: "We are coming to the conclusion here that war as an instrument of policy is no longer effective as it involves the major powers, that what we in military now can offer is mutual total destruction and therefore the role of the military is not one now of being prepared to a win a war but one of assisting politicians to avoid war." This, he went on, could only be done with a deterrent which "demonstrates clearly to Soviet Russia that they cannot so seriously damage our retaliatory capacity by a sudden devastating raid on North America that our capacity to retaliate would be impaired."[21] He was far from alone among the leadership at the Department of National Defence in such thinking. As Andrew Richter demonstrated in his 2002 study of strategic thought within the department during the first part of the Cold War, it placed much more emphasis on "the mutual nature of deterrence and the importance of retaliatory capabilities" and less on "the need for the United States to intimidate and/or defeat the Soviet Union through overwhelming military superiority."[22]

Not surprisingly then, Canadian strategists came independently in the mid-1950s to realize the importance of SAC survivability. In 1956 the department also officially concluded that security rested in nuclear deterrence through the "West's retaliatory forces" and that "[i]n the current phase of collective security, Canada's principal support of the West's retaliatory striking power is our contribution towards early warning and air defence on this continent."[23] The lack of defence in depth in Canada no doubt helps explain a somewhat more pessimistic tone about damage limitation among Canadian officials compared to US air defenders, who were "deep down in the system." None-theless, from the perspective of a US air defence planner in 1957, the different nuances between Canada and the US in thinking and public statements about the purposes of air defence had, for the moment, little to no practical impor-tance. The RCAF Air Defence Command would join its USAF counterpart in attempting to destroy Soviet bombers passing through the engagement zone in southern Canadian airspace, regardless of whether they seemed at the mo-ment to be heading for either US cities or SAC bases.

FROM CINCADCANUS TO NORAD

In 1954, the joint RCAF-USAF air defence planning group that had gathered at Colorado Springs asked itself rhetorically what needed to be fixed the most. "The answer," it concluded "is that forces deployed to defend against attack from one direction (for instance from the north) are not now under one com-mander, which imposes serious practical limitations in day-to-day training and in our capability to conduct a properly coordinated air battle in the case of actual attack."[24]

Just a few weeks earlier, the US military had taken a step to address the nagging problem in the coordination of its own national air defences, which arose from the interservice division of missions between the air force, which was responsible for fighter aircraft and longer-range missiles, the army, with its shorter-range missiles, and the navy, which had radar picket ships provid-ing offshore warning. Particularly troubling were the disputes between the air force and army's air defence commands over how missiles and fighter inter-ceptors should be coordinated in the event an air defence battle ever had to be fought.

The answer then, as well, was a single commander. The Joint Chiefs of Staff sought to resolve the quarrel by pretty much putting the air force in charge, giving the commander of USAF Air Defense Command additional responsibilities as commander-in-chief of a newly-created, joint Continental Air Defense Command (CONAD), with authority over the air defence efforts of all three US services.

Unlike the usual US command arrangements, CONAD could control sub-ordinate units directly, and did not need to issue orders directly through the headquarters of the service air defence commands. As Partridge, who was CONAD's second commander-in-chief (CINCONAD), explained the arrange-ments to a Congressional committee: "The air defense procedures are so vitally concerned with the time of reaction that in Continental Air Defense opera-tions, the units of the Army, Navy, and Air Force are operated directly by me and my subordinate commanders. In other words, the Army, Navy and Air

Force provide the units for air defense purposes. But the actual control of the units in the air battle is a responsibility which I must carry out as Commander-in-Chief of the Continental Air Defense Command."[25]

As CINCONAD, Partridge had operational control over the various air defence units; command over them, however, remained with their services. CONAD's operational control included such authority as specifying states of air defence alerts, establishing battle procedures, and directing the tactical air battle, should one ever occur. It did not include such matters as training, discipline, or logistics. Those all fell under the right to command.

For the first two years of its existence, CONAD was little more than the USAF Air Defense Command using different stationery. Not only was the same air force general the head of both, the headquarters staffs were largely the same, with air force officers holding almost all the key positions. Not surprisingly, the army remained unhappy. The Joint Chiefs sought to meet its objections in 1956 by disentangling CONAD from USAF Air Defense Command, giving each command a separate staff. Partridge stayed with CONAD. Some additional positions at CONAD headquarters were also given to army and naval officers. All this certainly did not mean there was now complete harmony in Colorado Springs. "While the three services debated and feuded in CONAD, Canada joined the air defense equation."[26]

This new structure built around an overarching, joint air defence command operationally controlling the units of three service commands and staffed by personnel from all three was, in fact, one that RCAF Air Defence Command could fit into well, as a fourth. The distinction between operational control and command that had been worked out in CONAD could be especially useful. If the RCAF's air defence squadrons were placed under a larger bi-national, continental organization, command over them could still remain in entirely Canadian hands.

Making things still easier, the RCAF's command was the only Canadian candidate to be fitted in. The Royal Canadian Navy had no continental defence radar ships and thus no air defence organization. The army had established an Anti-Aircraft Command in 1949 and located its headquarters close to the RCAF's Air Defence Command in St. Hubert. But it was closed in 1954–55 when the Canadian military opted for the RCAF's concept of area air defence and concluded that the close-in point defences that the army's efforts would provide Canadian cities were of little value. The army got out of continental air defence. It closed its anti-aircraft gun batteries and was never equipped with Nike surface-to-air missiles.

The RCAF did not have any bombers, giving it a professional outlook that also fit in especially well at Colorado Springs. After the Second World War, it had been obliged to shed its hopes of holding on to a strategic bombing role and instead had concentrated on fighter aircraft with air defence as its prime combat mission. Air defence was politically attractive to post-war Liberal governments. As Desmond Morton put it: "It would be visible to the Americans, popular with Canadians, easy on manpower and, for those who saw warmongers behind every gun, explicitly defensive."[27] Although CONAD had been transformed into an interservice command, it was still dominated by USAF fighter pilots. So it was only natural that CONAD and the RCAF would see things eye to eye, and all the more so as North American air defence efforts grew more integrated in the mid 1950s. Ties were natural and easy. It may even be that USAF officers at CONAD welcomed their RCAF counterparts to Colorado Springs if not as out-and-out allies, then as a bit of relief from their struggles with their army colleagues over ground-to-air missiles.

Beginning in the winter of 1954–1955, the two air forces set about to bring all of North American air defence under a single commander.[28] There was from the start considerable skepticism outside of Colorado Springs, especially from the military in Washington and civilians in Ottawa. The Joint Chiefs of Staff were not, at the outset, inclined to go along. While military-to-military relations with Canada were largely fine, from the perspective of the US military defence cooperation since the Second World War had not always gone as smoothly once the Canadian diplomats and politicians got involved. Although a common air defence command might be militarily a good idea, who knew what would happen once those same Canadian civilians got their hands on it? Might they not attempt to put limitations on its effectiveness? "Our experience in military planning with the Canadians," the Joint Chiefs of Staff wrote US Secretary of Defense Wilson in 1954, "has been that the Canadian military planners are unable to arrive at negotiated positions without agreement on a governmental level. A combined US–Canadian command would in all probability be equally restricted on the Canadian side." Therefore, any such command "would not seem sufficiently effective to warrant the expense in money and personnel involved." Still worse, the Canadians were well-known NATO enthusiasts and might try to subordinate a Canada–US command to it. That sort of thing, the Joint Chiefs of Staff warned Wilson, "might impose upon continental US defenses restrictions which would be militarily unacceptable."[29]

The St. Laurent government seemed no more enthusiastic about the idea than the US Chiefs. This was apparent in early 1955 when the chief of the air staff, Air Marshal C. Roy Slemon, apparently thinking he was speaking off the record at a Montreal gathering, wound up being quoted in the news to the effect that a Canada–US air defence command was "inevitable." Both Ralph Campney, the minister of national defence, and the chairman of the US Joint Chiefs of Staff promptly repudiated him in public.[30]

Nonetheless, the two air forces pressed on. This included misleading the Canadian government using the close ties that had grown up between the RCAF and Colorado Springs. The RCAF passed a message on to CONAD that the Canadian Chiefs were prepared to support a joint command, but because of political sensitivities in Canada they could not initiate the issue. If, however, the proposal were presented to the Canadian government as an American one in origin, they would be in a much stronger position to lend it their support. Partridge responded to the RCAF's proposal by enlisting the chief of staff of the USAF to convince the JCS to change their minds and allow the issue to be taken up with Ottawa. As a result, the US Chiefs concluded in late 1955 that "operational integration" of the Canadian and US air defence systems was desirable and should be proposed to the Canadians. But not a command, because "a combined Canada–US command is probably not acceptable to the Canadians at this time and should not be proposed."[31]

As a solution it was both ingenious, and far from forthright. If a combined command was something that might be difficult for Canadian civilians to accept – or, still worse, something that they might accept but whose military effectiveness they might try to hamper with political restrictions – there was no real reason to bring it up. What mattered was being able to use all of the continent's air defence resources rationally, as part of a single battle plan. It should, therefore, be possible to devise some sort of bi-national entity that would have operational control over the air defence forces of the two countries capable of operating with a minimum of delay without actually having to call it a command. The two militaries could set up such an entity themselves. To be sure, they both would need approval of their political masters. But since there was to be no command, there was no need for a formal agreement involving the diplomats.

All that remained was to work out some kind of arrangement for operational integration that avoided the creation of a formal command. A joint military study group was created and set to work. It provided the solution a year later, suggesting that operational integration should depend neither on a command nor an organization but on a person – a commander – to whom authority would be given to exercise operational control over all continental air defence forces.[32] The title it suggested for him was, "Commander-in-Chief, Air Defense Canada–United States" (CINCADCANUS). CINCADCANUS, the study group further recommended, should report directly to the US and Canadian Chiefs. There should be a deputy CINCADCANUS who would not be of the same nationality, meaning, in practice, a Canadian. CINCADCANUS should be supported by what was variously called in the report a headquarters or a staff – never a command. His chief tasks, exercised under the rubric of operational control, would be to provide for "the authoritative and timely employment of weapons, and to effect immediate reinforcement between commanders, regardless of nationality." The RCAF and US armed forces would retain command over their air defence commands and forces.

It was never in doubt, of course, who CINCADCANUS would be. The study group's report just made it more formal in recommending that CINCONAD don a new hat as CINCADCANUS. The CINCADCANUS staff, headquarters, or whatever it was to be except a command, would be built upon the CONAD structure already in place. Canadians, chief among them deputy CINCADANUS, would take places alongside the US air force, army, and navy personnel already in Colorado Springs. To the US air defence forces already being operationally controlled there, would be added the nine squadrons of the RCAF Air Defence Command, which would become the fourth command under its authority. To be sure, there were plenty of details still undetermined, especially since no formal Canada–US agreement was going to be signed. But these could all be worked out, it was assumed, once the new arrangements were in place. CINCADCANUS and his deputy would make some of the necessary decisions about their working arrangements themselves once they took up their new posts and submit others to the US and Canadian Chiefs.

In early 1957, the CINCADCANUS proposal was approved by the US Chiefs, the Canadian Chiefs and Secretary Wilson. Both Campney and Foulkes sent word to Washington that final approval by the St. Laurent government was soon expected at a meeting of the Cabinet Defence Committee scheduled for March. The issue never reached the committee, though. A general election had been scheduled for June and the Liberals had removed it from the committee's agenda.

When the Conservatives under Diefenbaker won the election unexpectedly, Foulkes pressed the outgoing Liberal government hard to approve the arrangements before it left office, thoroughly overemphasizing their urgency. The arrangements, he told Campney, constituted "an almost completed international agreement." Failure to approve them "would cause some doubts as to whether international agreements with Canada had continued validity," and might "bring about a serious deterioration in Canada–US military relations."[33]

When that did not work, Foulkes turned to the incoming government just as soon as it took office and pressed even harder. As he put it himself several years later, "unfortunately, – I am afraid – we stampeded the incoming government with the NORAD agreement."[34] At the time, of course, it was still the CINCADCANUS accord. In presenting it to the new prime minister and his defence minister, he minimized the political significance. Foulkes briefed Pearkes, stressing that the establishment of CINCADCANUS was just another step on the path of military cooperation upon which Canada and the US had set foot at the start of the Cold War. He argued that because the Liberals were about to approve the agreement when the election intervened, they could not oppose them.[35] When Pearkes was unable at first to obtain the prime minister's approval, Foulkes tried again, sending him a memo arguing that operational integration and the establishment of a new headquarters were just "further measures" in Canada–US air defence cooperation, allowing the two militaries to execute the already "agreed concept" of air defence and to improve upon "present arrangements."[36]

Pearkes was soon able to obtain Diefenbaker's approval. As Foulkes later recalled: "That afternoon, Pearkes took the paper with him up to the prime minister's office and he came back about an hour afterward and walked into my office, threw it onto my desk and said, 'There it is, approved.' I was stunned."[37] The further endorsement was sought of neither the Cabinet Defence Committee (which had not yet been constituted) nor the full Cabinet, except for an order-in-council appointing Slemon as deputy commander at the new headquarters and setting his salary. Although Diefenbaker was acting secretary of state for external affairs, he did not consult with officials of the Department of External Affairs before giving his approval and as will be discussed below, Foulkes left out that department's recommendations in his approach to Pearkes and Diefenbaker.

Pearkes and Wilson issued a press release on 1 August 1957 announcing the new arrangement. This brief statement explained that "as a further step" in defence cooperation, the two countries had agreed to a system of integrated operational control for their air defences. Command of those forces would remain in national hands. In a bow to reality, or perhaps just a slip, there was a reference to "an integrated command," although the terms "integrated headquarters" and "joint headquarters" were also used.[38]

The announcement left out the term "CINCADCANUS" entirely, the title of the new commander and his headquarters being unspecified. That was almost certainly no slip. That title had been an odd choice. Not only was it awkward, but its last four letters were also most unfortunate. Partridge certainly did not want to be called by it and recommended to the US and Canadian Chiefs in August that it be abandoned. He also pointed out that since, realistically viewed, what was in effect a new bi-national air defence command would be coming into existence within a few weeks, it might as well be called as such. He suggested "the *North American Air Defense Command*, abbreviated NORAD."[39] Both sets of Chiefs concurred. With political approval from Washington and Ottawa now in hand, and with the arrangements now safely in military-to-military channels and apparently beyond the reach of interfering Canadian civilians, the notion of the commander without a command could now be safely dropped.

NORAD, CONAD, AND THE CANADIANS, 1957–58

When NORAD stood up in September, Partridge became both CINCONAD and CINCNORAD. Slemon had just arrived to become DCINCNORAD.

Partridge applied two principles during 1957 and 1958 while setting up the newer command: giving priority to NORAD over CONAD, and integrating the Canadians fully into NORAD.

Partridge went so far at first as to propose in October 1957 to the Joint Chiefs of Staff that CONAD be disestablished entirely, leaving just NORAD.[40] This proposal produced considerable disagreement among the Chiefs. Not until January 1958 were they able to respond that a "national commander responsible to the US JCS for purely national matters" would still be needed. These "purely national matters," they told him, included air defence relations with Mexico and providing air defence for US defence installations in Greenland; the Canadian government had no interest in these relatively minor questions. They also included "the necessity of national channels for transmittal of certain classified material concerning purely national matters."[41] This cryptic formulation almost certainly referred to intelligence material that could not be shared with Canadians and information about the US defences, especially nuclear weapons, which similarly was not supposed to be shared.

An air defence commander did not necessarily need a full command, as the CINCADCANUS proposal had demonstrated. That concept might also be applied to the "national commander" the US Chiefs wanted to maintain. Partridge instructed his staff to prepare plans to replace CONAD not with a command, but with something he proposed to call "United States Forces NORAD."[42] The idea went nowhere, though, because the US Chiefs, responding to new defence legislation intended to strengthen the US command structure, decided that CONAD should be retained alongside NORAD. Therefore, parallel to the authority given NORAD to operationally control all US and Canadian continental air defence forces, CONAD was given in 1958 "operational command" (the term used in the new defence legislation) over all US continental air defence forces.

Partridge responded in late 1958 with a plan for single, fully integrated NORAD/CONAD headquarters. Its key provision was that there were to be no separate CONAD structures. Rather, when a CONAD, i.e. entirely US, matter came up, US personnel in the appropriate part of the NORAD/CONAD headquarters would handle it. These CONAD issues were not expected to be extensive. "NORAD will be predominant," Partridge told the JCS.[43] The chief of staff of the US Air Force, General Thomas D. White, shared this assessment. In a memo to the Chiefs on what he called "the peculiar status of NORAD and CONAD," he emphasized that operational control of continental air defence rested with NORAD. CONAD would be an operational command "only in the highly unlikely contingency of NORAD failure or dissolution." CONAD had become, therefore, "little more than an administrative convenience for US affairs which cannot properly be conducted by CINCNORAD."[44]

Canada, for its part, had no need to make equivalent provisions for a national commander at Colorado Springs because it needed no joint, (army, navy, air force) air defence command the way the US did. Inasmuch as Canada's sole air defence force was the RCAF, Canadian national command could be exercised, when necessary, through the RCAF Air Defence Command at St. Hubert.

Slemon later said that he had been surprised that "although we were a little partner making a relatively small contribution to the operational capability of the joint effort, our views were considered in exactly the same light as our partners, the Americans." Perhaps he was exaggerating somewhat. Nonetheless, it is clear that right from the start, Partridge placed Canadians in several key positions in the new command. These included deputy chief of staff for operations, a position Slemon saw as "the guts of our joint effort."[45]

Slemon's successor in Ottawa as chief of the air staff, Air Marshal Hugh Campbell, was also pleased with the NORAD headquarters arrangements. "The allocation to Canada of some of the key senior positions in the Headquarters is particularly advantageous since the incumbents can personally monitor and guard Canadian interests while, at the same time, they gain experience of future value to the RCAF," he wrote Foulkes in a 1958 report on developments at Colorado Spring. He also pointed out the good deal Canada seemed to be getting financially. Its contribution to NORAD headquarters consisted of 44 personnel (29 officers, 10 other ranks and four civilians). The Canadian officers constituted about 14 percent of those overall. That wasn't bad at all for a junior partner, especially considering that they were all within the headquarters itself. NORAD was hosted at Ent Air Force Base, which provided support services. These included, in Campbell's compendium, "the operation of a sizeable and expensive motor pool, aircraft pool and all the usual base facilities, including the officers' and other ranks' messes, hospital and dental clinic, base exchange, commissary, library, chapels, supply and maintenance section, security services, printing plant, etc." Fortunately, "to date there has been no suggestion that Canada should share in this rather large overhead and is consequently being treated very lightly in relation to what might be considered a more equitable share of the load in this respect."[46]

The cornerstone of Canada's new role in Colorado Springs was the DCINCNORAD position. Slemon was there not merely to represent Canadians' views at the highest levels in Colorado Springs and to report back to Ottawa on development in US air defence planning and operations. Nor was he there just to assist and advise CINCNORAD. In the CINC's absence, command would pass to him. That had been the understanding in the discussions leading up to NORAD's creation and it was later codified in the 1958 agreement. In the event of an attack he might be the one to issue the warning to

SAC and to Washington and the one to conduct the air battle. Partridge was determined that his DCINC be fully in a position to do so, using all the continental air defence resources available, despite even the tricky restrictions surrounding US nuclear air defence weapons.

Several savvy Canadian journalists, including James Minifie, who later published a book, *Peacekeeping or Powdermonkey*, that was highly critical of Canadian participation in NORAD, spotted in 1958 the potential flaw in the notion that Slemon could simply take over from Partridge in his absence. There were well-known legal restrictions in the US on providing information about nuclear weapons to foreigners. Wouldn't these extend to Canadians? It was obvious that Partridge had already received authority to use nuclear air defence weapons in an emergency. He had said so himself in an interview on the occasion of his becoming CINCNORAD. "[T]he President," he said in response to a question specifically about the MB-1, "has given his approval to use, without reference to anybody, any weapon at our disposal if there is a hostile aircraft in the system." Pressed on whether he needed to contact Washington, he responded, "No. We probably would be on the phone talking to people when the thing went off." [47] What would happen when he wasn't there? Could it really be that the Canadian deputy commander could order the use of nuclear weapons in US airspace?

The Pentagon tried to put the Canadian journalists off by releasing the brief statement that "Air Marshal Slemon, in accordance with agreement [sic] with the Canadians is Deputy Commander-in-Chief of NORAD, and in the absence of the Commander-in-Chief exercises all prerogatives of command in the event of war or any other time. This includes the use of nuclear weapons when authorized by the President."[48] This still did not answer the question of whether Slemon could employ the authority that Partridge apparently already had to order the use of nuclear air defence weapons. But the US government had no intention at the time of releasing further details either to the press or, for that matter, to any Canadian outside of Colorado Springs. The State Department decided not to tell the Department of External Affairs what the exact arrangements were and Slemon was not passing on such details to that department, either.[49]

The reality was that Slemon's position in the NORAD/CONAD command structure was paradoxical with respect to ordering the use of these weapons. While his legal authority was limited, his authority in practice would be great. President Eisenhower had, in fact, authorized the use of nuclear air defence weapons in 1956 and had "predelegated" further authority over them to CONAD.[50] NORAD had received no such predelegation authority upon its creation the next year, and would receive none until 1964. This indicates that only Partridge as CINCONAD (or in his absence, another US officer at CONAD) could authorize use; Slemon as DCINCNORAD could not.

However, State Department documentation also indicates that Partridge had further "delegated down" his authority to the several air defence division commanders in the US.[51] Moreover, the Pentagon, acting to implement the president's predelegation order, had set broad conditions for the use of nuclear air defence weapons. They "gave American air defense forces wide latitude to intercept and engage any 'hostile' Soviet aircraft, in large part due to the fact that they needed to be flexible to guide interceptor pilots in an encounter with a single Soviet aircraft or hundreds. Consequently, the predelegated authority could be exercised in minor incidents with hostile Soviet aircraft as well as in major attacks."[52] Slemon could declare an air defence emergency, which was one of the conditions under which US commanders could draw upon the predelgated authority and use the weapons.

The administration and US military wanted to make sure there were enough fingers on the trigger when it came to continental air defence nuclear weapons. They worried about a Soviet surprise attack, hence the predelegation. They believed that the MB-1s, with their high lethality, could make a significant contribution to limiting the effective scope of a Soviet attack. And they knew that the use of the continental MB-1s (and later, nuclear warheads on surface-to-air missiles) should not be seen by the Soviets as a hostile or escalatory act, inasmuch as they only could be used in North American airspace. In short, if Slemon could not legally authorize the use of nuclear weapons to destroy Soviet bombers, there was plenty of such authority elsewhere within the US air defence system to do so, as well as plenty of willingness. Should he ever have to conduct an air defence, he could count on the nuclear weapons being at his disposal.

That meant Slemon had to know about their capabilities, including such matters as their yield and radius of effect for weapon kill, even though such knowledge was supposed to be limited to Americans. He explained how this problem was solved, three months after he had arrived at Colorado Springs:

Pat Partridge got hold of me. He said, Roy, I'm supposed to be the Commander in Chief of NORAD and you're supposed to be the Deputy Commander in Chief. When I go out on a trip, inspecting units or go away to have a little fun, you have the responsibility and the authority. I can't go away on these trips and have any peace of mind because you don't know what the hell goes on with respect to the weapons. So, as of this minute, you are privy to all that is necessary with respect to the nuclear weapons. He never referred that to Headquarters or anyone. He made the decision right then and there and the word was passed on. I got a concentrated education on all these weapons from the staff and so on. He was never rebuked by his superiors and that guy took it on. It could have cost him his commission, because the security on those weapons is top.[53]

Arrangements were made in 1959 to give Canadians at NORAD official access to information about nuclear air defence weapons. Still, General Laurence S. Kuter, who became CINCNORAD in August 1959, later said that he, too, broke the law in continuing to give Slemon such information.[54]

THE 1958 NORAD AGREEMENT AND ITS SECRET COUNTERPART

In May 1957, while still only CINCONAD, Partridge had seen a weakness in the plan to integrate the Canadians and their air defences fully into the proposed new North American air defence arrangement: they might be withdrawn by their government at a critical moment. As he pointed out to the JCS, the discussions between the US and Canadian military establishments had been predicated on the assumption that an attack on either country would automatically involve the other. That assumption, though, "has not been recognized in any formal agreement between the two countries." It would be "intolerable," he said, "for either country to withdraw its forces or to make other than a maximum effort" in the event of an air defence emergency. So, he felt, "it is imperative that there be a binding agreement between the governments of the two countries recognizing the indivisible nature of the air defense of North America."[55] The US Chiefs told him to forget about it; a formal, more extensive agreement was unnecessary.[56] Things were under control. The military was working things out at the top. A formal agreement would only bring the Canadian civilians with their complications into the picture.

It certainly is hard to see how an international agreement locking Canadian forces irrevocably into bi-national operational control, as Partridge hoped, could ever be acceptable to Ottawa. But he had undoubtedly put his finger on a potential problem in Canada–US air defence cooperation. Government-to-government consultation in an emergency might be a way to help address it. The diplomats, especially the Canadians, had been quite interested in this possibility.

Just as Partridge had been shushed by the US Chiefs when he brought up the idea of a more formal agreement, when the Department of External Affairs championed that same issue later in 1957 it was sidelined by the Canadian Chiefs, or at least by Foulkes, their chairman. Separately from the military-to-military discussions over operational integration that had led to the CINCADCANUS proposal, Canadian diplomats had been trying since 1955 to reach an exchange of diplomatic notes with the State Department over political consultation between Washington and Ottawa in the event either believed that the chance of a Soviet bomber attack on North America was so high that the continental air defences needed to be put on alert. While progress was slow, the US was not unreceptive to the Canadian initiative, for Partridge was not the only US official who worried about what it might mean for air defence if Canada did not follow the US lead in a crisis. In 1956, the State Department wrote A.D.P. Heeney, Canadian ambassador in Washington: "our Government has independently been concerned with the problem of synchronization of alert measures in the face of compelling emergency, particularly in view of modern developments in warfare. The Canadian Government's parallel interest in this regard is, therefore, fully appreciated."[57]

If the Soviets attacked North America out of the blue, there obviously would be no time for much consultation, if any, between Ottawa and Washington. Under those circumstances, the air defence commands would simply issue the warning, alert their air defence forces on their own, and try to limit the damage. But it was unlikely that a nuclear war would begin that way. Likelier was a crisis with the Soviets, especially in Europe, that escalated into the use of nuclear weapons. In that event, there probably would be time. Decisions would have to be reached in both countries. Consultation could be useful in dealing with practical matters, such as alerting the civil defence systems of both countries at the same moment and, if possible, explaining the crisis to the publics in similar terms. Because Canada would be highly dependent on US information and intelligence sources, formal consultation through high-level channels, both military and diplomatic, could give Ottawa a better understanding of the overall international situation. It might also get a much better indication of what the US government was going to do.

All this ultimately would allow the Canadian government to make an informed judgment over whether to allow the Canadian air defences to go on alert, a sovereign right it would retain even under the NORAD arrangements, to the worry of General Partridge and others. Putting the air defences on alert would not necessarily be only a practical matter of self-defence. It could be seen by the Soviets as a signal. It could also be one of the last steps before the US launched a nuclear attack on the Soviet Union. Ottawa would want to make its own decisions. Washington would want Canadian defences on alert. The potential tension, already existing before NORAD was created, was built into it.

Canadian diplomats also hoped that agreed-upon bilateral consultation procedures would guarantee Ottawa special access with which it could to try to influence US decision making during the course of a grave crisis – perhaps up to and including a decision on the part of the US to use strategic nuclear weapons. "[A]s a leading member of NATO, Canada felt obligated to contribute where it could to the American deterrent, on which Western security depended. Nevertheless, Ottawa was determined that its alliance with Washington should not drag it into an atomic war without adequate consultation."[58] Ever since Harry S. Truman had said in an offhand remark that he would not rule out the use of atomic weapons in the Korean War, Canadian officials had worried. The Eisenhower administration's "massive retaliation" nuclear strategy made them worry even more.

When the CINCADCANUS proposals came to the fore with the St. Laurent government still in office, External Affairs argued that reaching a diplomatic agreement, emphasizing consultation, was still important. The CINCADCANUS and political consultation proposals had emerged from separate channels, the one military, the other diplomatic; it is not clear how External Affairs hoped to see them linked at that point, whether there should be one or two agreements, or whether a formal agreement on consultation would make an informal one on operational integration feasible. In any event, when Foulkes went to the newly elected Conservatives, the documents he took with him left out both political consultation and any need for a diplomatic agreement. All that was left for Diefenbaker to approve was an informal agreement on operational integration.

Diefenbaker later denied in his memoirs that Foulkes had stampeded him and that he had failed to grasp NORAD's importance right away.[59] But Basil Robinson, his foreign policy assistant at the time, was not so sure about this. In his own memoir of his service with the prime minister, he wrote: "How fully Diefenbaker understood what was proposed is not clear. He had been in office for only two weeks and had not received any detailed explanation." Robinson saw Foulkes' suppression of the importance of political consultation as having especially handicapped Diefenbaker. "Had the prime minister's attention been drawn to that issue, it would have helped him to appreciate the political advantage of using the air defence agreement to obtain a formal undertaking on consultation from the United States." Still, Robinson admitted, Diefenbaker may himself have thought that a formal agreement was unnecessary or would come later. "Whatever the explanation, it is strange that he failed to realize that issues of policy broader than military cooperation alone would have to be addressed immediately, and that, if this were not taken care of, the Liberal opposition, so recently in office, would be well placed to ask some awkward questions. NORAD might have started life somewhat later, but its birth would have been less painful."[60]

Even after NORAD was up and running in September, the Department of External Affairs pressed hard, over Foulkes' ongoing objection, for a diplomatic agreement formalizing it. This was a "matter of orderly practice" it argued. Moreover, it claimed, because of the new command's historic importance, it would be desirable to record formally the reason for its creation; this would be especially useful in answering questions in the House of Commons. And there remained, of course, the department's obsession with consultation. "An exchange of intergovernmental notes would give us another formal opportunity to record US recognition of the need for adequate consultation with

Canadian authorities on matters which might lead to the alerting of the air defence system. ... Geography and our willingness to cooperate effectively in joint continental defence efforts give us a special right to demand that US consultation with Canada be adequate at all times."[61]

The department did not have to press very long, though, for, with parliament about to open, Diefenbaker was now fully aware of the political difficulties he could find himself in because of his quick, informal approval of an informal accord. He told President Eisenhower in October that he wanted a government-to-government agreement. Shortly thereafter, the State Department and Department of External Affairs began negotiations on diplomatic notes.

The opening of those negotiations afforded the Conservatives a splendid defence against opposition charges that they had lackadaisically walked into NORAD. Stretching the truth, Pearkes told the House of Commons in November that it had been "considered desirable that the two commanders should get together and work out the exact details of their relations before any more formal agreement should be made defining exactly the role of the two commanders in relation to the civil power and that note is now in the course of study."[62]

The Conservatives relied on several other defences during the fall session of parliament. First, they charged that the arrangements had all but been approved by the outgoing Liberals, making their own quick decision nothing more than a sort of tidying up. This drew the explicit and accurate denial from the Liberals that either the Cabinet Defence Committee or the full Cabinet had ever considered the matter formally. While Partridge had worried that he, as the bi-national commander, might have too little authority in a crisis over Canadian air defences, many Canadians worried that he might have too much. The Conservatives handled the issue by dodging and fudging, and giving confused and contradictory answers, avoiding any clear and direct statement that CINCNORAD could, in a swiftly developing emergency, take Canadian air defence forces into battle without first consulting the Canadian government.[63]

Diefenbaker also fabricated a close NORAD relationship with NATO. It was politically irresistible to him. Viewed as part of NATO, NORAD could be seen as no new or great departure in Canadian defence policy that the Conservatives had walked into. Nor was it, so viewed, just a bi-national command in which Canada might be overwhelmed by the US, but was rather part of the much larger, multilateral alliance to which Canada already was committed by treaty. The door for such argumentation had been opened by the Pearkes-Wilson announcement, which had ended with the innocuous statement: "This bilateral arrangement extends the mutual security objectives of the North Atlantic Treaty Organization to the air defense of the Canada–US Region."[64] Meanwhile, the Canadian Embassy in Washington had reported that the State Department was at least open to the idea of actually making NORAD a NATO command.[65] But the US military remained adamantly, intractably, opposed to letting the Europeans get anywhere near North American defence.

The Department of External Affairs sought to restrain the Conservatives from simply trying to bring NORAD under the NATO aegis through the power of their own rhetoric. "It will not be possible," the undersecretary of state for external affairs warned his minister, "for Canada unilaterally to declare that NORAD is a NATO command; United States agreement to this concept would be essential and … the United States military are not prepared to implement such a concept at the moment."[66]

Diefenbaker, ignoring such advice, went on to make just such a unilateral declaration. Upon his return to Ottawa from a December 1957 NATO heads of government meeting in Paris, he informed the Commons that he had told the Paris gathering "and it was accepted as a fact" that the NORAD arrangements were "an integral part of the NATO military structure in the Canada–US region. … The NATO council will have full reports on everything we do, similar to the practice followed in all other NATO commands."[67] The Liberal opposition received these assertions with incredulity.

The US Joint Chiefs of Staff were, predictably, infuriated by them. Here was the very reason they originally had been so dubious about integrating US and Canadian air defence operations and why they had proceeded with the notion of a commander-without-a-command: while the Canadian military could be trusted in a North American air defence command, their civilian masters would interfere intolerably. The US Chiefs approved the text of a stern message to Wilson and Ottawa. NORAD, it said, "was established through bilateral agreement;" it "is not and should not be a NATO organization." While the alliance might be provided with general information on North American air defences, the draft message also said, the JCS would not countenance its being sent any plans.[68]

Before the message could be sent, Foulkes rushed to call on the chairman of the JCS, General Nathan Twining in order to prevent a head-on clash between the US Chiefs and the Diefenbaker government. The Canadian Chiefs certainly did not intend trying to make NORAD a NATO command, Foulkes told Twining, or to change the essentially bilateral nature of NORAD in any way. All they needed to do (as Twining later paraphrased Foulkes in a report to the US Chiefs) was to be able to "advise their government that they are fulfilling NATO regional responsibilities in their arrangements with the US," whatever that might mean.[69] The US Chiefs calmed down. The Canadian Chiefs went on to approve, like their American counterparts, the terms of reference or instructions for CINCNORAD which, despite their length, did not mention NATO once. If these terms had been publicly released, they would have punctured Diefenbaker's claims. But they were classified.

The May 1958 NORAD exchange of diplomatic notes, on the other hand, was both released to the public and larded with various general references to NATO, which the Diefenbaker government could use to persist in its claim that there was a relationship of sorts between the two.[70] It did not help when the NATO secretary-general, Paul-Henri Spaak denied, during the course of a visit to Ottawa, that NORAD was part of NATO. Not long thereafter the prime minister himself "seemed as tired as everyone else of trying to make the connection."[71] That summer, Eisenhower also visited Ottawa, and no doubt stunned Diefenbaker during a conversation at 24 Sussex Drive in which, according to the US record, he "suggested that it might be possible to translate NORAD into a NATO command. ... The prime minister seemed interested but did not press the point."[72]

The agreement, which was to expire in ten years unless brought to an end earlier by mutual accord, also codified the most important NORAD arrangements already in place. CINCNORAD would be responsible to the two sets of Chiefs and would operate according to an air defence concept, and other plans and procedures, all to be approved by the two governments. He would have operational control over the forces allocated to him. It was defined as "the power to direct, coordinate and control the operational activities of forces assigned, attached or otherwise made available." Command would remain in national hands; it included administration, discipline, internal organization and unit training. He and other commanders having operational control could move air defence forces temporarily from one area to another including across the border, while only national authorities could order a permanent change of station. Both governments would appoint both CINCNORAD and his deputy, who could not be from the same country. During the CINC's absence, command would pass to the deputy. The two governments would make arrangements for funding NORAD headquarters. CINCNORAD would consult with the two governments and, if necessary, obtain their permission when releasing public information.[73]

These provisions and ultimately NORAD itself were not very controversial when the agreement was put to a vote in the House of Commons in June 1958. It sailed through; only the eight CCF members, with a "visceral distrust of American military power" voting against it.[74] At the start of the debate, Lester B. Pearson, then leader of the opposition, said: "it is important to try to keep the house united on these matters and on this particular issue of continental defence there should not be any division between the parties. Indeed perhaps there would not have been any necessity for a debate of this kind if we had heard many months ago the kind of detailed statement about what NORAD meant and the arrangements that were being made under NORAD that we received this afternoon."[75]

Of course there was also a consultation pledge in the agreement. It was to be found in a single sentence which read: "The two Governments consider that the establishment of integrated air defence arrangements of the nature described increases the importance of the fullest possible consultation between the two Governments on all matters affecting the joint defence of North America, and that defence cooperation between them can be worked out on a mutually satisfactory basis only if such consultation is regularly and consistently undertaken."[76]

This broad and public dose of diplomatic language went hand-in-hand with a somewhat more specific pledge in a secret exchange of diplomatic notes between Ottawa and Washington on consultation that was reached later in 1958, bringing to fruition the negotiations between the Department of External Affairs and the State Department that had been underway for three years. The operative clause read:

> In a situation in which either Government concludes that alert measures are necessary or desirable, both in the USA and Canada, the two Governments agree to consult through the diplomatic channel and through the respective Chiefs of Staff of the two countries. Such consultation will precede the institution of alert measures by either Government except in the following extreme circumstances: if either Government considers an attack on North America to be imminent or probable in a matter of hours rather than days, consultation might, of necessity coincide or even follow the institution of separate alert measures by either Government. If either government is impelled by the time factor to take alert measures before initiating consultation, it agrees immediately to inform the other Government of the action taken and to consult with the other Government as soon as possible.[77]

The two pledges could be taken as a strong indication that in an emergency Ottawa would have Washington's attention. Ironically, Foulkes later firmly expressed this expectation, writing in 1961, that "as we are full partners in the defence of North America, we have to be consulted every time the US contemplates using force anywhere in the world."[78] But just as ironically, at the Department of External Affairs the primary authors of these consultation pledges had known better at the time. As they admitted in September 1957, "paper agreements will mean little unless there is a climate of opinion created in Washington's official circles which would ensure an almost automatic consultation with Canadian authorities on all matters affecting the continental air defence system."[79]

NOTES

[1] US Cong., House, Committee on Armed Services, Hearings, *To Authorize Certain Construction at Military and Naval Installations,* 83rd Cong. 2nd Sess., April 1954. 5151.

[2] *History, Air Defense Command, Jul-Dec, 1953.* Quoted in Kenneth Schaffel, *The Emerging Shield: The Air Force and the Evolution of Continental Air Defence, 1945–1960* (Washington: Office of Air Force History, US Air Force, 1991), 235.

[3] George Lindsey, "The Summer Study on Air Defence at Project Lincoln," September 1952. Quoted in Andrew Richter, *Avoiding Armageddon: Canadian Military Strategy and Nuclear Weapons, 1950–63* (Vancouver: UBC Press, 2002), 41.

[4] D. Arty, "Review of Air Defence," 14 October 1958. Department of National Defence, Directorate of History and Heritage, 112.1.003 (D14).

[5] For a complete discussion see Chapter 4, "The DEW and Mid-Canada Lines," in Joseph T. Jockel, *No Boundaries Upstairs: Canada, the United States and the Origins of North American Air Defence* (Vancouver: UBC Press, 1987).

[6] The details of these arrangements can be found in pages 50-58 of Jockel, *No Boundaries Upstairs* (see note 5).

[7] The text of the MB-1 agreement is to be found in *Documents on Canadian External Relations,* Vol. 23, 1956–57, Part II (Ottawa: Department of Foreign Affairs and International Trade, 2002), 77-78. See also Chapter 2, "Genies over Canada," in John Clearwater, *US Nuclear Weapons in Canada* (Toronto: The Dundurn Group, 1999).

[8] Staff Notes No. 443, 22 October 1958. Eisenhower Presidential Library, Ann Whitman File. Copy in David Cox research papers.

[9] Robert J. Watson, *History of the Office of Secretary of Defense,* Vol IV, *Into the Missile Age 1956-1960* (Washington: Historical Office of the Secretary of Defense, 1997), 423.

[10] Schaffel, 239 (see note 2).

[11] Quoted in Watson, 409 (see note 9).

[12] Schaffel, 224 (see note 2).

[13] "Interview with Gen. Earle E. Partridge, Commander in Chief, North American Air Defense Command," *US News and World Report,* 6 September 1957, 72-85.

[14] Quoted in Schaffel, 215 (see note 2).

[15] Quoted in Fred Kaplan, *The Wizards of Armageddon* (New York: Simon and Shuster, 1983), 134.

[16] JCS 1899/373, "Statement of Policy on Continental Defense," 13 December 1957. National Archives, Record Group 218, Files of the Joint Chiefs of Staff, CCS 381 US (5-23-46), Section 99.

[17] Quoted in Hanson W. Baldwin, "Nuclear Repellants," *New York Times,* 28 January 1958.

[18] Quoted in Schaffel, 258 (see note 2).

[19] Letter, Foulkes to prime minister, 18 November 1957. Department of National Defence, Directorate of History and Heritage, Raymont fonds, 213/869.

[20] Foulkes, as paraphrased in "Report by the Joint Planning Committee to the Chiefs of Staff Committee on the Review of Air Defence Against the Manned Bomber Threat," 14 May 1958. Department of National Defence, Directorate of History and Heritage, Raymont fonds, 58/1106.

[21] Letter, Foulkes to Brooke Claxton, 22 September 1955. Library and Archives Canada, R3306-0-1-E, Brooke Claxton papers, vol. 223.

[22] Richter, 69 (see note 3).

[23] Department of National Defence, *Canada's Defence Programme, 1956–57*, 3, 4.

[24] Quoted in "Seventeen Years of Air Defense," Historical Reference Paper no. 9, Directorate of Command History, Headquarters NORAD, 1 June 1963, 63.

[25] Quoted in Schaffel, 245 (see note 2).

[26] Schaffel, 246 (see note 2).

[27] Desmond Morton, *A Military History of Canada*, 4th Edition (Toronto: McClelland and Stewart, 1999), 240.

[28] For a more detailed discussion of engineering of NORAD by the air forces, 1954–1958 see Chapter 5, "The Creation of NORAD," in Jockel, *No Boundaries Upstairs*.

[29] Memorandum, JCS to secretary of defense, "Proposed North American Continental Defense Organization" approved in JCS 1541/94, 11 June 1954. Files of the Joint Chiefs of Staff; Freedom of Information Request.

[30] *Montreal Daily Star,* 7 June 1955 and House of Commons, *Debates*, 3 June 1955 IV, 4346-47.

[31] JCS 1541/102 5 December 1955, including "Report by the Chief of Staff, US Air Force, to the Joint Chiefs of Staff on a combined Canada–United States Air Defense Command," memo, Partridge to USAF chief of staff, 21 October 1955, memo USAF Headquarters to Partridge, 9 September 1955, and "Note to the Holders." National Archives, Record Group 218, Files of the Joint Chiefs of Staff, CCS 092 (9-10-45).

[32] "Integration of Operational Control of the Continental Air Defenses of Canada and the United States in Peacetime," appendix to "Eight Report of the Canada–US Military Study Group," 19 December 1956, which in turn is an appendix to JCS 1541/112, 25 February 1957, "A Memorandum by the Chief of Staff, US Air Force, on the Integration of Operational Control of the Continental Air Defenses of Canada and the United States in Peacetime." National Archives, Record Group 218, Files of the Joint Chiefs of Staff, CCS 092 (9-10-45) sec. 43.

[33] Aide-memoire, from Foulkes for Campney, 12 June 1957, "Integration of Operational Control of Canadian and Continental United States Air Defence Forces in Peacetime." Department of National Defence, Directorate of Heritage and History, Raymont fonds, 73/78.

[34] Foulkes testimony in House of Commons, Special Committee on Defence, *Minutes of Proceedings and Evidence*, 22 October 1963, 510.

[35] Reginald H. Roy, *For Most Conspicuous Bravery: A Biography of Major-General George R. Pearkes, V.C.* (Vancouver: University of British Columbia Press, 1977), 290. Jon B. McLin, *Canada's Changing Defense Policy* (Baltimore: The Johns Hopkins Press, 1967), 44-46.

[36] Aide-memoire, 23 July 1957, "Integration of Operational Control of Canadian and Continental US Air Forces in Peacetime." Department of National Defence, Directorage of Heritage and History, chief of the defence staff files, "Answers to questions on NORAD."

[37] Quoted in Roy, *For Most Conspicuous Bravery*, 289.

[38] *US Department of State Bulletin*, XXXVII, 19 August 1957, 306.

[39] Message CINCONAD to Chairman of the Joint Chiefs of Staff and Chairman, Canadian Chiefs of Staff. National Archives, Record Group 218, Files of the Joint Chiefs of Staff, CCS 092 (9-10-45) sec 44. Also *Seventeen Years of Air Defense*, 65.

[40] *CONAD and NORAD Historical Summary, July-December 1957*, 6. Directorate of Command History, Headquarters NORAD. Copy in NORAD/USNORTHCOM History office.

[41] JCS decision on JCS, 1541/132, 10 January 1958. National Archives, Record Group 218, Files of the Joint Chiefs of Staff, CCS 092 (9-1045).

[42] *NORAD and CONAD Historical Summary, July-December 1958,* Directorate of Command History, Headquarters NORAD/CONAD. Copy in NORAD/USNORTHCOM History office.

[43] Ibid.

[44] Memorandum by the chief of staff, US Air Force for the JCS on CINCNORAD and CINCONAD Relationship, JCS 1541/184, 3 March 1959. Quoted in David Cox, *Guarding North America: Aerospace Defense During the Cold War, 1957–1972.* NORAD Special Historical Study, n.d. Chapter 2.

[45] Quoted in Schaffel, 252-53 (see note 2).

[46] Memo, chief of the air staff to chairman, Chiefs of Staff, "NORAD Establishment," 5 March 1958. Department of National Defence, Directorate of History and Heritage, Raymont fonds, 58/1106.

[47] See note 13.

[48] As reported in a memorandum, Foulkes to minister of national defence, 12 June 1958. Department of National Defence, Directorate of History and Heritage, Raymont fonds, 6/87.

[49] State Department: Memo, Frederick W. Jandrey to Murphy, "Canadian Embassy Inquiry Regarding Article Entitled 'Air Defense Unit has No Atom Curb …'" 9 October 1958 and Memorandum, Porter to Dale, 13 October 1958. George Washington University, The National Security Archive, document 01343. The undersecretary of state for external affairs was told by his department that "We have no exact knowledge of what authorization CINCNORAD does have. A/M Slemon told Mr. Bryce earlier this year that CINCNORAD would in fact be able to use nuclear weapons

without the express authority of the President." Department of External Affairs, "Memorandum to the Under-secretary, Re: Acquisition of Defensive Nuclear Weapons by
Canada," 14 November 1958. Department of National Defence, Directorate of History and Heritage, Raymont fonds, 73/223 file 2509.

[50] The definitive article on this subject is Peter J. Roman, "Ike's Hair-Trigger: US
Nuclear Predelegation, 1953–60," *Security Studies* 7, No. 4 (Summer 1998), 121-64.

[51] Jandrey to Murphy (see note 49).

[52] Roman, 138-39 (see note 50).

[53] Text of interview with A/M Slemon, 20 October 1978. Department of National
Defence, Directorate of History and Heritage, 79/128.

[54] Circular memo from Department of Defense and Atomic Energy Commission,
Joint Atomic Information Exchange Group, "Transmittal of Fact Sheet to Canadian
staff at NORAD," 15 December 1959; text of USAF oral history interview with General Laurence Kuter. 1974. Copies of both in David Cox research papers.

[55] Memorandum, CINCONAD to chief of staff USAF (as JCS executive agent for
CONAD), 14 May 1957, reprinted as Appendix to JCS 2019/226, 6 June 1957, "Memorandum by the Chief of Staff, US Air Force to the Joint Chiefs of Staff on Air Defense
of Canada and the United States." National Archives, Record Group 218, Files of the
Joint Chiefs of Staff, CCS 381 (1-24-42) sec 74.

[56] SM-543-57 to CINCONAD, 24 July 1957. National Archives, Record Group
218, Files of the Joint Chiefs of Staff, CCS 381 (1-24-42) sec 74.

[57] Note, Robert Murphy, députy undersecretary of state to Heeney, 4 December
1956. Department of National Defence, Directorate of History and Heritage, Raymont
fonds, 217/992.

[58] Greg Donaghy, "Nukes and Spooks: Canada–US Intelligence Sharing and Nuclear Consultations, 1950–1958." Unpublished paper.

[59] John Diefenbaker, *One Canada: The Memoirs of the Right Honourable John G.
Diefenbaker,* Vol 3, *The Tumultuous Years, 1962-1967* (Toronto: Macmillan of Canada,
1977), 17-18.

[60] Basil Robinson, *Diefenbaker's World: A Populist in Foreign Affairs* (Toronto:
University of Toronto Press, 1989), 19-20.

[61] DEA Briefing paper "Meeting of Consultation, September 30, 1957." Foulkes
copy. Department of National Defence, Directorate of History and Heritage, 73/1223
file 2509.

[62] House of Commons, *Debates*, 4 November 1957 (1957–58) I, 702.

[63] For a good overview see McLin, 48-59 (see note 35).

[64] See note 38.

[65] Robertson to External Affairs, 6 November 1957, in J.L. Granatstein, *A Man of
Influence: Norman A. Robertson and Canadian Statement, 1929-68* (Ottawa: Denau,
1981), 317.

[66] Memorandum, Jules Léger to secretary of state for external affairs, 2 December 1957. Department of National Defence, Directorate of History and Heritage, chief of defence staff files, "Answers to Questions on NORAD file."

[67] House of Commons, *Debates,* 21 December 1957 (1957–58) III, 2721-22.

[68] JCS 1541/134, 25 February 1958, "Canadian View of NORAD as a NATO Organization," National Archives, Record Group 218, Files of the Joint Chiefs of Staff, CCS 092 (9-1045) sec 48.

[69] JCS 1541/139, 29 April 1958 "Memorandum by the Chairman of the Joint Chiefs of Staff for the Joint Chiefs of Staff on Canadian View of NORAD as a NATO Organization." National Archives, Record Group 218, Files of the Joint Chiefs of Staff, CCS 092 (9-1045) sec 49.

[70] "North American Air Defense Command: Agreement effected by Exchange of Notes," 12 May 1958 US *TIAS* 4031 (9 UST 538); *Canada Treaty Series* 1958, No. 39.

[71] Mclin, 55-56 (see note 35).

[72] "President's Trip to Canada." Memorandum of Conversation, 8 July 1958. Meeting at 24 Sussex. *Foreign Relations of the United States, 1958–1960,* Vol VII, Part 1 (Washington: USGPO, 1993), 692-94.

[73] See note 70.

[74] David Cox, *Canada and NORAD, 1958-1978: A Cautionary Retrospective* (Ottawa: The Canadian Centre for Arms Control and Disarmament, 1985), 18.

[75] House of Commons, *Debates,* 10 June 1958 (1958) I, 1000.

[76] See note 70.

[77] Note, Robert Murphy, deputy undersecretary of state to Heeney, 10 November 1958, copy in Department of National Defence, Directorate of History and Heritage, Raymont fonds, 217/992.

[78] Charles Foulkes, "Canadian Defence Policy in a Nuclear Age," *Behind the Headlines* 21, No. 1 (May 1961), 12.

[79] See note 61.

CHAPTER TWO

AIR TURBULENCE, 1958–1968

ARROW, BOMARC, SAGE, AND VOODOO

A month after NORAD stood up in Colorado Springs, the roll-out ceremony for the CF-105 Arrow supersonic interceptor was held at the AVRO plant in Malton, Ontario. The two events had seemed to go hand in hand. "The Arrow was an assurance that Canada, traditionally one of the most air-minded nations in the world, would do more than simply hold its end up in the NORAD compact. It would provide NORAD not only with a highly qualified Deputy Commander and the support of a strong RCAF, but also with an aircraft that gave promise of being the finest, most sophisticated interceptor in the world."[1] A year and a half later, the Arrow was cancelled by the Diefenbaker government, throwing Canadian air defence planning into disarray and leaving the RCAF to wonder whether its influential role in NORAD might be short-lived.

Diefenbaker had an excellent reason to cancel the Arrow: it would cost far too much. When it was first being planned as the replacement for the subsonic CF-100, only its airframe was to be developed in Canada. The engine, air-to-air missile, and fire control system were all to be bought "off the shelf" elsewhere. For a variety of reasons, a switch had to be made to developing the engine and air-to-air missile in Canada, and to providing Canadian funding for the development of a fire control system in New Jersey, all at greater cost. Meanwhile, the number of aircraft to be acquired dropped sharply from well over 400 to just over 100, driving the price per unit up sharply. The original plan had been to equip all nine regular air defence squadrons with Arrows, and to establish eleven auxiliary squadrons with them. When it was discovered that reserve pilots could not easily be trained to operate the CF-105, the auxiliary squadrons were dropped.

If CF-105s could be sold to the Americans or the British, the cost per aircraft could be driven back down. The government gave this a try and failed. In retrospect, the foreign sales attempt looks a little naïve, especially with respect to the US. To be sure, the USAF had, from time to time, made vague expressions of interest in the Arrow. Nonetheless, while the CF-105 may well have been the best interceptor in the world, the US aircraft industry was developing comparable supersonic interceptors of its own. "Any realist would understand that the American government would be subject to strong pressure to put its taxpayers' money into American-built aircraft."[2]

In 1958, the Canadian military leadership, having grown alarmed at the cost increases, was prepared to give up the Arrow in favour of a cheaper, US-made supersonic interceptor. Most of the Canadian Chiefs – not including the chief of the air staff – informed the government in August that they had "grave doubts" about proceeding with the project.[3] As Foulkes later explained that decision: "The Chiefs of Staff came to the conclusion that it did not make military sense to purchase aircraft at a cost of $8 million each when we could maintain aircraft with similar performance from the end of an American production line at something about $2 million."[4]

Taking their advice, Diefenbaker released a statement the next month announcing that the Arrow was under review, and that the SAGE system and Bomarc missiles would be added to Canada's defences. But he shied away from simply pointing to the aircraft's increased cost. He also claimed that it was obsolete in the face of the new threat to North America posed by ICBMs and the decline of the bomber threat. "The government has concluded," the statement said, "that missiles should be introduced into the Canadian air defence system and that the number of supersonic interceptor aircraft required for the RCAF air defence command will be substantially less than could have been foreseen a few years ago, *if in fact such aircraft will be required at all* in the 1960s in view of the rapid strides being made in missiles by both the US and USSR" (emphasis added).[5] This seemed to imply that the Bomarc, because it was a missile, was some kind of response to the ICBM. That was not true, of course; the Bomarc could only attack bombers.

More serious was Diefenbaker's assertion that air defence fighter aircraft might not be needed at all in a few years. Neither the US nor Canadian military believed this. To be sure, the still-expanding US air defence system was about to peak as the threat to North America shifted to ballistic missiles. As its official USAF historian put it, "With the ICBM heralding a new age in warfare, some observers in Congress and the Defense Department began to fear that funds spent on bomber defense were funds wasted."[6] In response to such skepticism, the US Defense Department devised in 1959 a new air defence master plan that cut back on planned improvements. The number of new Bomarc squadrons was reduced and a more austere SAGE program introduced. The most advanced supersonic interceptor under development, the F-108, was cancelled, and the number of interceptor squadrons began to fall. Nonetheless, other new supersonic interceptors continued to enter the US inventory.

The Department of National Defence saw a special role for the CF-105 in the defence of SAC, even as ICBMs became a threat. Its Defence Research Board worried in 1958 that a small, diversified surprise raid by the Soviets could destroy SAC on the ground. Such a raid would include advanced bombers attempting to sneak through the DEW and Pinetree/Permanent radars. Against them, the air defence needed better identification capabilities. "Improvement of present identification resources means provision of more and better supersonic armed identification aircraft. This is where a need for the CF-105 arises."[7] The board thought that fewer than 40 aircraft were needed though, which meant that the price per unit would be unbearably high. The RCAF agreed that improvement in identification at the edge of the air defence combat zone was needed. But it argued in 1959 for six squadrons of Arrows, totalling 72 aircraft, not counting replacements. Meanwhile, NORAD encouraged Canada to acquire nine squadrons.

The Canadian and US military's insistence on the importance of supersonic interceptors was made publicly quite clear for Canadians when Slemon, with Partridge standing next to him, issued a November 1958 public statement in Colorado Springs in reaction to the debate in Canada that had broken out upon Diefenbaker's September statement. A manned interceptor, he said, was an "unescapable requirement for as long as we can see."[8]

The case that the military continued to make both publicly and privately for a manned interceptor still did not stop Diefenbaker from reiterating in his February 1959 announcement of the cancellation of the Arrow that the interceptor had been made obsolete by the advent of ICBMs. As he put it, "the threat against which the CF-105 could be effective has not proved to be as serious as was forecast ... It is considered that the defence system of North America is adequate to meet this threat."[9]

Why did Diefenbaker feel twice compelled to offer a justification for the cancellation that would put him at odds with the Canadian military, not to mention put him in a position where he had to defend the deployment of the Bomarc and SAGE systems at the same time he was arguing that the bomber threat would soon be passing? He knew that the cancellation would deliver an all but fatal blow to the Canadian aircraft industry. Pressure on the government was enormous. The Arrow's supporters argued that the aircraft's high price was one worth paying in order to save jobs in the short run and the industry in the long run. Diefenbaker may have especially wanted to strengthen his case against such claims by arguing that not only was the cost too high, but the product of little use. "There is no purpose manufacturing horse collars when horses no longer exist," he said at another point in the debate.[10] Jon B. McLin, in his classic study of Diefenbaker's defence policies, offered a more complex explanation. He concluded that the prime minister could not bring himself to the "recognition, psychologically and politically difficult, that Canada could no longer pay the price which advancing technology exacted to remain a producer of the more sophisticated military equipment. Unwilling to recognize the loss of power and prestige involved, the politically sensitive Diefenbaker obscured the issue."[11]

The Chiefs of Staff, with the important exception of the head of the RCAF, had been with Diefenbaker on the Arrow's cancellation. Once that decision had been taken, both the military and the government had to consider whether to acquire a US-built interceptor. In his cancellation announcement, Diefenbaker said that "no decision" had been made and that the defence minister and the Chiefs were "engaged in further studies of the various alternatives for the improvement of our defences."[12] The Canadian Chiefs dutifully turned to the consideration of four options, all of which proceeded from the premise that new interceptors were needed at Canadian bases, whether or not they were operated by the RCAF:

(a) acquiring 100–150 US-built interceptors for the RCAF with which to replace the CF-100s;
(b) replacing the RCAF air defence squadrons across Canada with USAF ones;
(c) stocking bases across Canada so that the USAF squadrons could use them in an emergency; and
(d) having USAF aircraft on readiness at Canadian bases.

Pearkes and the Chiefs came to the quick conclusion that they could not support (b) and (d); "for both political and military reasons it was unacceptable to have US squadrons on Canadian bases."[13] Acquiring a new interceptor and stocking bases for the Americans, the remaining options, were complementary. While the deployment of US fighter aircraft in an emergency to Canada was a well established aspect of Canada–US planning, there was no prestocking for entire American squadrons.

The RCAF may well have worried that it was about to be hoisted upon its own NORAD petard. The close cooperation that had grown up between it and the USAF, culminating in NORAD, meant that options (b), (c), and (d), which would leave the RCAF without its own fighter aircraft, were not inconceivable. Diefenbaker might want to go for them. Yet they would undermine the RCAF's position at Colorado Springs. A horrified Air Marshal Hugh Campbell, chief of the air staff, wrote Pearkes that if the RCAF was left without its own interceptor, "Canada could no longer be a full partner in NORAD but would have to assume a much more junior position. It would be difficult to justify senior command positions. ... if Canada was not providing any effective weapons in the air defence system."[14]

The Canadian Chiefs were not alone in their opposition to giving up RCAF interceptors. Neither the USAF nor defence officials in Washington were at all eager to see the US squadrons completely replace Canadian ones at Canadian bases. They were quick to propose in late 1959 that 66 F-101 Voodoo supersonic interceptors, already ordered and budgeted for the USAF, be diverted instead to the RCAF. Because of their range and speed, the F-101s were especially suited to identify and attack bombers at the edge of the combat zone. The USAF would replace them for its own purposes with an inferior plane, the F-102, which it would deploy "deep down in the system." The US proposal initially went nowhere. "The reason," Slemon told Kuter, "is that it constitutes a major political headache, following as it does in the wake of cancellation by the government of the CF-105. ... Procurement now of US interceptors of roughly the same performance as the 'Arrow' would place the Canadian government in an embarrassing spot, regardless of the nature or extent of any US–Canada cost-sharing arrangement."[15]

With a bit of time, the embarrassment began to fade. More importantly, the new Kennedy administration presented an extremely attractive package to Ottawa in 1961, which replaced an earlier proposed arrangement whereby the Canada would buy the 66 Voodoos and the US would in return buy Canadian-made transport aircraft. The 1961 swap or "Triangular" agreement, as it was called, had three elements: The RCAF would be furnished with the 66 Voodos. In return, Canada would not pay cash but would take over sixteen Pinetree radars that had been operated by the US and assume financial responsibility for five more that were being manned by Canadians but paid for by the US. Finally, F-104 Starfighter aircraft were to be built in Canada and made available to European NATO allies, with the US paying two thirds of the cost and Canada the other third. Thus this single agreement solved the problem of a supersonic interceptor for the RCAF, decreased the US military presence on Canadian soil to the gratification of Canadians worried about sovereignty, and brought some new business to the Canadian aircraft industry that had been so badly battered by the Arrow cancellation.

As the RCAF was painfully aware, the 66 Voodoos were significantly fewer than both the 100–150 supersonic interceptors the military had last hoped for and the CF-100s that they would replace. RCAF headquarters warned Air Defence Command in 1962 that because the inventory was "only 66 ... our attrition must be held to the absolute minimum with no unnecessary risks taken such as operating from fields with inadequate facilities."[16] The aircraft were divided over five squadrons, a reduction from the nine with CF-100s. The broad geographic distribution of Canadian interceptor squadrons was not changed. One Voodoo squadron was located at Comox, the others in southeastern Canada, including one at Chatham, New Brunswick. NORAD proposed to the RCAF in 1959 that its fighter aircraft be spread across the country to fill in the gap on the prairies. Specifically, it suggested that Canadian interceptors be deployed to Namao, Saskatoon and Gimli. But the RCAF rejected the idea, saying that it would stick to the longstanding Canadian pattern in order "to concentrate our air defence forces to provide protection for our main industrial areas on the West Coast and in the East and to rely on US forces to provide protection across the Prairies and Western Ontario."[17]

Although the overall number of interceptors would fall, the capability of the Canadian air defence system would be significantly enhanced by the combination of CF-101s, Bomarcs and SAGE. Unlike the CF-100s they would replace, the CF-101s, like the Bomarcs, would take advantage of SAGE. To accommodate the extension of SAGE into Canada, NORAD established new air defence operational boundaries in 1961 (see Map 5). The one Canadian SAGE centre at North Bay, which was located in an underground complex opening in 1963, was given responsibility for controlling operations in a vast area named the Northern NORAD Region, covering all of the Northwest Territories and the Yukon, the northern parts of the prairie provinces, a small piece of Ontario, all of Quebec and all of Atlantic Canada, except for a small piece of New Brunswick on the Maine border. "Northern NORAD Region," a 1962 RCAF Air Defence Command Staff Paper said, "lies athwart the main avenue of approach for Soviet bombers. The weapons systems and control headquarters within these areas would stand in the way of enemy bomber forces attacking the continent. Indeed, they form the main, northern outer-defensive shield of North America."[18]

But its size was misleading. Fighter aircraft could only operate in the vicinity of the ground environment provided by CADIN/Pinetree radars in southern Canada. Most of the region was allocated to a Hudson Bay Sector, which was entirely without such radars and had been formed largely just to fill in the map. A similar decision had been made to form a Denver Sector in the centre of the continent, where no air defence was needed and where NORAD headquarters itself was located. Nonetheless, the Northern NORAD Region included much of what counted for the RCAF, namely four of the five CF-101s squadrons as well as the Canadian Bomarcs which were located at North Bay and La Macaza, Quebec, twenty-eight at each base. It also included the USAF air defence interceptors in Newfoundland and would soon be expanded to include northern Maine, where a USAF air defence squadron was located. As the map also shows, the rest of Canada was controlled from transborder regions and sectors headquartered in the US. These were commanded by USAF officers. RCAF officers were placed on the appropriate headquarters staff, just as USAF officers also served in the Northern NORAD headquarters. All the air defence regions with headquarters in the US were simultaneously designated CONAD regions which would allow US officers at

Colorado Springs to operationally command them outside of the NORAD structure if necessary and thus without the participation of their Canadian colleagues.

THE RELATIONSHIP GOES SOUR: NUCLEAR AIR DEFENCE WEAPONS IN CANADA

The Canadian and US military had every expectation in 1958 that the air defences in Canada soon would be equipped with nuclear weapons. On the agenda were MB-1 Genies for the US fighter interceptors at Goose Bay and Harmon Air Force Base, Newfoundland and for whichever advanced interceptor, Arrow or US-built, that the RCAF acquired; and nuclear warheads for the RCAF's Bomarcs, without which the missiles were useless.

To US officials, reaching an agreement with Canada on the Newfoundland interceptors at first seemed relatively easy. After all, Canada had just agreed to US interceptors carrying MB-1s flying into Canada in an emergency; equipping US interceptors already located there with them looked like a natural extension. Few practical difficulties were expected. Washington assumed that the weapons would remain entirely in US legal custody on the US-leased bases in the province where they would be protected by US forces. In recognition of Canadian sovereignty there would have to be joint responsibility for their use; this could be accommodated readily through agreed upon NORAD plans and procedures.

On the other hand, equipping Canadian fighter aircraft and Bomarcs at Canadian bases with the weapons looked trickier. However, the Eisenhower administration, which shared the military's expectations for the extension of nuclear air defence weapons into Canada, had a daring solution to the problem. President Eisenhower was prepared simply to turn them over to Canada, giving it legal custody as well as full authority to use them without having to seek any further permission from Americans. He approved a December 1958 National Security Council policy directive that held, "Whether or not the Canadians themselves request actual custody of and authority to use nuclear warheads, such custody and authority will be required for optimum effectiveness if we are to assure an operationally-ready and full effective continental defense posture."[19] The administration was willing to seek an amendment of the US Atomic Energy Act or a treaty with Canada to make this possible.

This striking decision was in line with two conclusions about continental defence the Eisenhower administrations recently had reached that were reiterated in the presidential decision. The first was that it was important to make sure that there were fingers on the trigger of nuclear air defence weapons. This consideration had led to the president's "predelegation" of authority to CONAD in 1956. In a sense, the president was now prepared to predelegate authority to Canada, as well. The National Security Council directive observed that "[t]he evolving threat to continental security and the exposed geographic position of Canada with regard to this threat, together with the complexity of existing and future weapon systems generate a requirement for reduced reaction time which can be met only if Canada has actual custody and authority to use the nuclear warheads in question ... In the case of any fast-reaching air defense missiles system, the utility of the weapons would be degraded if involved bilateral procedures delayed weapon launching."[20]

The second conclusion was that Canada–US defence ties were special: "our North American continental defense arrangements with Canada were established outside of the NATO structure; and the peculiarities of geography, the defense structure which we have established, the purely defensive role of the weapons under consideration, and the partnership of the United States and Canada in this defense undertaking, provide a reasonable and logical basis for according Canada a favored-nation status."[21] Washington had every reason to have confidence in its Canadian partner. The steady improvements in Canadian air defences and Canada–US air defence cooperation that had been authorized during the first part of the decade by the St. Laurent government had continued under the new Diefenbaker government, beginning with its swift and decisive action on NORAD and followed within a year by its approval of CADIN/Pinetree, SAGE, and Bomarc. There was no reason to expect major difficulties with it over nuclear air defence weapons.

The December 1958 decision was the high-water mark in Washington of continental defence relations. Cooperation with Ottawa in NORAD would never again be seen there as both so close and so important.

The Eisenhower administration's idea of simply turning the weapons over to Canada died quickly. The Canadian government did not want its own nuclear weapons. Diefenbaker told parliament in February 1959: "Believing that the spread of nuclear weapons at the independent disposal of individual states should be limited, we consider that it is expedient that ownership and custody of the nuclear warheads should remain with the United States."[22] With no clean transfer from the US to Canada, negotiations between the two over the weapons would have to be conducted in the complicated legal, political, and military thicket of joint responsibility. Practical ways would have to be found to reconcile US legal custody and ownership with Canadian sovereignty, affecting how the weapons would be stored, protected in storage, released for potential use, and used.

Still, there was yet no reason yet for Washington to believe that an agreement with Canada could not be reached. Every indication, including the rest of Diefenbaker's February remarks, was that the Canadian government was not unreceptive to nuclear air defence weapons in Canada. As Basil Robinson later recalled of the period, "the Diefenbaker government was consciously heading in the direction of acquiring nuclear weapons for its own forces, both in Canada and in Europe and of allowing US forces stationed at or using bases in Canada to store nuclear weapons and equipment on them. The questions for discussion with the Americans and the NATO authorities in 1958 and 1959 had mostly to do with the how and the when rather than with the whether or the why."[23]

The Diefenbaker government's attitude to defence was about to change radically, though. The first indication of this change was Ottawa's abrupt decision at the end of August 1959 to terminate Canadian participation in a long-planned NORAD air defence exercise called "Operation Skyhawk," which was to be held in October. In this extensive exercise, SAC bombers would attempt to penetrate the NORAD air defence as if they were Soviet, necessitating the closing of all civil air traffic in North America for several hours. The Canadian withdrawal meant that it could not be held. Frantic diplomatic efforts on the part of Washington, including a personal appeal to Diefenbaker from Eisenhower, were of no avail. The US government was left frustrated, puzzled (especially since Canadian officials had participated in the planning for "Skyhawk"), and greatly irritated.

Diefenbaker's new secretary of state for external affairs, his good friend Howard Green who had been appointed in June, was the decisive voice in arguing for withdrawal from the exercise. Green was able to convince the cabinet that "Operation Skyhawk" was needlessly provocative to the Soviets, especially on the eve of a visit to the US by the Soviet leader, Nikita Khrushchev, a conviction from which it could not be budged even by Eisenhower's assurance, "I do not myself see anything provocative in such a defensive exercise and from the point of view of my coming talks with Mr. Khrushchev, [it] should have no adverse effect."[24]

Green was deeply worried about Cold War tensions, skeptical about nuclear deterrence, and committed to nuclear non-proliferation and disarmament. As McLin summarized his outlook:

[S]ince there was little enough that Canada could do to promote disarmament, it was all the more important, according to his view, that it do what it could: set a good (non-proliferating) example by refraining from acquiring or storing nuclear weapons on its soil. It is curious that Green attached more importance to keeping nuclear weapons – whether for US or Canadian forces – out of Canada, where they could only be used defensively, than in refusing such weapons for Canadian forces in Europe, where their function could be called offensive and even provocative. He was apparently motivated more by a concern for the purity of Canadian soil than by a desire to reduce the risks of war.[25]

The complicated negotiations with the US over the details of exercising joint responsibility over various nuclear weapons systems – "the how and the when" – gave him excellent opportunities to throw monkey wrenches in at every turn. His highly experienced undersecretary, Norman Robertson, who largely shared his views on the weapons, backed him up expertly. The stall tactics involved proposing an unworkable formula for "joint control" of weapons in Newfoundland which would have undermined US legal custody. There was also extensive exploration of details. "At one point, for example, Mr. Green became very concerned about the costs of the food consumed by American personnel stationed on Canadian bases."[26] They also involved the creation of unwieldy linkage. US and Canadian officials reached a draft agreement in 1960 on the interceptors in Newfoundland, the easiest of the nuclear questions, which could have served as a precursor to the more difficult agreements on providing weapons for the Canadian forces. In a brilliant tactical move, Green, with Diefenbaker's support, convinced the cabinet that the Newfoundland accord should be held in abeyance until all bilateral nuclear matters had been settled. In the meantime, it was decided, the government would follow the progress of international disarmament negotiations and attempt where it could to foster it. This approach, aimed at a "package deal" as it was called, afforded more opportunity for endless delay. The list of weapons under consideration was formidable. Not only were there the nuclear air defence weapons, but the US also had requested permission to store high-yield nuclear bombs at Goose Bay for the use of SAC and nuclear anti-submarine weapons at Argentia, Newfoundland, for the US and Canadian navies. Ottawa was engaged as well in negotiations with Washington over equipping the Canadian army and air force in Europe with nuclear capability.

Ranged against Green was Pearkes, who was replaced in October 1960 by Douglas Harkness as minister of national defence. Harkness was an equally tenacious supporter of nuclear weapons. Until the end of the Diefenbaker government a little over two years later, the cabinet remained deadlocked with Green at External Affairs on one side and an increasingly frustrated Harkness at National Defence on the other.

The stalemate meant no weapons, which seemed to suit Diefenbaker fine. The prime minister fudged and hedged over the issue in private discussions with US officials, including the new US president, John F. Kennedy, as well as in public, much as he had done in 1957 after his quick approval of NORAD, and in 1959 after the Arrow cancellation. A Kennedy aide said after the first discussion between the two leaders that Diefenbaker had "confused the hell" out of the president over the weapons, which was no doubt the intent.[27] Robinson observed that "[f]rom the prime minister's standpoint, Green's campaign against nuclear weapons had afforded time and scope for continued improvisation, a phrase which offers a kindly description of Diefenbaker's conduct of the nuclear weapons issue." The improvisation would last over two years. Towards the end of the Diefenbaker government this reached almost farcical proportions when a desperate prime minister (at the suggestion of the Department of External Affairs) endorsed the possibility of training and preparing the RCAF to be able to use nuclear weapons with its CF-101s and Bomarcs, but keeping the weapons themselves in the US, whence they would be flown into Canada in the event of an emergency. When that method of keeping Canadian soil pure proved impractical because of the time that would be needed to transport and install the weapons, a search was made to identify "missing parts" which, instead of entire nuclear weapons, could be kept south of the border and brought in when necessary. For a while, the candidates to be made missing included a cable on the MB-1 and a plug on the Bomarc warhead. The US sought to accommodate Ottawa by investigating the "missing part" option but found that it, too, would take too much time. More seriously, as US Secretary of State Dean Rusk later revealed, there would be "the chance of an actual nuclear explosion in the process of putting [the] pieces into the weapons ... under circumstances of great urgency."[28]

The Liberals came out in 1960 as opposed to nuclear weapons, especially those for the RCAF in North America. They offered a clear cut strategic argument, one based on grounds other than the purity of Canadian soil. Their spokesmen, opposition leader Lester B. Pearson and defence critic Paul Hellyer, said that efforts at damage limitation through active air defence would soon be hopeless because of ICBMs. "If the United States wishes to continue that kind of protection, let the United States do so," Pearson told the House of Commons. "Let us withdraw from that direct form of continental defence."[29] For the Liberals, this meant no nuclear air defence weapons for the RCAF but still keeping the CF-101s, while limiting their role to the identification of attacking bombers. The Bomarcs, on the other hand, which needed nuclear warheads to work and could not be used in the identification role, would be abandoned altogether. Diefenbaker and others derided the Liberal policy as "bird watching."[30] Canadians would just identify the targets and leave the shooting to the Americans. However, the Liberals' skeptical take on damage limitation was in line with much of the recent strategic thinking on the issue within the Department of National Defence by Foulkes and others; their emphasis on the need to identify bombers without the capability to destroy them was quite similar to the case that the Defence Research Board had made for replacing the CF-100 with an advanced, supersonic interceptor.

Canada–US relations deteriorated in large part because of the nuclear dispute, and were made worse by the now-legendary mutual dislike of Diefenbaker and Kennedy and their calamitous encounter during the president's 1961 visit to Ottawa. The Kennedy administration, frustrated at the obviously obstructive delays in the negotiations, did what it could to push the Diefenbaker government into deciding. At one point Washington attempted to make the transfer of the Voodoos to Canada conditional on their being equipped with MB-1s, but dropped the effort on the recommendation of CINCNORAD, who feared a delay. Simply getting the interceptors in place as swiftly as possible at their northern bases was urgent, he told Washington, so urgent in fact that NORAD had supported their being reassigned from USAF squadrons. Ottawa would eventually come around on the nuclear issue, he seemed sure, for as he told Washington, it was "inconceivable" to him "that the RCAF, when the uncertainty is removed concerning their acquisition of adequate carriers, would fail to use the most effective warheads that their carriers could handle."[31] Yet meanwhile, the Bomarcs that the RCAF had already acquired still had no warheads.

DELAYED ALERT: THE CUBAN MISSILE CRISIS

With Washington and Ottawa still unable to resolve their dispute over nuclear weapons, the Cuban missile crisis made their relationship much worse. On 22 October 1962, Diefenbaker received President Kennedy's special envoy, Livingston T. Merchant, a former ambassador to Canada who informed him of the contents of a television address Kennedy would be making in just a few hours and passed on a short message from the president. Merchant also had the CIA officer who accompanied him show the prime minister a set of aerial photographs. The US government, having discovered that the Soviet Union had put nuclear-armed missiles in Cuba, would confront the Soviets by insisting that the missiles be removed and by placing a blockade (which it called a "quarantine") on offensive military equipment going to the island.

Merchant had the mistaken impression, which he reported to the US State Department, that after a rough start the session had gone reasonably well. The prime minister had seemed especially impressed by the photographic evidence. So it came as a shock in Washington when later that evening, after the president's address, the prime minister gave an address of his own in the House of Commons in which, far from expressing solidarity with his American ally, he seemed to question the truth of its claims. An international team, Diefenbaker said, should be sent into Cuba to investigate. That was the advice he had been prompted by External Affairs to give Kennedy on Cuba had he been consulted by the president as to what steps should be taken.

But he had not been consulted. Diefenbaker's pique came in large part from his suspicion and dislike of Kennedy and an anxious determination not to be pushed around by Americans. "We were not a satellite state at the beck and call of an imperial master," he later wrote, describing his reaction to Merchant's visit.[32] He worried that the emotional Americans might have gone too far in confronting the Soviets. Overall, his reactions were in line with "the normal Canadian approach when trouble flares in the world: don't resort to violence, bring the UN into the picture and make sure that Canadian policy is decided in Ottawa."[33]

Diefenbaker had a reasonable expectation to be consulted by Washington that had not been met. In simply informing Ottawa of the steps it was on the verge of taking, the Kennedy administration had not been able to honour the pledges of consultation with Ottawa the US government had made in the NORAD agreement and the 1958 agreement on consultation, as well as in a third agreement, entered into in 1959, and a fourth one entered into in 1960, both to be discussed below. This also played an important part in his reaction.

What Merchant told Diefenbaker did not come as a complete surprise to the prime minister. Canadian officials in Washington had caught wind of a crisis over Cuba and had also been informally told what was going on, whereupon they had passed the word on to Ottawa. Canadians at NORAD also knew about the impending crisis and appear to have let Ottawa know. At the start of his meeting with Merchant, Diefenbaker did not know precisely which steps Kennedy was about to announce or the extent of the evidence the administration had accumulated. But, according to Robinson, "he had had more than twenty-four hours to get steamed up about what he was to be told and perhaps also what he would be asked to do. Despite what he had learned in advance, it would have been completely out of character if he had not been upset at being presented with the evidence of the Soviet missiles and the outline of the president's plans, at a stage when he could do little more than acknowledge their receipt."[34]

The failure to consult with Ottawa had not been because of a lack of time. No rapidly developing emergency had precluded consultation, nor were there fears of an immediate attack. The administration, particularly its specially constituted "ExComm," had deliberated for an entire week after the presence of the missiles had been confirmed. Nor had Canada been simply overlooked or deliberately snubbed, as bad as relations between Washington and Ottawa were. Rather, the deliberations and decision making in Washington had been conducted in deep secrecy, which the administration had seen as absolutely essential. One US staff-level advisor later recalled: "It should be stressed, as many have observed, that the ability to devote an entire week of deliberation and decision free of public pressure and free of Soviet action or interaction, was crucial. It was also unique; no other past crisis has had, and none in the future can be expected to have, such a lengthy period for decision free from external and domestic political pressures."[35]

Diefenbaker had not been alone. No other ally was taken by the Kennedy administration into its deliberations. Other allied leaders were informed of the US decision just about the same time he was. Canada was supposed to be special, though. According to the Department of External Affairs at the time of the NORAD negotiations, Canada's geography and its participation in North American air defence were supposed to give it a "special right" to be consulted in an emergency by Washington. The Cuban crisis might be seen as putting an end to that supposition.

That conclusion was not embraced by Ottawa, though, which continued to view emergency consultation as an important part of the NORAD arrangements. A memo written by "D.B.D." just a few weeks after the crisis for R.B. Bryce, clerk of the Privy Council, warned that "the oversimplified view that the crisis showed the NORAD Agreement to be unworkable is an unfortunate one and should be dispelled if possible." It made the convincing argument that the crisis had been of a completely unexpected kind.

> The NORAD Agreement does not seem to have worked properly during the crisis mainly because it was not designed for this sort of emergency when the US took the initiative after a period of secret planning. The Agreement is designed to operate in a situation in which evidence accumulates of a danger of attack on North America resulting from the deliberate planning for such an attack by the Soviets or from a worsening situation that may get out of control. From the Canadian point of view the Cuban crisis was in a sense interpreted as a worsening international situation that might get out of control, and therefore our decision to increase the readiness of our air defence forces would seem, from our point of view, to have been taken at about the right time. But the US Government had quite a different viewpoint of the crisis which for them was being planned for before Canada even knew of it and in which the alerting of air defence forces was probably regarded as part of the posture the US wanted to assure from the outset. *In these circumstances proper consultation as required by the agreement is impossible* (emphasis added).[36]

In other words, Canada was not so special that it would be consulted by Washington under any circumstances, including the extraordinary ones that had just occurred, but was still special enough to count on being consulted in the event of the kind of Cold War crisis that was more probable and so might still occur.

While Washington was unable to meet its NORAD commitments to Ottawa, Colorado Springs observed the NORAD procedures scrupulously, especially those related to Canadian sovereignty and independence of action. The relationship between NORAD and CONAD proved particularly useful not only for that, but also for simultaneously allowing the US air defence forces to respond to national command by going on higher alert, while keeping the Canada–US command structure at Colorado Springs in operation despite the differences in alert status.

At the insistence of Diefenbaker, CINCNORAD's authority in the event of alerts had been further worked out. On 15 July 1958, because of a crisis in the Middle East, CINCNORAD had placed both US and Canadian air defence forces on an alert condition of "increased readiness" that had lasted, with diminishing intensity, for two weeks. The Canadian government, including the prime minister, was upset. While raising the alert status undoubtedly fell under CINCNORAD's authority, the Canadian government argued that he should do so on his own only in the event of imminent or actual Soviet attack. Otherwise he should turn to the two governments for permission. Tensions later in the year between the US, the Soviet Union, and China over Quemoy and Matsu Islands in the Taiwan Straits left Diefenbaker still worrying about CINCNORAD's authority. Extensive discussions between Washington and Ottawa over NORAD followed by a secret agreement reached in October 1959 resolved the issue, to Ottawa's apparent satisfaction. In addition to the stipulation that CINCNORAD would raise the alert status on his own only in the event of a real or immediately anticipated attack – and not just in the event of an international crisis – the agreement included another pledge of government-to-government consultation, the third one now after the two reached in 1958. In 1960, there were refinements in still another exchange of notes.[37]

That stipulation was respected on the evening of 22 October 1962 when the US armed forces, including US continental air defence forces, went on alert (DEFCON 3) during President Kennedy's address. General John K. Gerhart, CINCNORAD, did not put RCAF air defence forces on alert. Moreover, the US air defence alert was ordered not by NORAD, but by CONAD.[38]

Shortly thereafter, Slemon telephoned RCAF headquarters on behalf of General Gerhart, informing it of the US action (including the fact that there was a CONAD alert) and passing on Gerhart's urgent request that the RCAF's air defences forces be put on equivalent alert. Diefenbaker recalled in his memoirs that Merchant had made the same request to him during their encounter. But this is not credible, inasmuch as Diefenbaker also recalls being told by Kennedy that the US plan was for only Canadian forces to be alerted, and not those of the US, because that would be less provocative to the Soviets.[39]

Slemon passed on two other requests from CINCNORAD during his call to Ottawa. One was that RCAF air defence aircraft be moved to their dispersal bases, just as USAF aircraft had been. The other was that the Canadian Voodoos and Bomarcs be equipped with nuclear weapons. This last request, which was hedged with disclaimers that it was not immediately urgent and that Gerhard was hoping to get the opinion of the Canadian Chiefs before making it formal, must have come as quite a surprise. Air Vice Marshal Annis, the vice chief of the air staff, naturally wondered whether the chairman of the Chiefs of Staff and Harkness would think "now is the time to raise this question."[40]

In the wake of Slemon's call, Air Chief Marshal Frank Miller, who had replaced Foulkes as chairman of the Chiefs of Staff Committee, went to see Harkness, who in turn asked Diefenbaker for permission to put the Canadian air defences on alert, in accordance with CINCNORAD's request. The issue of dispersal of the RCAF aircraft seems to have been subsumed by the question of going on alert. It is not clear whether Miller told Harkness and Diefenbaker about the request to arm the Canadian air defences with nuclear weapons. The matter was not directly pursued any further, though, for the rest of the crisis. According to Annis, Miller contacted Slemon, telling him that while arming the Voodoos and Bomarcs with nuclear tips was going nowhere, "perhaps a way of introducing that question up here" would be for Slemon to arrange for a request to be made for Ottawa to allow the arming of the USAF interceptors in Newfoundland with nuclear weapons.[41] Slemon obliged; the RCAF passed on to the Canadian Chiefs the next day an official request from Gerhart that the Newfoundland interceptors be armed with such weapons. The RCAF's chief of staff wrote, either punctiliously or archly, (it is impossible to tell) that the request had come from "CINCNORAD (or CINCONAD, if you preferred)."[42] This request for nuclear air defence weapons in Newfoundland seems not to have been pursued further; here the record also is unclear.

Harkness had every expectation that the prime minister would give his quick approval to putting the forces on alert and was stunned when Diefenbaker demurred, putting it off to a cabinet meeting to be held the following morning. At that session, and at a subsequent one on the morning of the 24th (the day the quarantine went into effect), Harkness was unable to obtain its permission. There was a substantial cabinet split. Although most of the ministers eventually came to support the defence minister, Diefenbaker blocked the way, firmly supported by Green. Harkness later recalled that at this second session, "I made a final effort with a rather angry outburst that we were failing in our responsibilities to the nation and *must* act, which produced an outburst from the Prime Minister to the effect that he would not be forced into any such action."[43]

Despite the different alert levels, NORAD/CONAD headquarters continued to function and to exercise operational control over both US and Canadian air defence forces. The Canadians remained on duty, although in an uncomfortable position. Orders to US forces related to the US alert were to be issued by US officers acting as CONAD. Had there been a Soviet attack, CINCNORAD would then have raised the Canadian alert level on his own authority and conducted the air battle.

This is not to say there were no command problems. These arose principally in the regional air defence headquarters. US interceptors in northern New England were in the Northern NORAD region, headquartered at North Bay. Upon the initiation of the US alert, CONAD directly ordered them moved to dispersal bases elsewhere, without proper notification to or consultation with the Canadian regional commander. After the crisis, arrangements were made to have the interceptors controlled by a US regional headquarters in the event of another CONAD alert. In the Wisconsin headquarters of the 30th region, which also straddled the border and whose fighter aircraft were all located in the US, the situation grew "especially stressful" as Canadian and US officers sorted out who should do what.[44]

Such difficulties, and the overall impact of the government's decision not to let the military go on alert, were minimized by Harkness' covert circumvention of the prime minister and cabinet. After Diefenbaker turned down his first request, the defence minister simply authorized on his own the Canadian military to take such steps that it could that would move it to higher alert but not draw the attention of the public and the prime minister, such as cancelling leaves. As he explained later: "These measures accomplished the majority of the purposes of an alert – i.e. to get into a state of preparedness to meet an attack – but did not reassure the United States and our other allies, as the declaration of an alert would have done, that we were prepared to fight."[45] According to Robinson, Diefenbaker may have known what was going on and turned a blind eye to it. "Not much escaped the Diefenbaker antenna."[46]

Later on the 24th, after the quarantine had gone into effect, the Department of National Defence received word about the most recent Soviet military preparations and also learned that SAC and the US Navy had gone to a still higher state of alert (DEFCON 2). Nuclear war now seemingly closer, Harkness went to Diefenbaker once again. "This time he succeeded. Diefenbaker was convinced that Canada's security was now gravely endangered by the reported preparations of the Soviet Union."[47] While the formal proclamation of the Canadian alert was delayed until the next day, with Canadian permission now in hand, NORAD went on DEFCON 3 that evening, two days after CONAD, and would remain on alert until the confrontation with the Soviet Union was over.

Afterwards, the Diefenbaker government was sometimes accused of having left the air approaches to the northeast open during those two days. With the revelation that the RCAF had gone on de facto alert, as approved by the minister of national defence, that charge lost much of any sting it may have had. But it was always overblown. Even if the Canadian air defences, including the four new Voodoo squadrons that were operational at the time, were not on alert, Diefenbaker never withdrew them from their normal NORAD duties and CINCNORAD could have moved them to a higher status had he judged an attack imminent. Potentially more telling is the charge that the government left the northeast inadequately protected throughout the crisis by not having agreed earlier to nuclear air defence weapons for the Voodoos, Bomarcs, and the Newfoundland interceptors. That depended on whether attempting damage limitation still made sense. The air defenders said yes. Others, including the bird-watching Liberal Party, had said no.

NUCLEAR RESOLUTION

According to the historian John English, the Cuban missile crisis "stiffened Canadian spines, including some in Diefenbaker's cabinet."[48] Almost as soon as it was over, the cabinet, pushed hard by Harkness, agreed to the reopening of negotiations with the US over nuclear weapons.

For much of the Canadian public, Kennedy emerged from the crisis as the hero of the day who had stood Soviet blackmail down. Diefenbaker's hesitations and the delayed Canadian alert were, by contrast, troubling. Public discussions over how Ottawa had conducted itself during the crisis soon turned into a renewed nuclear debate. There was a strong shift in attitude, noticeable in both the press and in public opinion polls, toward the acquisition of nuclear weapons for the Canadian forces at home and in Europe. This was only strengthened by the public remarks of the outgoing NATO commander, General Lauris Norstad, who said during a January 1963 visit to Ottawa in response to questions from the press that Canada was reneging on its commitments. The next day CINCNORAD, who was visiting North Bay, also made it into the papers, quoted as saying (to his later objection that he was misquoted) that the lack of nuclear warheads for the Bomarcs was "a chink in the North American polar shield."[49]

The most surprising change of attitude was Pearson's, which he announced a few days after Norstad's visit. It was not that the Liberal leader had changed his views on strategic value of nuclear weapons in Canadian hands. Rather, he said, it was a matter of keeping promises: "As a Canadian I am ashamed if we accept commitments and then refuse to discharge them." The government, he went on, "should end at once its evasion of responsibility, by discharging the commitments it has already accepted for Canada."[50]

Norstad's reproach and Pearson's turnaround together placed the Diefenbaker government under heavy pressure. The prime minister still was not giving in, though. On the contrary, he was determined to resist what he saw as a conspiracy between Pearson and Kennedy, his sworn enemy. He also continued to believe that despite the country's shifting views, there was still an anti-nuclear majority with him.

Diefenbaker budged, though, after Harkness threatened to resign if there was continued delay. A special cabinet committee was struck where Harkness tried to pin the government down. The committee found that an agreement should be reached with the US on nuclear air defence weapons and that Canada had committed itself to acquiring weapons in Europe, although there was a need for further clarification from NATO. After the full cabinet endorsed the committee's recommendation, Harkness awaited the major address Diefenbaker was to give on that subject.

That speech to the House of Commons, given on 25 January, was "a two-hour masterpiece of obfuscation filled with illusions, delusions and confusions."[51] At the start, the prime minister, in line with the cabinet conclusions, conceded for the first time that Canada had nuclear commitments. He revealed the confidential negotiations with Washington that had been underway since the end of October, and said they were based on finding ways to move nuclear air defence weapons swiftly into Canada. Then he waffled and hedged once more, implying Canada might not have to meet those commitments. His pretext was a recent meeting at Nassau between Kennedy and British Prime Minister Harold Macmillan to which he had wangled an invitation for himself at the end, for lunch. Kennedy and Macmillan had put an emphasis at their meeting on conventional weapons and on a possible NATO multilateral nuclear force. This called into question, Diefenbaker suggested, the need for Canada to acquire nuclear weapons for its forces in Europe. As for air defence weapons for the RCAF in North America, he tried the same kind of argument he had used to explain the cancellation of the Arrow in 1959: The British had agreed at Nassau to replace their nuclear bombers with US-built Polaris ballistic missiles. This meant that bombers were becoming obsolete; so was North American air defence.

Harkness took the extraordinary step of issuing on 28 January, as a press release, a "clarification" of the prime minister's remarks. He again tried to pin the government down by emphasizing the first part of the speech, where Diefenbaker had dealt with commitments. It meant, Harkness said, Canada was obligated to acquire nuclear weapons, and that Ottawa would meet that obligation. Diefenbaker refused to endorse his minister's "clarification," leading to opposition calls for Harkness' resignation.

An even more extraordinary press release was issued in reaction to Diefenbaker's speech by the State Department in both Ottawa and Washington on the 30th, its text having been approved by the US ambassador to Canada, the secretary of state, and the president's national security advisor. It called Diefenbaker a liar. "The agreements made at Nassau have been fully published. They raise no question of the appropriateness of nuclear weapons for Canadian forces in fulfilling their NATO or NORAD obligations." It challenged his good faith in the new negotiations over air defence weapons. These talks were only "exploratory" and "the Canadian government has not as yet proposed any arrangement sufficiently practical to contribute to North American air defence." And it argued that the need for more conventional forces did not eliminate the need for nuclear weapons: "A flexible and balanced defense requires increased conventional forces, but conventional forces are not an alternative to effective NATO or NORAD defense arrangements using nuclear-capable weapons systems."[52]

Harkness resigned on 4 February, taking two other ministers with him. The minority Conservative government, besieged and crumbling, was defeated on a non-confidence motion made by Pearson the next day. McLin notes that "[t]he ensuing election campaign was waged not so much on the specific defense issue as on the question of the Diefenbaker government's general incompetence to govern. Its handling of defense policy was a relevant, but only a partial point; however, it did loom always in the background and intruded unexpectedly into discussions of other issues from time to time." [53] Diefenbaker tried to capitalize on congressional testimony by the US Secretary of Defense, Robert McNamara, about the Bomarcs, coincidentally released during the campaign. While McNamara underlined the protection they could provide, albeit at a high financial cost, he also said that they would at the very least draw Soviet attacks away from other targets. This left the way open for the prime minister to charge that the Liberals, by arming the Bomarcs, would turn Canada into a nuclear decoy. The Liberals of course replied that it was Diefenbaker who had acquired them.

Diefenbaker was also convinced that NORAD was conniving with the Kennedy White House during the campaign. He charged that Canadian groups were brought to Colorado Springs to be "propagandized" by Slemon. Whether or not that is true, NORAD certainly did not fall silent while the campaign was underway. Gerhart took an opportunity to tell reporters that the Canadian Bomarcs were ineffective without nucear warheads. Two weeks later NORAD headquarters, taking a leaf from the State Department's book, issued a press release in response to a Halifax speech by Diefenbaker in which the prime minister had said that the Bomarcs should be retrofitted to use conventional warheads.[54]

Pearson, for his part, believed that Canadian reaction to the State Department's press release had cost him several seats in the 8 April 1963 election, and with them, a majority government. He went off to a meeting with the president at the Kennedy family compound in Hyannis Port the next month where he confirmed his intention to honour Canada's nuclear commitments.

However, Pearson also told Kennedy that he was not yet ready to discuss any new nuclear obligations. The US was hoping to open negotiations with Canada over the dispersal of USAF fighter interceptors, capable of using nuclear air defence weapons, to nine remote Canadian air bases and storing the nuclear weapons for them in Canada. NORAD was growing increasingly worried about the vulnerability of USAF interceptors to ICBM attack, in large part because many of them were deployed at the same bases as SAC bombers and SAGE installations, which would be struck first. While the immediate plan was for interceptors on ready alert at their home bases in the US to be able to fly to their Canadian locations in the event of warning of attack, NORAD's ultimate goal included continuous dispersal, whereby a portion of the interceptors would routinely be located at their Canadian bases. The USAF considered it both undesirable and impractical to have the fighters ferry nuclear weapons to their proposed Canadian dispersal bases. Four of these would soon be equipped for storage of nuclear weapons for the RCAF, now that the new Pearson government was about to clear the way; new nuclear facilities would have to be built at the others.

Kennedy agreed at Hyannis Port to pull interceptor dispersal from the bilateral agenda while the two countries dealt with the other, now-longstanding nuclear issues. Even after these were essentially settled, Pearson still hesitated to take up dispersal. His "own inclination to avoid any extension of Canada's nuclear role was strengthened by the opposition to nuclear weapons expressed by several Quebec Cabinet ministers" in early 1964.[55] At Pearson's behest, the new US president, Lyndon B. Johnson, again pushed the issue off the agenda. NORAD's continued anxiety over the growing vulnerability of the interceptors to ballistic missile attack meant that the issue would not go permanently away, though.

In August 1963 the two governments reached an agreement on nuclear weapons for the Canadian forces in North America and Europe. This was followed the next month by one on the Newfoundland interceptors. The nuclear weapons for the Bomarcs and the Voodoos would be in the legal custody of the US and the physical custody of the US military at Canadian bases. Their use would have to be authorized by both governments. On the US side, this was covered by the predelegation procedures for nuclear air defence weapons. Liberal defence minister Paul Hellyer established for Canada in March the equivalent to predelegation, called "prior authorization." He gave the military permission to use nuclear air defence weapons in an emergency, defined as an event "where warheads have impacted or where there is other clear and unmistakable evidence that an attack against the North American region has been launched."[56]

Hellyer's step was a temporary measure while the two governments conducted negotiations on a permanent agreement governing both authorization for use and government-to-government consultation in the event of an emergency. Far from being convinced by the Cuban missile crisis that pursuit of consultation with Washington in an emergency would be fruitless, the Department of External Affairs seized the opportunity to consolidate all the earlier consultative arrangements into one omnibus accord and to codify the procedures that were to be used to keep the two governments in contact on continental defence in a variety of circumstances, especially if NORAD's state of readiness needed to be raised or if nuclear air defence weapons were to be used. The resulting September 1965 secret agreement provided for regular consultations between senior civilian and military representatives at six month intervals. It also provided special meetings in the event of "a situation if increasing international tension which could give rise to hostilities involving North America" and "emergency consultation" in the event of an "urgent" risk of attack. "Emergency consultation" would be conducted by teleconference and would include the most senior officials, namely the president, secretary of state, secretary of defense, chairman of the US Chiefs, prime minister, secretary of state for external affairs, minister of national defence, chief of the defence staff and CINCNORAD.[57]

The starting point for the negotiations had been to set the conditions for authorizing the use of the Bomarcs and Genies by the Canadian forces. The 1965 agreement provided a bi-national or NORAD regime for such use, in two senses. First, CINCNORAD was to be authorized to order their use. The designation in the agreement of CINCNORAD and not CINCONAD meant that in the commander's absence the DCINC or any other senior Canadian officer at NORAD in temporary command could use this authority. Second, both governments set out in the agreement the circumstances to which CINCNORAD's authority to order the use of nuclear air defence weapons extended. These included an imminent attack, an actual attack and a long list of "emergency circumstances," such as nuclear explosions of unknown origin occurring in North America or a nuclear attack on NATO forces in Europe.

Pointedly, the list did not include single intrusions into North America by an unknown or hostile aircraft. The US had preferred to trust CINCNORAD's judgment in such a case and, as the Canadian negotiators had to admit, "In fact the record over a number of years of the US Air Force in dealing with repeated intrusions of US airspace, particularly by Soviet aircraft in Alaska, without recourse to weapons of any sort provides a good deal of reassurance as to both the effectiveness of US control procedures and the good judgment and restraint of US commanding officers."[58] Nonetheless, the Canadian government had reserved to itself the right to order the use of nuclear weapons in such circumstances.

Nuclear air defence weapons in the US had been under a unilateral CONAD regime. In a fairly audacious move, the Canadians, led by their forceful chief negotiator Ross Campbell, an assistant undersecretary of state for external affairs, had proposed – and then all but insisted – that with Canada about to become a nuclear air defence partner, the NORAD regime also cover the weapons in the US. To be sure, as Campbell had pointed out, "[t]he draft agreement of course recognizes that the US is and must remain free to use its own forces in its own airspace as it may consider necessary to its own defence."[59] So what the Canadians had proposed for the nuclear weapons in the US came down to a NORAD/CONAD regime. Normally, the NORAD provisions would apply. But the US, under the Canadian proposals, could still opt out. For example, even though the NORAD arrangements did not delegate authority to use nuclear weapons against single intruders, CINCONAD might order the destruction with a nuclear weapon of a single unknown aircraft off, say, the coast of Maine.

This was but the extension to nuclear air defence weapons of how the NORAD/CONAD relationship already functioned. Reflecting this, the proposed language had been so general that it covered more than just nuclear weapons. It had stated that each government retained the right to use unilaterally forces it had placed under CINCNORAD's operational control and to use the NORAD command and control facilities in doing so, to the extent necessary. It probably was not legally necessary to include it, especially after the Cuban missile crisis had shown that the means for unilateral US action not involving Canada were pretty much in place at Colorado Springs. But it was reassuring for the US Chiefs.

At stake for the Canadian side had been its standing. A NORAD regime for all North American nuclear air defence weapons, even one which could be overridden, seemed to mean for the Canadian negotiators that Canada was a full partner, with more complete access to US planning, thinking and intelligence, and a greater say in the decision making, both within the command and through consultation.

The US Chiefs, who had wanted to keep the CONAD regime, had resisted. The Canadian negotiators, backed up by the Pearson government, had remained equally firm. The diplomats had cabled Paul Martin, the secretary of state for external affairs:

> The essence of the CDN argument is that it would be difficult for any CDN govt to accept a formal agreement, even a secret one, which explicitly admits that the concept of an integrated command under joint control, which was intended to make NORAD something more than an alliance, is one which the USA in practice rejects since it wants joint control in CDA only while retaining national control in the USA ...

> To give way on this matter, now or later, would encourage the USA to expect us in negotiation on other matters to accept one-sided arrangements in response to the argument of preponderant USA strength and responsibilities. The USA may be sensitive, bearing in mind their relations with other allies, to any suggestion that it wishes to treat in an inequitable manner the only ally with which it has a fully integrated command on a bilateral basis.[60]

The matter finally had to be decided by President Johnson, who sided with the Canadians. The September 1965 agreement applied the NORAD regime to both US and Canadian nuclear air defence weapons, although it included the generally worded opting-out clause for unilateral US action outside NORAD and, for good measure, a supplementary exchange of letters providing a broad interpretation of the US right to do so. The agreement remained secret as long as such weapons were in Canada. Public statements by Canadian officials about the Bomarcs and Genies usually emphasized that the permission of both the president and prime minister was necessary for NORAD to use them. While this was true, such accounts left out that standing permission had already been given by both of them.[61]

THE CHANGING AND EXPANDING THREAT

The Pearson government sought in its 1964 defence white paper to put a firm end to the notion, of which Diefenbaker had been so fond, that as the missile threat grew, Canada might soon get entirely out of air defence. It observed that "a downtrend in continental air defence forces seems likely, yet, short of total disarmament, one cannot foresee the day when Canada will not be directly involved in some form of air defence operations." The great uncertainty was what kind of missile defences the US would deploy. If the continent could be protected against ballistic missile attack, a reinvigorated air defence would also be in order. "It seems probable, however, that, failing the wide-scale deployment of [missile defence] the proportion of Canada's resources directed to air defence will gradually decline through the balance of the decade.[62]

By the time the white paper had appeared, the decision already had been taken to reduce the number of CF-101 squadrons to three, located at Comox, BC, Bagotville, Quebec and Chatham, New Brunswick, each with eighteen aircraft; this number would drop over the next few years. Four Pinetree radars were closed. The next year Ottawa decided, over CINCNORAD's objections, to close the Mid-Canada Line. The decline in the bomber threat, the expansion of Pinetree coverage, and the improvements that SAGE had made in the value of Pinetree radar data had rendered the Mid-Canada line marginal.

At the end of 1964, McNamara put US air defence forces on the downward path the Canadian white paper had anticipated. He wrote President Johnson: "At present, with no defense against ballistic missiles and only the beginning of a viable civil defense posture, our anti-bomber defenses could operate on only a fraction of the damage inflicting forces in a determined Soviet attack." Such an attack, the secretary's analysts had calculated, would cost 90–120 million Americans their lives. Deep cuts in air defence would increase that number "by perhaps 1 to 6 million persons; the Chief of Staff of the Army believes the difference would be less than 1.5 million in the most plausible situations and I agree with his judgment." Therefore, McNamara concluded, "it no longer appears to be necessary or useful to retain our large interceptor force at its present size." Over the objection of the US Chiefs, McNamara proposed to the president cutting the number of fighters from the 1,225 planned for 1969 to 732. There were to be other cuts. The airborne and sea-based extension of the DEW Line would be closed, the warning time they provided no longer needed. The Permanent radar system would be thinned out. And production would be put off of the "improved manned interceptor," the hypervelocity F-12, then under development by the USAF, which NORAD had seen as the heart of its future interception capability.[63]

The air defence system still posed several gnawing problems.[64] Its ground control environment (the Permanent radars and the SAGE centres with their controllers) was vulnerable to ICBM attack. It was weak against low-flying bombers, because ground radars were limited to line-of-sight detection, which cut off at the horizon. Fighters were still locked into the engagement zone in southern Canada instead of being able to meet the enemy further out as it approached. And, even after McNamara's 1964 cuts, its vast warning and ground control networks (including both the DEW Line and Permanent radars), as well as its hundreds of fighter interceptors, cost a lot of money for marginal protection.

To address these problems, the USAF devised a thorough overhaul, the most important details of which McNamara announced in January 1968. It had four elements. First, much of the radar coverage would be phased out in the central and southern US. Around the edge of the country the military would depend on a new cooperative arrangement with the civil aviation authorities for radar coverage. The Pinetree radars in Canada would continue to provide a northward extension. Second, powerful new over-the-horizon backscatter (OTH-B) radars would be deployed. Their detection range extended out to almost two thousand miles and because their beam "bounced" off the ionosphere, they were expected to be capable of detecting low-flying aircraft. Just a few OTH-B stations would be needed to provide coverage to the east, west, and south. Because of the aurora borealis it was unlikely that OTH-B could provide northward coverage; tests were needed. Nonetheless, the DEW Line would still be closed because of the third element of the plan, the deployment of airborne warning and control system (AWACS) aircraft in the high north, equipped with large, powerful scanning radars, and the displays, computers, and communications which would enable a crew of human controllers to identify targets and guide fighter aircraft to conduct interceptions. If, as expected, a northward OTH-B could not function, three AWACS aircraft in continuous flight above northern Canada would do. They would have excellent low-altitude detection capability. Just as importantly, many more AWACS aircraft, sent aloft in an emergency, could take over from the vulnerable ground environment and move the air battle further north.

The final element of the plan was an improved manned interceptor. Over the furious objections of NORAD, McNamara opted not for the F-12, which had a tremendous range and speed allowing it, in conjunction with AWACS, to take the battle far to the north, but the less capable F-106X. According to David Cox, this "decision on the F-12 marked the final turning away not only by Defense Secretary McNamara but also by his successors from any determined and sustained effort to deploy an effective defense against the manned bomber."[65]

In short, the Pentagon was planning a thinned out, although less vulnerable air defence, with better detection capabilities and much of its radar and control facilities airborne, and oriented more towards the northern periphery, which itself would be moved aloft northward. Senior officials in Ottawa reacted positively. Pearson was told by the departments of external affairs and national defence that "[t]he principal value of the new air defence system is that it will improve the protection of the western deterrent." There were also for Canada "certain clear supplementary advantages. Having the air battle well to the north of the present limits would significantly increase the protection to the Canadian population."[66] That was probably a bit of an exaggeration, given the new system's limited capabilities. There is no record of how Pearson, who had once endorsed "bird watching" and had opposed active air defence by Canada as being futile, reacted.

There were other anticipated advantages. The Canadian Bomarcs could go by the mid-1970s. So could the DEW Line, meaning the Americans would leave the Canadian Arctic. On the other hand, the CF-101s and the Pinetree radars would still be needed. However, since 1966 the Department of National Defence and the Ministry of Transport had been investigating whether their surveillance radars in southern Canada could be integrated, which if implemented, would be not unlike the cost-saving military/civilian radar integration that the US had just announced.

The US plan also raised several questions for Canada. In a study for the Department of National Defence, George R. Lindsey pointed to three in particular.[67] The first was whether F-106X squadrons would be based or dispersed in Canada. Interceptor dispersal remained a sensitive issue. The USAF had revived its request, which had been pushed off the agenda by Presidents Kennedy and Johnson, to disperse nuclear-capable interceptors to Canada. It was now on the cabinet's agenda. Second, the same question concerning basing in Canada could be asked about the AWACS. Strikingly, though, officials in Ottawa seem not to have asked themselves if Canada should pay for any of the costs of the AWACS aircraft in light of the extra protection which the government had concluded they would give Canadians. Finally, it still remained to be determined whether OTH-B would work in the Canadian north. "For the moment," Pearson had also been told, "the new system is more of a concept than a detailed plan and because of this it will be some time before the extent of potential Canadian involvement is clear."[68]

As the threat to North America shifted, McNamara needed to address not only whether to downgrade air defence but also whether to deploy missile defence. Right after the 1960 elections which brought the Kennedy administration into power, the US Army pushed hard for an enormous deployment of its Nike-Zeus ballistic missile defences, protecting areas in both the US and Canada. The military had already discussed Canadian protection. Even while the Eisenhower administration was declining to fund Nike-Zeus in the late 1950s, Partridge had taken the initiative to consider where in Canada Nike-Zeus sites should be located, drawing a lesson from the initial US planning for Bomarc. As he wrote Foulkes in 1958: "Had we got together with the Canadians in the early planning stages for BOMARC, the Canadians feel that some of our BOMARC installations, notably in the northwest, could well have been located farther north, in Canada, and thus would have provided a great deal more protection for populated areas of Canada. We, therefore, feel quite strongly that we should approach the siting of our anti-missile firing units on a North American rather than a United States basis."[69] The next year, NORAD drew up plans to deploy Nike-Zeus sites in Canada in 1965 to protect Ottawa and Toronto, with a site near Montreal to be added in 1966 – all pending approval by the two governments.[70]

Initially, the US Army got no further under the Democrats than under the Eisenhower Republicans. McNamara resisted its missile defence push, largely because of the costs and his doubts that the system would work. The army's program was then reconfigured as a layered defence, called Nike-X, combining the longer range Nike-Zeus interceptor with a shorter-range Sprint missile. Both would carry nuclear warheads. McNamara's resistance hardened, though, as he swung around to skepticism about active defences to embrace the "'defence is a dangerous thing' argument."[71] It could only provoke an arms race between the US and the Soviet Union and could incite one side to strike early with nuclear weapons out of fear that the other would do so and then sit protected behind its defences.

That view was decidedly not shared by the US Chiefs, who unanimously wanted a missile defence, or by many members of the US Congress, especially after it was revealed that the Soviets were deploying their own missile defences. "In spite of McNamara's best efforts, the political pressure for deployment of an American missile defense system had reached the point in late 1966 where President Johnson was no longer willing simply to rubber stamp the recommendations of his secretary of defense."[72] Johnson leapt, however, at a compromise McNamara suggested, namely inviting the Soviets into arms control talks while putting money into the budget for missile defence if the talks failed. The exploratory discussions held in June 1967 at Glassboro, New Jersey, failed. The Soviet premier, Alexei Kosygin, upon listening to McNamara's explanation of the dangers of missile defences, turned red in the face, pounded the table, and declared, "Defense is moral; offense is immoral!"[73]

In an odd September 1967 address, McNamara announced the deployment of a limited missile defence system, named shortly thereafter "Sentinel" and based on the Nike-X. Most of the speech was devoted to the "'defence is a dangerous thing' argument'" which must have left the secretary's audience at first convinced that he was about to announce that there would be no missile defence. McNamara went on to say, however, that the new system was primarily intended to provide protection not against Soviet missiles – for that would be dangerous – but against the Chinese, who had just detonated a hydrogen bomb. He added that the new system would also have some limited utility against an accidental missile launch by the Soviets, and inasmuch as it protected US missiles, it might make a contribution to strategic stability. As he later admitted, he had seized upon Sentinel's role in protecting against the Chinese in order to leave himself free to warn against building a heavier system directed against the Soviets.

The Pearson government had only recently put the Bomarc, CF-101 and Newfoundland fighters nuclear issues behind it, and still had the USAF fighter dispersal question before it. The last thing it wanted to deal with was negotiations with the US over nuclear-tipped Nike-X missiles on Canadian soil. In March 1967, Hellyer obtained from McNamara the assurances that no elements of the system being contemplated would need to be located in Canada. In September, just a week before he announced the Sentinel system, McNamara took pains to assure Hellyer once again. Hellyer was also told at the September meeting that as a "by-product" the system would provide protection to all of southern Canada from Quebec City westward.[74]

Even if no sites were to be put north of the border, the "'defence is a dangerous thing' argument" that had been raised in the US and endorsed by McNamara still resonated in Canada. It was compatible with the longstanding skepticism about active strategic defence and worries about strategic stability. The prime minister particularly subscribed to the view that missile defence could lead to an arms race. A few days after McNamara's address, he expressed at a press conference in Ottawa his "regret" with the US decision, saying that it could lead to a "new dimension" in the arms race and making it clear to the public that Canada would not be participating.[75] This left Canada in active air defence but out of active missile defence, with implications for NORAD renewal in 1968.

Whatever NORAD's role was to be in missile defence, it had been involved in warning of missile attacks since the BMEWS system had become partially operational in 1960. On 5 October of that year, when CINCNORAD was away, Slemon impressed both the NORAD combat operations staff and the US Joint Chiefs of Staff with his calm reaction to the brand new system's fishy warning that a Soviet missile attack was underway. Rather than sound the alert, he ordered quick and intense checking. It later turned out that the system needed to be better calibrated, for radar pulses had been bouncing off the moon.

After technical studies, NORAD began in 1967 to adapt its computer pro-
gramming so that its missile warning could be accompanied by an "attack
assessment" of which targets in North America incoming Soviet ballistic missiles were about to strike. Inasmuch as ballistic missiles, unlike manned
bombers, could not change their course, it was possible to determine their
targets before impact, using computers that relied on tracking data from
BMEWS. The US Joint Chiefs of Staff instructed CINCNORAD in 1968 that
in the event of an attack he should report "the name of the attacking country,
and whether the attack was probably directed against SAC forces only, urban/
industrial complexes only, or a combination of both."[76]

NORAD's new responsibility for attack assessment was in keeping with
the shift in US nuclear strategy, launched by McNamara at the start of the
Kennedy administration. The nuclear targeting plan at the end of the Eisenhower administration had provided for a blanket attack on just about every
city in the Soviet Union, China and Eastern Europe, as well as military targets, which would have all but invariably resulted in hundreds of millions of
deaths. In the Kennedy administration's 1962 targeting plan, McNamara sought
to build in flexibility through a variety of targeting options and the possibility
of a "controlled response" in the event of nuclear war. Having NORAD provide an assessment of the nature of a Soviet attack might possibly allow the
US president to respond appropriately without having to resort to indiscrimi-
nate slaughter.

NORAD's role in the US search for flexible targeting options was scarcely
noted in Canada at the time. The JCS mandate to NORAD to provide an attack assessment was not public. By mid-decade, McNamara was publicly
emphasizing a different aspect of his strategy, "assured destruction," which
caught more attention and could be taken as compatible with Canadian no-
tions of deterrence and stability. Assured destruction was, however, not the
targeting plan, but rather a measure of what US strategic forces in their total-
ity should be able to achieve; that is, the destruction of the Soviet military and
Soviet society. Within the context of assured destruction, "McNamara never
abandoned his belief in the necessity for flexibility" and no substantive changes
were made during his time in office to the 1962 plan.[77]

In 1961 the US Chiefs added detection and tracking of satellites in earth
orbit to NORAD's existing responsibilities for air defence and missile warning. A Space Detection and Tracking System (SPADATS) brought together,
under NORAD's operational control (and CONAD's operational command),
the efforts of the U.S air force and navy, and soon thereafter those of the
Canadian military, as well.

Unlike the situation with the BMEWS sensors, which were located entirely
outside Canada, Canadian territory and the Canadian military almost immediately had a role to play in SPADATS. The USAF had a surplus Baker-Nunn

space surveillance camera to give the RCAF, which installed it at Cold Lake, Alberta. It was one of only five in existence. Such cameras gave especially good positional data for tracking satellites. At Prince Albert, Saskatchewan, the RCAF and the Defence Research Board operated a radar laboratory that also contributed information to SPADATS. It was well positioned for the early detection of Soviet satellites in polar orbit.

NORAD had made a number of arguments as to why it should be the command where the space detection and tracking efforts of the various armed services should be centralized. It was already scheduled to receive a computer that would predict satellite orbits, with a view towards limiting the number of false alarms by the three BMEWS radars. More importantly, NORAD argued that watching over objects in space was nothing short of an essential extension of its longstanding responsibility to warn of an attack on the continent. Kuter's formulation of this in a June 1960 message to the US Chiefs is worth citing, for it heralds the emergence of integrated air and space warning and attack assessment as NORAD's most important function:

> The expanding nature of the threat has materially reduced the time available for decision to alert the nation and take defensive and retaliatory action. Our very survival may depend upon our ability to make vital decisions in a matter of minutes. To accomplish this, it is mandatory that all air and space be under continuous surveillance reporting to a single responsible commander who can correlate, evaluate, and establish the credence of complementary sensors and intelligence information ... Time will not permit the conferencing of more than one agency to determine the existence and proximity of attack on the country. Therefore, all sources of early warning and information must be integrated and under the control of one responsible commander who can provide the appropriate alarm to military commands and government authorities.[78]

In late 1962 there were strong intelligence indications that the Soviets might have the capability to deploy nuclear-armed satellites. Such weapons would be able to strike with little warning. This must have been especially alarming after the Cuban missile crisis to the Kennedy administration, which authorized the USAF to quickly deploy an anti-satellite (ASAT) system, supplanting a less versatile army system further under development. The ASAT system was built at Johnson Island in the Pacific out of modified Thor missiles, equipped with nuclear warheads. It became operational in 1964.

The Johnson Island interceptors were dependent on NORAD's SPADATS to reach their targets. However, the ASAT system was not placed under CINCNORAD's operational control but rather only under CINCONAD's operational command. The US Chiefs were not opposed in principle to ASAT eventually becoming a NORAD mission. On the contrary, they saw it logically as still another extension of NORAD's role in the protection of the continent. But for the moment at least there were security restrictions which prevented Canadians from having access to information about US military space projects, except SPADATS. This would have to be worked out. Moreover, with the negotiations over consultation and authorization of Canadian nuclear weapons still incomplete, and with the memory of the Diefenbaker government's conduct during the Cuban missile crisis still fresh, the US side would want to have a lot clarified with Ottawa before it entrusted to NORAD a nuclear-armed weapon for whose use there almost certainly would be no time for government-to-government consultation. The issue, soon intertwined with that of NORAD's role in missile defence, spilled over into the preparations to negotiate about the NORAD agreement, set to expire in 1968.

THE 1968 RENEWAL: AEROSPACE DOUBTS ON BOTH SIDES

The 1958 NORAD agreement and CINCNORAD's classified terms of reference referred only to air defence. Over the subsequent decade the strategic defence of North America had become complex with respect to capabilities, the roles of the Canadian and US militaries, and the responsibilities of the two main commands at Colorado Springs. Capabilities had been added to detect and track ballistic missiles and to detect, track, and destroy satellites. As announced by McNamara, there was soon to be a limited missile defence. The Canadian military still played a role in air defence, which was shrinking. It had also acquired a capability to detect and track satellites. But it played no direct role in detecting and tracking missiles or in destroying satellites, and the Pearson government had made it clear that it would also play none in missile defence. The US Chiefs had insisted on the retention of CONAD, wisely as it had turned out. NORAD and CONAD both had responsibility for air defence, missile detection and tracking, and satellite detection and tracking. CONAD alone had responsibility for the anti-satellite weapons and for planning for missile defence.

There were attempts to bring the terms of reference and agreement up to date to reflect NORAD's expansion beyond air defence. In 1963, Gerhart, whose responsibilities by then included BMEWS and SPADATS, proposed that the terms of reference be changed from "air defence" to "aerospace defence." Both the US and Canadian Chiefs reacted positively. But it was soon evident to the military that the diplomats and other civilians would have to be brought in, for such a change would make the CINC's terms of reference broader than the 1958 agreement, the framework upon which his command rested, and would also touch on the interests of several other agencies. The proposal bogged down. Meanwhile, the US Chiefs had grown cautious about dealings with Ottawa while the longstanding negotiations with it over nuclear air defence weapons were still underway.

With those negotiations complete in 1965, the US Chiefs dropped their caution and proposed that parallel discussions be conducted between the diplomats on the agreement and the Chiefs on the terms of reference with a view towards giving NORAD the aerospace defence mission. This would not only recognize that with BMEWS and SPADATS the command already had acquired roles beyond air defence, but could also point the way for it to have operational control over both ASAT and any future missile defence. That met with an enthusiastic response from the chief of the defence staff in Ottawa, who also reported, probably inaccurately, that the Canadian government was disposed to look favourably on the formal expansion of NORAD's responsibilities. General Earl G. Wheeler, chairman of the US Chiefs, thereupon concluded optimistically in early 1966 about the terms of reference that "it may be a relatively simple matter, subject to higher authority, to convert the language ... from 'air defense' to 'aerospace defence.' The more difficult problem will probably be concerned with the resources to do the job."[79]

That was far too optimistic. As the Johnson administration moved, under pressure from the Chiefs themselves and members of Congress toward deploying a missile defence system, there was new reluctance in both Washington and Ottawa towards further expanding NORAD's role. Among the most reluctant was the US Army, which had developed the Nike interceptors and which would be responsible for the operation of the missile defence system. The army was not especially concerned about Canada, but rather about the USAF, which dominated NORAD. Elsewhere in the US defence department there was some real skepticism about the involvement of Canadians in space and missile defence. The assistant secretary of defence for international security affairs wrote in early 1967: "we have been loath to approve earlier recommendations for amendment of the NORAD mission to include aerospace defense owing to policy problems posed by potential demands for multinational operational control of space and missile systems and the potential loss of flexibility in US decisions concerning the operational deployment of emerging space and missile systems."[80] Such doubts about Ottawa may have been encouraged by the lengthy negotiations with it over consultation and authorization of use of nuclear weapons.

With the formal negotiations over renewal of NORAD in sight, the US and Canadian Chiefs as a matter of course asked General Raymond J. Reeves, who had become CINCNORAD in August 1966, for advice. At the same time, the US Chiefs separately asked him as CINCONAD to address, in effect, the skeptical views that had arisen in Washington about the expansion of the NORAD mission. They solicited his comments on two alternative command structures: one in which NORAD would be given the expanded mission and one in which it would be limited to air defence, with space and missile defence being given to another command with another commander. Reeves reacted sharply, opposing any splitting off of missions. He wrote the US Chiefs in January 1967 that "air and missile defenses must be directed by a single individual and this individual must be CINCNORAD." Otherwise there would be confusion and a loss of effectiveness. Reeves also stressed the importance of the basic precept, established almost a decade before under Partridge, that NORAD should be the primary command, with CONAD to be used only when necessary.[81]

The US Chiefs sided with Reeves, telling McNamara that they supported NORAD renewal and the expansion of its mission. The secretary of defense was not prepared to go that far. As he told Hellyer in April and the US Chiefs in May, the issue of whether NORAD would operationally control missile defences could be put off to after renewal. That became the basis of the US negotiating position. On 6 September 1967 the US ambassador in Ottawa sent a diplomatic note to the Canadian government proposing that the renewal "specifically exclude antiballistic missile defense and leave the subject to possible later joint action."[82] Twelve days later McNamara announced the deployment of the limited missile defence system.

The 1958 agreement had sailed through the House of Commons, its rational scarcely questioned. No one was expecting a repeat with the 1968 renewal. A public debate had broken out in Canada out about NORAD. Canadian attitudes towards defence cooperation with the US recently had turned decidedly cool, largely as a result of the war in Vietnam. Paul Martin, the secretary of state for external affairs, was along with Hellyer the most important supporter in the Pearson cabinet of NORAD renewal. He had to admit to Pearson in a May 1967 memorandum (endorsed by Hellyer) that the Vietnam War "has given rise in Canada to misgivings concerning possible Canadian involvement in US foreign policy. This in turn appears in some cases to have led to questioning of the nature of our continental defence cooperative arrangements with the US, in particular NORAD. NORAD, moreover, is linked for many with the nuclear issue which remains sensitive and has been enhanced by the current debate in the US over the deployment of a possible anti-ballistic missile defence."[83]

Around the cabinet table itself there were voices calling for a rethinking of Canada's alliances and nuclear commitments, and for an "independent" foreign policy. Their champion was Walter Gordon, the minister of finance.

The prime minister had his own misgivings about renewal. He wondered whether the pre-1957 Canada–US air defence arrangements, which functioned without a joint command, might not be revived. Martin argued in response that the operational integration that NORAD had been created to provide was still the most effective way to provide for the air defence of North America without sacrificing Canadian sovereignty. As he put it, "there is no alternative to NORAD which would not involve a substantial reduction in military effectiveness unless defence forces were to agree in advance to US control of air defence forces and facilities and to deployment of US air defence forces as necessary in Canada."[84]

Pearson had once openly been a "bird watcher" and so might not have been very impressed by arguments of air defence effectiveness. But Martin also warned Pearson that NORAD had become the linchpin of several other defence arrangements with the US, which would have to be renegotiated if the agreement were to lapse. For starters, there was the 1965 authorization of nuclear air defence weapons that, at the firm insistence of Ottawa, had been directly linked to NORAD, especially to CINCNORAD. The possibility of re-opening that issue must have made Pearson shudder. The extensive arrangements on consultation in the 1965 accord would also have to be revisited. The Voodoos had been provided to Canada on the specific condition that they be allocated to NORAD operations. There were the defence production sharing arrangements with the US to think about as well, as they were of considerable economic benefit to Canada. "One of the principal reasons for these arrangements was US acknowledgements that Canada's contributions to continental defence warranted a fair share in continental defence development and production ... The lapse of the NORAD Agreement could increase the pressures in the US for radical modification, if not termination, of these arrangements."[85] Martin turned these arguments into the case he would make to cabinet for renewal.

Pearson's greatest worry about NORAD was that it might involve Canada in missile defence. While the struggle in the US over Nike-X was underway, he continually put the brakes on the negotiation of NORAD renewal until Hellyer heard from McNamara that Canadian territory would not be involved. Even that did not assuage the worries of "Gordon and company" in cabinet who would agree to NORAD renewal only if it included a provision specifically exempting Canada from any commitment to missile defence, as well as a method for Ottawa to terminate the agreement on one year's notice. Such a provision would be reassuring to the prime minister, too. That became in September 1967 the basis for the Canadian negotiating position.[86]

Precisely why "Gordon and company" wanted the reservation on missile defence put into the renewal agreement is somewhat mysterious. Not only was the Sprint system to be built entirely in the US, but, as Martin also emphasized, the NORAD agreement itself could not oblige Canada to participate. It was a command and control arrangement, nothing more. Each country decided which forces it would deploy, and which ones it would put under NORAD's operational control.

The missile defence reservation may have been intended just as a gesture of Canadian foreign policy independence and as a public expression of firm disapproval of the US plan. On the other hand, it may be that Gordon and the other ministers (including the prime minister) believed that, the terms of the agreement notwithstanding, NORAD membership somehow still made Canada vulnerable to being lured or pressured into missile defence. They may have feared military machinations in Colorado Springs. Or perhaps they worried that Canada could be called upon by Washington to sign up for missile defence in order to be a "real" NORAD partner. Still, in terms of its practical and legal effects, an opting-out clause would be a gimmick, nothing more.

Not much if any attention at all seems to have been paid by the Pearson cabinet to Canada's existing role in space surveillance and CINCNORAD's hopes that the command would be given operational control over the US nuclear-armed ASAT weapon. The ASAT system was located far from Canadian soil and, quite unlike the case with missile defence, there had been no real controversy in either the US or Canada after Johnson's announcement of the deployment.

In January 1968, with the negotiations over NORAD renewal in the final stages, Reeves asked the US Chiefs to change the name of CONAD to the Continental *Aerospace* Defense Command and to endorse a similar name change for NORAD. The new names undoubtedly would better reflect the two commands' functions. At the same time the USAF took the step of changing the name of its Air Defense Command, to *Aerospace* Defense Command (ADCOM). Reeves emphasized that the proposed new names for CONAD and NORAD would not themselves necessitate any changes in the missions of the two commands. The Chiefs said no to both changes.[87] The term "aerospace" had become too hot to handle. It could be seen as indicating, especially to Canadians, but also to the US Army and in the Pentagon, that NORAD would get the missile defence mission. The Chiefs knew that Reeves' argument worked in reverse. Missions could be changed without new command names. That was how NORAD received responsibility for BMEWS and SPADATS and how CONAD had been given responsibility for the ASAT weapon. The Chiefs eventually could assign the new missile defence and reassign the ASAT weapon, regardless what the commands were called.

The US side accepted the Canadian negotiating proposals. The 12 May 1968 NORAD renewal specified that the agreement would "not involve in any way a Canadian commitment to participate in active ballistic missile defence."[88] This came to be known as the "ABM clause." Either country could terminate the agreement on one year's notice. Unlike the original ten-year term, the renewal was limited to five years. That made sense given how quickly both offensive and defensive weaponry was changing.

Those were the only changes. The 1958 text was otherwise left intact, creating a strange situation. On paper, in its renewed charter, NORAD was still only an air defence command, as if BMEWS and SPADATS did not exist. The only mention the renewal made at all of ballistic missiles – now the main threat to North America and a chief preoccupation of NORAD in its efforts to warn of and assess an attack – was to say that Canada was not committed to missile defence.

NOTES

[1] Murray Peden, *Fall of an Arrow* (Toronto: Stoddart Publishing, 1987), 66.

[2] Ibid., 93.

[3] Memo, Chiefs of Staff to Cabinet, quoted in "Aide Memoire for the Minister, Replacement of CF-100s," 5 December 1959. Department of National Defence, Directorate of History and Heritage, Raymont fonds, 1/14.

[4] House of Commons, Special Committee on Defence, *Minutes of Proceedings and Evidence,* 22 October 1963, 510.

[5] Copy in Jon B. McLin, *Canada's Changing Defense Policy* (Baltimore: The Johns Hopkins Press, 1967), 225-28.

[6] Kenneth Schaffel, *The Emerging Shield: The Air Force and the Evolution of Continental Air Defense, 1945–1960* (Washington: Office of Air Force History, US Air Force, 1991), 260.

[7] Defence Research Board, "Defence Against the Manned Bomber," July 1958, Department of National Defence, Directorate of History and Heritage, Raymont fonds, 1/14.

[8] Quoted in Reginald H. Roy, *For Most Conspicuous Bravery: A Biography of Major-General George R. Pearkes, V.C.* (Vancouver: University of British Columbia Press, 1977), 319.

[9] House of Commons, *Debates*, 20 February 1959 (1959) II, 1221.

[10] Quoted in Peden, 148 (see note 1).

[11] McLin, 84 (see note 5).

[12] See note 9.

[13] Foulkes, "Notes on Improvements in Air Defence," 18 February 1959. Department of National Defence, Directorate of History and Heritage, Raymont fonds, 1/12. Also "Aide Memoire for the Minister: replacement of CF.100s," 5 December 1959. Same source, 1/14.

[14] Memorandum, Campbell to minister "Canadian Posture in Air Defence," May 1960. Department of National Defence, Directorate of History and Heritage, Raymont fonds, 1/14.

15 Memorandum, Slemon to CINC "F-101Bs for the RCAF" 23 January 1960. Department of National Defence, Directorate of History and Heritage, Raymont fonds, 1/14.

16 Letter, AVM D.M. Smith for chief of the air staff to air officer commanding ADC, 16 January 1962. Library and Archives Canada, R112-0-2-E, Files of the Department of National Defence, 3120-2 Vol 6.

17 Memorandum chief of the air staff to Chiefs of Staff Committee, "Air Defence Plan NADO 59-69, NADOP 59-63," 9 February 1959. Department of National Defence, Directorate of History and Heritage, Raymont fonds, 202/88.

18 Air Defence Command Staff Paper, "The ADC Concept of Operations Under Nuclear Warfare Conditions," 12 December 1962. Library and Archives Canada, R112-0-2-E, Files of the Department of National Defence, 3120-2 vol. 7.

19 "Canadian Access to Nuclear Weapons in Peacetime," Annex/Section E, to NSC 5822/1, "Certain Aspects of US Relations with Canada," 30 December 1958. *Foreign Relations of the United States, 1958-1960*, Vol VII, Part 1 (Washington: USGPO, 1993), 740-74.

20 Ibid.

21 Ibid.

22 Quoted in David Cox, "Canada and NORAD 1958-1978: A Cautionary Retrospective," Aurora Paper 1 (Ottawa: The Canadian Centre for Arms Control and Disarmament, 1985), 28.

23 Basil Robinson, *Diefenbaker's World: A Populist in Foreign Affairs* (Toronto: University of Toronto Press, 1989), 107.

24 Letter, Eisenhower to Diefenbaker, 1 September 1959. FRUS, 767 (see note 19).

25 McLin, 236-37 (see note 5).

26 Cox, 33 (see note 22).

27 Quoted in Knowlton Nash, *Kennedy and Diefenbaker: Fear and Loathing Across the Undefended Border* (Toronto: McClelland and Stewart, 1990), 94.

28 Quoted in Jocelyn Ghent-Mallet, "Deploying Nuclear Weapons, 1962–63," in Don Munton and John Kirton (eds.), *Canadian Foreign Policy: Selected Cases* (Scarborough: Prentice Hall Canada, 1992), 104.

29 House of Commons, *Debates*, 4 August 1960 (1960), 7606.

30 "The proposed policy has wittily been dubbed 'a policy for bird watchers,' but bird watchers have more strength and stamina." James Eayrs, *Northern Approaches: Canada and the Search for Peace* (Toronto: Macmillan, 1961), 43.

31 *NORAD/CONAD Historical Summary, January/June 1961*. Directorate of Command History, Headquarters NORAD, 51. Copy in NORAD/USNORTHCOM History Office.

32 John Diefenbaker, *One Canada: The Memoirs of the Right Honourable John G. Diefenbaker*, Vol 3, *The Tumultuous Years, 1962–1967* (Toronto: Macmillan of Canada, 1977), 82.

[33] Robert W. Reford, *Canada and Three Crises* (Toronto: Canadian Institute of International Affairs, 1968), 214.

[34] Robinson, 285 (see note 23).

[35] Raymond L. Garthoff, *Reflections on the Cuban Missile Crisis* (Washington: The Brookings Institution, 1987), 30.

[36] From "D.B.D," Privy Council Office, "Memorandum for Mr. Bryce: Lessons of the Cuban Crisis," 20 November 1962. Department of National Defence, Directorate of History and Heritage, Raymont fonds, 113/2503.

[37] Letter, Canadian ambassador to US secretary of state, 30 September 1959 and reply, 2 October 1959. Letter, Canadian minister to Department of State, 11 January 1960 and reply, 14 January 1960. Department of National Defence, Directorate of History and Heritage, Raymont fonds, 217/992. Details on the July 1958 alert are in "North American Air Defence Command Historical Summary, January-June 1958" [sic], Directorate of Command History, NORAD. Copy in NORAD/USNORTHCOM History Office.

[38] "NORAD/CONAD Historical Summary, July-December 1962," Directorate of Command History, Headquarters NORAD/CONAD, 1 April 1963. Copy in NORAD/ USNORTHCOM History Office.

[39] Diefenbaker, 82 (see note 32). The account in this paragraph continuing into the next two is largely based on four documents: (1) "Conversation between VCAS [Annis] and AOC ADC," 25 October 1962. Library and Archives Canada, R112-0-2-E, Files of the Department of National Defence, Acc 83-4/216, Vol 47 file S-003-114 pt 4. (2) "Thursday, 25 October–A/V/M Annis VCAS" same file. (3) "Requests from CINCNORAD," attached to memo, C.R. Dunlap, chief of the air staff to chairman, Chiefs of Staff Committee, "NORAD State of Alert – Request from CINCNORAD," 23 October 1963, Department of National Defence, Directorate of History and Heritage, Raymont fonds, 113/2503. (4) Memo, Dunlap to chairman Chiefs of Staff Committee, 23 October 1962, "Nuclear Weapons for USAF Air Defence Forces in Canada" same file. My thanks to Peter Haydon of Dalhousie University for providing me with copies of the first two documents.

[40] "Conversation between VCAS [Annis] and AOC ADC" (see previous note).

[41] Ibid.

[42] Memo, Dunlap to chairman, Chiefs of Staff Committee, "Nuclear weapons for USAF Air Defence Forces in Canada" (see note 39).

[43] Harkness, "The Nuclear Arms Question and the Political Crisis Which Arose from it in January and February 1963," 19-27 August 1963. Library and Archives Canada, RG 32 B19, Harkness Papers, Vol 57, Jan-Feb 1963. My thanks to Peter Haydon of Dalhousie University for providing me with a copy of this document.

[44] Schafel, 253 (see note 6). Also NORAD/CONAD Historical Summary, January-June 1963. NORAD/CONAD Directorate of History, 1 November 1963. Copy in NORAD/USNORTHCOM history office.

[45] Harkness (see note 43).

[46] Robinson, 288 (see note 23).

[47] Jocelyn Ghent-Mallet and Don Munton, "Confronting Kennedy and the Missiles in Cuba, 1962," in Don Munton and John Kirton (eds.), *Canadian Foreign Policy: Selected Cases* (Scarborough: Prentice Hall Canada, 1992), 89.

[48] John English, *The Worldly Years: The Life of Lester Pearson Vol II: 1949–1972* (Toronto: Vintage Books, 1993), 248.

[49] Quoted in Nash (see note 27).

[50] Quoted in English, 250 (see note 48).

[51] Nash, 235 (see note 27).

[52] Quoted in McLin, 163 (see note 5).

[53] Ibid., 164.

[54] Nash, 291 (see note 27).

[55] Greg Donaghy, *Tolerant Allies: Canada and the United States, 1963–1968* (Montreal and Kingston: McGill-Queen's University Press, 2002), 101-02.

[56] Quoted in John Clearwater, *US Nuclear Weapons in Canada* (Toronto: The Dundurn Group, 1999), 26.

[57] Exchange of Notes on Authorization and Consultation, 17 September 1965. Department of National Defence, Directorate of History and Heritage, Raymont fonds, 207/350.

[58] Letter, Ross Campbell to Air Chief Marshal Miller, 3 June 1964. Department of National Defence, Directorate of History and Heritage. Raymont fonds, 207/349.

[59] Ibid.

[60] Cable, 23 June 1964, "Kirkwood-Cameron Telecon Jun 23, Authorization and Consultation." Department of National Defence, Directorate of Heritage and History, Raymont fonds, 207/349.

[61] The September 1965 agreement provided that such authority would be given. In accordance with its terms, Pearson granted authority to NORAD and Johnson to both NORAD and CONAD.

[62] Minister of National Defence, *White Paper on Defence*, March 1964.

[63] Office of the Secretary of Defense. "Memorandum for the President, Subject: Recommended FY 1966-1970 Programs for Strategic Offensive Forces, Continental Air and Missile Defense Forces, and Civil Defense," 3 December 1964.

[64] This paragraph and the next draw heavily on Owen E. Jensen, "The Years of Decline: Air Defense from 1960 to 1980," in Stephen J. Cimbala, *Strategic Air Defense* (Wilmington, Delaware: SR Books, 1989), 23-47.

[65] David Cox, *Guarding North America: Aerospace Defense During the Cold War, 1957-1972*. NORAD Special Historical Study, n.d. Chapter 9.

[66] "Memorandum for: The Prime Minister, North American Air Defence-Implications for Canada of Proposed Modernization," 24 January 1968. Department of National Defence, Directorate of History and Heritage, Raymont fonds, 19/344.

[67] G.R. Lindsey, "North American Aerospace Defence Plan for 1975," 31 January 1968. Department of National Defence, Directorate of History and Heritage, Raymont fonds, 219/110.

[68] See note 66.

[69] Extract of letter, Partridge to Foulkes, 3 July 1958, attached to letter, Foulkes to Jules Leger, undersecretary of state for external affairs, 21 July 1958. Department of National Defence, Directorate of History and Heritage, Raymont fonds, 23/819.

[70] Joint Ballistic Missile Defence Staff, "US Warning and Active Defence against ICBM," 27 October 1959. Department of National Defence, Directorate of History and Heritage, Raymont fonds, 213/870.

[71] The term is Lawrence Freedman's, *The Evolution of Nuclear Strategy,* Third Edition (Houndsmills: Palgrave Macmillan, 2003), 238.

[72] Donald R. Baucom, *The Origins of SDI, 1943–1983* (Lawrence: University Press of Kansas, 1992), 31.

[73] Quoted in ibid., 34.

[74] "Notes on a Meeting Held at the Pentagon ... 11 September 1967 between Hon. Paul Hellyer and Secretary Robert McNamara." Department of National Defence, Directorate of History and Heritage, Raymont fonds, 219/110.

[75] *New York Times*, 24 September 1967.

[76] Continental Air Defense Command, *Command History 1968,* 1 May 1969. Copy in NORAD/USNORTHCOM History Office.

[77] Desmond Ball, "The Development of the SIOP, 1960–1983," in Desmond Ball and Jeffrey Richelson (eds.), *Strategic Nuclear Targeting* (Ithaca: Cornell University Press, 1986), 70.

[78] Message, CINCNORAD to JCS, cited in *NORAD and CONAD Historical Summary, Jan-Jun 1960.* Copy in NORAD/USNORTHCOM History Office.

[79] Quoted in Cox, Chapter 9 (see note 65).

[80] Quoted in ibid.

[81] Continental Air Defence Command, *Command History 1968*, 1 May 1969. Copy, NORAD/USNORTHCOM History Office.

[82] Quoted in Cox, Chapter 9 (see note 65).

[83] "Memorandum for the prime minister: Future of NORAD," 19 May 1967. Department of National Defence, Directorate of History and Heritage, Raymont fonds, 19/343.

[84] Ibid.

[85] Ibid.

[86] Donaghy, 117-18 (see note 55).

[87] CONAD *Command History 1968* (see note 81).

[88] "Agreement between Canada and the United States of America," *Canada Treaty Series* 1968, No. 5.

CHAPTER THREE

TRUDEAU AND AEROSPACE DEFENCE, 1968–1981

SOVEREIGNTY AND "STABLE MUTUAL DETERRENCE"

Pierre Trudeau came to power in 1968 determined to reshape Canadian defence policy. Given "Trudeau's belief that Canada's natural military role was in North America rather than in Europe," the review of defence policy his new government launched almost immediately after taking office raised far more skeptical questions about Canada's involvement in NATO than its role in NORAD.[1] In April 1969 the prime minister announced its outcome, which entailed cuts in the Canadian Forces in Europe and a set of four priorities which constituted, the prime minister said, a "philosophy of defence." They favoured tasks at home. The first was "protection of our sovereignty," to which Trudeau added the dictum: "To the extent that is feasible, we shall endeavour to have those activities within Canada which are essential to North American defence performed by Canadian forces." North American defence in cooperation with the US was itself the second priority. NATO and international peacekeeping were relegated to third and fourth place.[2]

The Canadian military in NORAD felt the impact almost immediately of the new emphasis on sovereignty. From Ottawa the vice chief of the defence staff wrote the Canadian who was deputy of chief of operations at NORAD: "As you are aware, the matter of command of NORAD formations which have responsibility for Canadian airspace has become a particularly sensitive matter in Canada, particularly since the PM's April 3 policy statement ..." NORAD was at the moment reconfiguring its regional boundaries. Populous southern Ontario was still controlled by air defence headquarters in the US. Ottawa suggested that Canadian sovereignty would be enhanced if it were put under the authority of North Bay. There were, to be sure, no Canadian fighters in the immediate area. No matter, the vice chief said, the transfer to North Bay could be nominal, not real. "It is our understanding that this can be done without affecting operational effectiveness by simply arranging a working agreement between the two commanders concerning which division would actually operate in that area."[3] NORAD rejected the pretend transfer, leaving southern Ontario both nominally and actually in US regions.

After the announcement of the defence review's outcome, Trudeau set about fleshing out what the first two priorities meant in order to provide a sort of subsidiary philosophy of North American defence. In November 1969 he asked the cabinet to agree that "[i]n normal peacetime circumstances, the guiding principle in respect of Canadian sovereignty in the context of North American defence is that weapons systems in Canadian territory should be manned by the Canadian Armed Forces."[4] At the same time, Trudeau asked for cabinet endorsement of "the principle, as part of the public policy posture of the Canadian government, that Canadian territory be used solely for purposes which are defensive in the judgment of the Government of Canada."[5] Over at the Department of National Defence, the prime minister's proposal produced a certain amount of puzzled irritation. After all, weren't *all* Canadian defence efforts defensive? An indignant Ramsey Withers, a colonel and a future chief of the defence staff, wrote the then-chief that "since we have neither ever openly stated nor implied that Canadian territory would be available for *other* than defensive purposes, political opponents might conclude that the proposed policy statement indicated a change of heart and, furthermore, indicated that we had had nefarious arrangements with the United States in the past!" (original emphasis)[6]

The confusion was in part terminological. By "defensive" Trudeau meant in support of nuclear deterrence. As he explained, "the concept can be put succinctly by expressing an old maxim in slightly different terms: The capacity to counter attack is the best defence." In one sense there was nothing new to this proposal as a basis for Canadian defence policy. Defending the US nuclear deterrent, or at the least providing warning so that it could be used, was a Canadian air defence task that stretched back to the beginning of the 1950s. However, Trudeau now sought to place that task in a new context, that of *stable mutual* deterrence. As he also put it, "[b]y participating in North American defence with the US, Canada is directly involved in nuclear strategy which is now based on the concept of stable mutual deterrence. The essence of this system is that each of the super powers is deterred from striking the other first with strategic nuclear weapons because each retains the capability, after absorbing a first strike, to counter with a second strike of sufficient force to inflict unacceptable devastation in retaliation."[7]

Trudeau's thinking about deterrence was not unique. It was another version of the "'defence is a dangerous thing' argument" that had had the upper hand in debates over nuclear strategy since the late 1960s. The growth of the Soviet missile arsenal undoubtedly had put an end to US nuclear superiority and left the US population vulnerable. The Johnson administration itself, by foregoing the deployment of a thick missile defence for the thin Sentinel, had accepted the situation. Its argumentation in public about deterrence often was not unlike Trudeau's. Philipp Bobbitt observed in a study of deterrence that "[i]n their anxiety to build a constituency for arms control, President Johnson and Secretary McNamara made the American position appear more absurd than it in fact was, sometimes depicting the American strategy as a kind of suicide pact, with only one devastating option available to fend off a Russian attack."[8] The new Nixon administration had just gone somewhat further in accepting urban vulnerability, scrapping in March 1969 the plan for Sentinel in favour of a "Safeguard" missile defence system to be built in small increments and designed not to protect cities but US ICBMS.

Nonetheless, the US, despite its vulnerability to Soviet attack, simply could not abandon the possibility of its striking the Soviets first with strategic nuclear weapons. Pledges to do so in the event of a Soviet attack on Western Europe constituted a cornerstone of the NATO arrangements. US strategy and targeting options reflected this. "Extended deterrence," it was called. Trudeau had focused only on central deterrence.

In other words, the US could never accept the idea of stable mutual deterrence as Trudeau seemed to mean it. But would a Canadian commitment to the principle mean anything concrete in terms of North American defence cooperation? That was not at all clear, even to the prime minister. As he admitted, "The proposal gives rise to challenging questions as to its form, content, presentation, implementation and interpretation. Satisfactory answers to these questions will have to be sought in detail before it can be finally determined whether the proposal should be adopted."[9] Nonetheless, the cabinet duly endorsed Trudeau's principles pertaining to both sovereignty and deterrence. They constituted guidelines for the government's white paper, *Defence in the 70s*, which appeared in 1971.

Since the 1950s, Canadian air defence efforts had been concentrated in southwest British Columbia and in eastern Canada. All Canadian fighter interceptors, as well as the Bomarcs, were still in those regions. Air defence operations over the Prairies were undertaken by the USAF while off the east coast they were undertaken by both the Canadian air force and the USAF. This would begin to change, *Defence in the 70s* said, in the name of sovereignty. The government would improve its capability, using existing resources, to identify intruders in peacetime Canadian airspace. "Although from a strictly air defence point of view, it may make little difference whether the aircraft is Canadian or US, from a national point of view the Government believes that normal peacetime identification should be performed by Canadian aircraft."[10] It put the emphasis on the approaches off eastern Canada. While the white paper did not say so, this mainly meant intercepting and identifying Soviet bombers. In 1968 the Soviets had stepped up flights of small groups of long-range bombers along the coasts of North America, regularly approaching the coasts of Newfoundland and Labrador. Occasionally they flew into the Canadian air defence identification zone. NORAD presumed that they were intended to search out any gaps in radar coverage and test its reaction time. The Canadian government had adopted a policy of not challenging the Soviets in public on the intrusions. CINCNORAD had responded to them in 1968 by placing CF-101s at Chatham and US aircraft at Loring Air Force Base, Maine, on identification alert. When the early warning radars detected approaching Soviet bombers, these interceptors would fly northward to meet them, relying on bases in Newfoundland and Labrador for refuelling. After the Canadian government's decision to Canadianize this identification, the Loring aircraft would only back up the CF-101s. Canada also took over from the US operation of an air defence radar station in Newfoundland and another in Labrador.

The white paper announced, as well, that CF-104s from the training squadron at Cold Lake would be relied upon to conduct interception and identification missions in the Prairies, where there never had been Canadian fighter coverage. The CF-104s, which were flown operationally by the Canadian Forces in Europe, were being converted from a nuclear bombing role to ones with conventional weapons. These included air-to-air weapons which would give them modest air defence capabilities.

In the wake of the white paper's injunction about interception with Canadian aircraft, Air Defence Command moved in the early 1970s to redeploy its real air defence interceptors, the Voodoos, so that they would have greater coverage of Canadian airspace. Bagotville in the east and Cold Lake in the west were to be the two main interceptors bases. Detachments of fighters were to be located at Comox, Chatham and Val d'Or (which would provide Canadian fighter coverage over southern Ontario), while interceptors would be deployed irregularly to Winnipeg, Portage la Prairie and Moose Jaw on the Prairies as well as to Goose Bay and Gander in support of the continuing Soviet aircraft identification operation. CINCNORAD approved of all this, because "it improved NORAD's peacetime posture, would not adversely affect deployment plans and increased flexibility by exercising additional bases."[11]

The Ministry of Transport (MOT), on the other hand, was unenthusiastic about Air Defence Command's growing role in the protection of national sovereignty. MOT was responsible for the civilian air traffic control radars. The discussions that the Department of National Defence had conducted with it since 1966 about establishing a single national surveillance system serving the needs of both departments had not gotten far.

The MOT did not believe that there was a very great need for fighter interceptors to be able to intercept and identify civilian aircraft. As a January 1973 report reflecting its views put it, "the principal foreign civil users of Canadian airspace are either commercial carriers engaged in international air transport services whose aircraft, normally, in their own interest, comply with the applicable regulations, or operators of lighter aircraft, mainly from the United States, a large proportion of which fly outside controlled airspace under visual flight rules. Neither of these kinds of foreign traffic presents air traffic control problems essentially different from similar Canadian traffic, nor do they pose any major problems of enforcement in the event of infractions of Canadian regulations, since, in most instances, where the offending pilot cannot be prosecuted in Canada, the Ministry of Transport can rely on co-operation of the civil air authorities of the state of registry."[12]

Transport also downplayed the usefulness of the military in responding to hijacking. It was true that "in recent years, the growing number of incidents of hijacking of airliners by groups of political extremists, or by criminals for purposes of personal gain, and of the use of airliners for other acts of terrorism, have given rise to a new set of problems regarding the lawful uses of national and international airspace, for which solutions are urgently being sought both nationally and internationally." Nonetheless, "it appears evident that, apart from shadowing of hijacked aircraft to ensure that rescue action can be promptly taken in the event of a crash or forced landing or for purposes such as to assist in locating hijackers who may escape by parachute for which interceptor aircraft may be employed, such incidents seldom can be countered effectively in the air and that this too is an area, although a particularly difficult one, which must be dealt which mainly through law enforcement activities at airports and elsewhere on the ground."[13]

Given this skeptical take on the role of Air Defence Command in controlling civil aviation, it is not surprising that the Ministry of Transport admitted that it had little interest in expanding civil-military radar integration. Its own radar system was "adequate for the purposes of en route air traffic control" and while it could not detect and identify infractions, these would be "rare." So it did not "in its present planning foresee a need" to build a joint system with the military.[14]

In the United States, on the other hand, the MOT's equivalent, the Federal Aviation Administration, saw things differently. It was able to reach agreement with the USAF in 1973 on a new cooperative civil-military arrangement for radar to replace the Permanent radars. The pursuit of such an arrangement had been announced by McNamara years before. Dubbed the Joint Surveillance System, it was to ring the US, including along the border with Canada. Ironically, this step taken by the US government to improve the enforcement of US sovereignty had the additional effect of dropping a way to improve national control of Canadian airspace right into the Canadian military's lap. The SAGE centres were aging and expensive. Of the six in the US, four controlled NORAD regions extending into Canadian airspace. Under the plans for the new Joint Surveillance System, all six in the US would be replaced with four new control centres using updated technology. This provided the Canadian air force with the opportunity, which it seized, not only to replace the SAGE centre at North Bay but to build a second new Canadian centre. With the two it could take over control of all Canadian airspace within the coverage of air defence radars, putting thereby an end to the regions that included US and Canadian airspace. While the original plan was to put one centre at North Bay and the other at Canadian Forces Base Namao, near Edmonton, both were eventually located at North Bay.

The 1971 white paper dutifully expressed Trudeau's principle that the role of Canadian Forces in North America was to be only defensive and in support of "stable mutual deterrence." "Each side," it said, "now has sufficient nuclear strength to assure devastating retaliation in the event of a surprise attack by the other, and thus neither could rationally consider launching a deliberate attack."[15] However, this led to no changes in air defence policy. If Trudeau and his colleagues were at all tempted to move to a "bird watching" approach, they did not act on it. The Voodoos would continue to be armed with nuclear weapons. Their operations, the white paper said, defended the US nuclear deterrent, would reduce the weight of the attack, and helped dissuade the Soviets from expanding their long-range bomber fleet. The government did, though, take the opportunity to announce in the white paper the retirement of the vulnerable and obsolete Bomarcs.

The emphasis on "stable mutual deterrence" in *Defence in the 70s* can be taken as the expression of a consensus that had crystallized not just in the Trudeau government but in Canada more broadly as to the most appropriate role for US strategic nuclear weapons. Just as importantly, it reflected the way many Canadians preferred to view their closest involvement with such weapons. "A catastrophic war between the super powers constitutes the only major threat to Canada ..." the paper pointed out. "Canada's overriding defence objective must therefore be the prevention of nuclear war by promoting political reconciliation to ease the underlying causes of tension, by working for arms control and disarmament agreements, and by contributing to the system of stable mutual deterrence."[16] Thus the Canadian air defence and Canadian foreign policy, especially efforts encouraging arms control, could be joined. So could self interest and international service. Geography placed Canada in a precarious position between the Soviet Union and the US. But it also conferred upon it, and upon its air defence forces, the role of helping to prevent war by contributing to stable *mutual* deterrence through the protection of the US nuclear deterrent. So conceived, Canada's role in NORAD was not to serve the Strategic Air Command but to help protect global stability. Mutual deterrence, in turn, could even be seen as freeing Canada from the burden of its ties with the US. As the eminent commentator John Holmes observed in the mid-

1970s, "it may seem increasingly as if we were protected not by the US deterrent but by the system of deterrence itself, which enables not only Canada but all lesser powers to pursue their contribution to world politics relatively free of the threat of oblivion."[17] .

In 1972 the US and the Soviet Union entered into the Strategic Arms Limitation Treaty (SALT) as well as the Anti-Ballistic Missile Treaty. The latter limited each country to two missile defence sites, so located that they could not provide a nation wide defence. The two countries would remain vulnerable to each other's ballistic missile strikes. The Canadian approach to "stable mutual deterrence" appeared thereby to have been vindicated.

THE 1973 RENEWAL AND THE YOM KIPPUR ALERT

Just a few days before the ABM Treaty was signed, General Seth J. McKee, CINCNORAD, sent the US Chiefs and General F.R. Sharp, chief of the Canadian defence staff, his recommendations for the negotiations over the renewal of the NORAD agreement, which would expire in May 1973. At the top of his wish list was addressing the longstanding anomaly in the command's name and mission statement. McKee, like his predecessor, wanted "aerospace" in both.[18] He could count on the support of the US Chiefs.

McKee also wanted the agreement to be renewed for ten years, and for the 1968 "ABM clause" in it to be taken out, presumably because it was an even greater anomaly after the 1972 ABM Treaty had been signed. McKee may also have wanted the clause out in order to make it easier for him to make the case that NORAD eventually should be given operational control over the Safeguard missile defence system when it was up and running. Just because Canada was not participating directly in the operation of the system did not necessarily mean that Canadians at NORAD headquarters could not be part of its operational control. Given the touchiness of this subject, not just in Canada but also in the US because of the army/air force rivalry over missile defence, approval of this recommendation would be much iffier.

McKee also asked that the two governments consider putting into the public NORAD agreement the paragraph contained in the secret 1965 agreement on nuclear authorization and consultation that affirmed the right of both countries to take independent military action and to make use of the NORAD command and control structure to do so. While it is not possible to say what prompted him to make this suggestion, it certainly appears prescient given that scarcely over a year and a half later the US was to make use of this right.

None of CINCNORAD's suggestions for the 1973 renewal went anywhere, for the process of revising the accord was brought to a halt in autumn, 1972. General Sharp suggested then to the US Chiefs that because of the uncertainties besetting the future of North American air defence, the NORAD agreement be frozen and extended for only a short period. As Bud Drury, the acting minister of national defence was told, "[a]lthough the NORAD Agreement does not bind either country to a specific contribution in terms of personnel and equipment, it would obviously make little sense to discuss the renewal of NORAD in the absence of any agreed judgment on the future need to an integrated air defence system and on the size and composition of our forces."[19]

The air defence modernization program announced by McNamara in 1967 still constituted the framework for US air defence planning. At issue was how much the US was prepared to invest in it. The Nixon administration was obviously grappling with the issue. While it was being told by McKee and the USAF that their analysts expected the number of Soviet bombers to remain the same and be improved in quality, the intelligence agencies believed that the number would decline over the decade. There was disagreement within the military over the role bombers would play in any Soviet attack on the US. There was also disagreement over whether it made sense to maintain much of an active air defence for such goals as complicating a Soviet attack, discouraging the Soviets from developing new bombers, and limiting the damage to US cities in the event deterrence failed.

The just-signed ABM Treaty intensified the dilemma. Now that it had been decided that there was to be no missile defence "roof," how robust should the North American air defence "walls" be? Unlike the case with missile defence, the Soviets had always refused to negotiate any limits on air defence. There might soon be negotiated limits on the number of bombers, though, that could affect the level of air defence. The ABM Treaty had been accompanied by an interim Strategic Arms Limitation Treaty. While it addressed only ballistic missiles, and so left the door at least temporarily open for the Soviets to increase the number of manned bombers, the follow-up negotiations between the Soviets and the Americans were to encompass all strategic launchers, including the bombers.

On the other hand, there was some pressure in the US to improve the aging, reduced air defence, and not just from NORAD. Two Congressional committees held hearings on the state of the national air defences, including the House Armed Services Committee's Investigating Sub-committee, which sprang into action when a Cuban airliner landed in October 1971 at New Orleans, having gone undetected by NORAD. After hearing alarming testimony by McKee and others, the subcommittee concluded that "the existing US air defense is virtually useless … Because of the failure to maintain a viable US air defense system, sovereign US airspace cannot be effectively protected from intrusions of foreign aircraft, civil or military."[20] Whether Congress was prepared to spend the money to rebuild it extensively was still very much an open question, though. The hearings showed members divided over the issue.

The US defense department readily agreed to the Canadian proposal for a short-term NORAD renewal, "motivated not so much by concern for Canadian sensitivities as by its own uncertainty over the future of air defence," as Drury was also told.[21] The agreement was renewed by the two governments in May 1973 for two years, as it was, meaning the 1958 text with the 1968 ABM clause stood.[22] Even though NORAD had become an aerospace defence command, and as much as its CINC wanted to call it such, both governments were prepared to put its future on hold while one of them figured out what it wanted to do about the declining air defences.

The Canadian government took the occasion of the 1973 renewal to obtain – once again – assurances from Washington about its commitment to consultation. The impetus for this had come from Trudeau. Upon receiving a briefing in 1969 about the 1965 arrangements for consultation and authorization of the use of nuclear air defence weapons, he called for a review of the procedures. When that never occurred, he delayed approval of the NORAD renewal in spring 1973. With the expiry date looming, there was a quick review first among Canadian officials and then between Canadians and Americans. Both sides pledged allegiance to the 1965 accord and promised to improve the communications facilities which its consultative arrangements would depend upon.

Those arrangements were not invoked by Washington several months later when on the night of 24 October 1973 US forces around the world, including US aerospace defence forces, were placed on DEFCON 3 alert for the first time since the 1962 Cuban missile crisis. Attempts had failed to negotiate a cease fire in the Yom Kippur War that had broken out between Israel and the Arab states two weeks before; the Soviet Union threatened to intervene militarily on behalf of Egypt, which was facing crushing defeat. The US alert was intended to warn the Soviets off. There was a crucial difference between the Cuban missile crisis and Yom Kippur alerts. "In 1973, unlike 1962, neither civilian nor military authorities believed that escalation to nuclear war was at all likely. The DEFCON 3 alert was a military action intended as a political signal to the Soviet Union and was so understood by American military commanders. Because there was little expectation of actual use of military force, the strategic alert was ordered at a relatively low level by the central authorities and was executed in a relatively *pro forma* fashion by military commanders."[23] The alert ended late the next morning. The Soviets accepted a UN resolution to send a peacekeeping operation in to supervise a cease fire.

CINCNORAD did not place Canadian air defence forces on alert and the government of Canada was not requested by him to do so, as it had been in 1962. As in the first few days of the Cuban missile crisis, CONAD (and USAF's Aerospace Defense Command, which in 1962 had been Air Defense Command) went on higher readiness. NORAD did not. Canadian officers in the Cheyenne Mountain combat center were caught up in the alert, though.

Lieutenant-General W.K. Carr, deputy chief of the defence staff, later told a parliamentary committee, in response to a question about the alert, "... as you saw in Colorado Springs, the staff on duty is a completely integrated staff and it could be on a midnight shift, for example, in this particular case, that the duty director, even though he represents the CINC, could well be a Canadian. Should the US forces, as they did in this instance, decide to declare an increased readiness condition worldwide, he as a representative wearing his NORAD hat, would have to relay the CINC's instructions to the America forces which were part of really the CONAD command ..."[24]

No attempt was made by the US government to consult Ottawa about the alert. Because US officials saw escalation to nuclear war as being quite unlikely, the consultation provisions in the 1965 agreement were not applicable. The US was obliged, however, by the same agreement, to inform the Canadian government "immediately" upon deciding to use the aerospace command and control facilities for a unilateral purpose. That did not happen, either. Word was informally received in Ottawa about it during the evening via the Canadian NORAD regional headquarters at North Bay. The chief of the defence staff, General Jacques Dextraze, decided it was not necessary to wake up James Richardson, the minister of national defence, who was not told about the alert until the start of business the next day, eight hours after the word had originally come in.

The Yom Kippur alert led to two policy changes. Richardson told the House of Commons that procedures had been established to require the chief of the defence staff to inform the minister "automatically and immediately" in the event of any future unilateral US alert.[25] Second, as Carr also told the parliamentary committee, there were new rules about how a Canadian officer at NORAD should conduct himself under such circumstances. "The regulations now stipulate – and they were amended to make them more clear after this particular incident – that whereas he must do his initial action, because time delay cannot be accepted, he immediately is replaced by an American officer."[26] No such decision was reached after the Cuban missile crisis, when it had been accepted that Canadians could continue to function at NORAD even while CONAD was on alert. Presumably a different conclusion was reached in 1973 because the alert was intended solely to signal resolve and not to prepare to defend.[27] This provision compelling Canadian officers to leave their posts at NORAD could have put them in an excruciating position if there ever again was a unilateral alert like 1962 when nuclear war truly seemed a possible outcome of the crisis. No such alert ever came again.

Except to make these two changes, Ottawa reacted with equanimity. There is no indication that the Trudeau government was upset with the Nixon administration, the way Diefenbaker had been with Kennedy. The alert was over almost before Ottawa knew it. Ottawa may have also been glad not to have been consulted or officially informed by Washington this time. Having to take a stance on the US alert might have had an impact on Canada's ability to participate in the UN peacekeeping operation undertaken at the war's end.

WARNING AND ASSESSMENT, AND THE 1975 RENEWAL

Secretary of Defense James Schlesinger put an end to most of the uncertainty surrounding the future of continental air defence when he announced in February 1974 that "[w]ithout an effective antimissile defense, precluded to both the US and the USSR by the ABM Treaty of 1972, a defense against Soviets bombers is of little practical value."[28] He revealed that deep cuts were to be made in the US air defences: the number of interceptor squadrons was to be reduced from twenty-six to twelve, of which six would be regular USAF and six Air National Guard. The remaining Nike Hercules missile batteries would be closed. Plans for a dedicated air defence AWACS force, a centrepiece of the McNamara modernization plan, were scrapped. Instead, the USAF would acquire a general purpose AWACS force largely for use overseas, although aircraft might be made available in an emergency for North America. On the other hand, the consolidation of civilian and military radars into a system around the periphery of the US would continue and so would the plan to put in place over-the-horizon backscatter radars looking further out. Upon taking office the year before, Schlesinger had wanted to make even deeper cuts but had been talked out of it by the USAF and the Chiefs.

The purpose of the remaining US air defences shifted decisively. As the USAF chief of staff put it in the wake of Schlesinger's announcement: "We are now maintaining an air defense posture to provide surveillance and warning – to maintain the sovereignty of our airspace from intrusion or overflight. This differs from earlier air defense posture which was oriented to defending against a bomber attack."[29] Any case to be made in favour of a robust North American air defence was further weakened later in 1974 by the Interim Agreement between the US and the Soviet Union reached at Vladivostok, which placed a ceiling on intercontinental delivery vehicles of both sides of 2400, including heavy bombers. This removed much of the incentive for the Soviets to expand their bomber fleet, inasmuch as for each new bomber a missile would have to be removed from service.

The shift in purpose, and the dismantling of most of the US air defence forces, led to changes in the solely US part of the command structure at Colorado Springs. With the closing of the Nike Hercules batteries, the US Army was getting out of North American air defence. As a result, it closed its air defence command in early 1975. The US Navy's air defence command having been shut down several years before, only the USAF's ADCOM was left. The USAF had explored the possibility of closing ADCOM and transferring its shrinking assets to the Strategic Air Command and the Tactical Air Command. Instead, it had consolidated ADCOM headquarters with those of CONAD and NORAD, saving money and resulting for a while in a triple-hatting of the commander as CINCNORAD/CINCONAD/CINCAD.

However, the closing of the army's air defence command meant that CONAD no longer qualified as a unified command, that is, one with several service commands under it. Accordingly, the Pentagon disestablished CONAD in June 1975 and recognized ADCOM as a specified command. That meant it would both retain its identity as a USAF entity and assume CONAD's functions; the commander was down to two hats as CINCNORAD/CINCAD. ADCOM was one of two commands over which NORAD had operational control, the other being the Canadian Forces Air Defence Group. There was a military reorganization during 1975 in Canada as well, in which the air force structurally re-emerged as Air Command, and the air force commands, among them Air Defence Command, were renamed groups.

The US could also employ ADCOM for national purposes, just as CONAD had been used. NORAD remained the primary command. The US Chiefs directed that CINCAD would exercise operational command over US air defences "only in the event of action by Canada and the United States which makes it impossible for CINCNORAD to exercise this assigned responsibility."[30]

The relationship between NORAD and its "twin" at the Colorado Springs headquarters remained a useful way to provide for Canadian participation at Colorado Springs in the command and control of most – but not all – North American aerospace defence activities. Thus when the US Safeguard missile defence system became operational in 1974 it was under not the operational control of NORAD, but rather only under the operational command of CONAD. This authority passed to ADCOM in 1975 where it remained until the Ford administration decided that Safeguard was unnecessary and closed it in 1976.

With North America completely vulnerable to Soviet missile attack except for the very limited protection provided to missile fields by the Safeguard system, and with it becoming increasingly vulnerable to bomber attack, NORAD's responsibilities for warning and assessment became increasingly important functions. As early as 1972 a perceptive Senator John Aird, the chairman of the Canadian section of the Permanent Joint Board on Defence, had noticed this. After the board visited both SAC and NORAD headquarters he wrote Trudeau that "I was struck by the extent to which SAC and authorities in both countries are dependent upon the intelligence and warning information supplied by NORAD and its strategic warning network, part of which is located in Canada. Although many Canadians tend to think of NORAD solely in terms of bomber defence, I was most impressed by the extent to which activities at NORAD headquarters are devoted mainly to the intelligence and warning aspects of aerospace and ballistic missile defence."[31]

Just a few months before Aird's visit to Colorado Springs, NORAD's new computer program for missile attack assessment became operational. It would draw upon data from both missile detection and tracking radars to plot the North American targets of an incoming Soviet missile attack, thereby allowing NORAD to make a more detailed assessment of the nature of the attack and to pass that assessment swiftly on in the few minutes before the missiles impacted. The US Chiefs approvingly noted that "in most ICBM raid scenarios the new program could be expected to give a high confidence assessment of the attack pattern and would provide the National Military Command system with an added attack assessment capability."[32] During the 1970s, NORAD's capabilities were enhanced by the USAF's deployment of Defense Support Program (DSP) satellites capable of detecting the infrared radiation in a missile's exhaust trail soon after its launch, and by radar installations on the US east and west coasts which could track submarine-launched ballistic missiles. Map 6 shows the full array of US land-based missile detection and tracking sensors in 1981, none of which were located in Canada.

NORAD's more sophisticated capabilities to assess a Soviet attack dovetailed into revisions of US nuclear strategy which re-emphasized the possibility of limiting nuclear exchanges. While the Trudeau government settled into the comforting notion of stable mutual deterrence, the Nixon administration openly struggled to find ways to reassure America's overseas allies that the United States was still prepared to engage its strategic nuclear arsenal on their behalf, despite the vulnerability to devastating attack into which it had been locked by the ABM Treaty. At a January 1974 press conference, Schlesinger announced a new strategic approach, which entailed preparations for nuclear strikes on individual Soviet missile silos and military bases, as well as military industries, on a smaller scale than had previously been provided for. As he later elaborated, "If, for any reason, deterrence should fail, we want to have the planning flexibility to be able to respond selectively to the attack in such a way as to (1) limit the chances of uncontrolled escalation and (2) hit meaningful targets with a sufficient accuracy-yield combination to destroy only the intended target and to avoid widespread collateral damage. If a nuclear clash should occur – and we fervently believe it will not – in order to protect American cities and the cities of our allies, we shall rely into the wartime period upon reserving our 'assured destruction force' and persuading, through intrawar deterrence, any potential foe not to attack cities."[33] These limited options were embodied in National Security Decision Memorandum (NSDM) 242, which Nixon signed in early 1974.

The "Schlesinger doctrine" as it was often called, was no great innovation in US strategy. McNamara had sought limited options in nuclear targeting. Nor was it an abandonment of deterrence. On the contrary, as Schlesinger took pains to emphasize, "[t]o the extent that we have changed our targeting doctrine, we have recoupled US strategic forces to the security of Western Europe and as long as we have that coupling action, I think we have strengthened deterrence – reduced the risk of war."[34]

But it was not the Trudeau government's notion of stable mutual deterrence, which assumed that because of parity in nuclear weapons and the lack of a missile defence neither the Soviet Union nor the US rationally could resort to the use of strategic weapons against one another. The "Schlesinger doctrine" sought to demonstrate how the US might indeed be able to do just that in the event of a Soviet attack on US allies abroad.

The Nixon administration expected NSDM-242 to generate considerable controversy. Some critics did indeed charge that it was completely unrealistic to believe that nuclear war could be limited, that by emphasizing limiting options the administration had made it too easy to start a nuclear war, and that the Soviets would fear that the US was out to obtain the capability to disarm it in a first strike, which could touch off an arms race and put an end to the SALT negotiations. But the attack on the "Schlesinger doctrine" was subdued largely because it was hard for the US critics to argue against flexibility and limited options *per se*, especially since, as they had to concede, these had been a feature of US nuclear strategy since the McNamara years.[35]

No doubt largely because there was such little debate over NSDM 242 in the US, it drew little attention in Canada. North of the border, it in fact went almost completely unnoticed that there were some important differences in how the two governments conceived of nuclear deterrence. As a result, as the expiry of the two-year 1973 NORAD agreement swiftly approached, there was also all but no realization in Canada that how Canadians tended to view NORAD was also at odds with what the command was becoming. For most Canadians, NORAD was still largely a continental air defence command (as Aird had pointed out) as well as, in effect, a simple tripwire which could precipitate the launching of a US nuclear strike designed to obliterate the people of the Soviet Union. For the US military, NORAD's air defence tasks had become peripheral while its growing responsibilities to both warn of and assess Soviet nuclear strikes on North America gave it a role in a US nuclear deterrent strategy that held out the option of limiting nuclear war, should it ever break out.

The House of Commons committee that studied NORAD renewal in 1974–75 took no notice in its April 1975 report of the recent revisions in US strategy and their implications for NORAD and there is no indication that senior officials of the Trudeau government did so, either. The committee did recommend, based upon what it had heard about the Yom Kippur alert, that the agreement be amended to include provisions "ensuring that, in the event of a US national alert – as distinct from a NORAD alert – Canadian officers on duty at NORAD headquarters should be replaced immediately by US personnel to the extent that these Canadian officers were performing CONAD command functions." The US side had no objection to this. It was prepared to put into agreement language partially based on that found in the 1965 secret agreement, along the lines suggested by CINCNORAD at the time of the 1973 renewal. Inasmuch as arrangements had already been made after the Yom Kippur alert to allow Canadians to be pulled immediately from duty in Colorado Springs under such circumstances, the Trudeau government did not feel that such a "disassociation clause" as the bureaucrats called it, was needed in the agreement.[36] So the matter was dropped.

Officials at the Department of External Affairs first thought that the downgrading of US air defences announced by Schlesinger might make the 1975 NORAD renewal difficult. Canadians might be skeptical about the continuing need for the joint command. "It seems more and more likely," the Department's Defence Relations Division concluded in November 1974, "that the question of renewing the NORAD agreement will be the subject of a good deal of public debate and we will require arguments that are more acceptable than those used in the past."[37]

But the reverse was true. Just a couple of weeks later Trudeau blurted out at a press conference held in the Canadian Embassy in Washington, "I guess it would be pretty safe to speculate that NORAD probably will be renewed."[38] NORAD just was not very controversial any more; the 1975 renewal for five more years went through without a fuss. NORAD seemed to be supporting "stable mutual deterrence" and the pressure was off Canada to participate in strategic defence. There was to be no missile defence (beyond the single site) into which Canada might be dragged and not only were continental air defences to be downgraded as NORAD abandoned any attempt to significantly blunt a bomber attack and turned to air sovereignty as the prime task, but the regional air boundaries were to be redrawn along national lines.

The command remained, as the Trudeau cabinet was told, an efficient and economical way to coordinate the remaining air defences the two countries would be deploying. There were also other benefits: "Through NORAD we are kept fully informed of the air defence activities of the USA, we have access to the product of missile detection and warning systems, and we benefit from the consultative process to which the USA is bound." Just as importantly, NORAD, whatever its functional value, had become in its eighteen years of existence a fixture of Canada–US relations and thus seemed to have become a symbol not to be trifled with. "The USA is known to place considerable importance on the principle of continued Canadian cooperation in the area of North American air defence through renewal of the NORAD Agreement and Canadian willingness to do so would have a positive impact on

Canada–US relations generally. Conversely Canadian refusal to renew the Agreement could well have an adverse effect on various aspects of our relations with the USA."[39]

General Lucius D. Clay, like his two immediate predecessors as CINCNORAD, pressed the negotiators in 1974–75 for a modernization of the agreement. He got further than they did. For the first time the agreement was significantly rewritten. To be sure, there still was to be no new name for the command. Nor was the Canadian ABM clause to be taken out. Removing it may not have been of much importance for Clay, though, inasmuch as there was not to be much of a missile defence. On the other hand, even though NORAD was still to be called an air defence command, the 1975 agreement recognized that strategic missiles had replaced bombers as the major threat to North America. Still, in a nod to Canadian strategic sensibilities, the agreement said that in recent years there had been an "enhancement of mutual deterrence." While the earlier agreements had mentioned only air defence, the 1975 text acknowledged for the first time this had changed, providing a fairly realistic summary of what the command was actually doing: "In addition to performing the airspace surveillance and control functions related to air defence, NORAD will continue to monitor space activities of strategic and tactical interest and provide warning of aerospace activities that may threaten North America." Similarly, while NORAD's mandate in the earlier agreements had been solely to provide air defence, the renewal set out three new "primary objectives" for it:

(a) to assist each country to safeguard the sovereignty of its airspace;
(b) to contribute to the deterrence of attack on North America by providing capabilities for warning of attack and for defence against air attack;
(c) should deterrence fail, to ensure an appropriate response against attack by providing for the effective use of the forces of the two countries available for air defence.[40]

AIR DEFENCE PLANNING

The 1975 renewal also said that "[s]ince surveillance and control in peacetime are expected to assume increasing importance, each Government has decided to establish a joint civil-military system to carry out these activities in conjunction with the air defence operations of NORAD."[41] It was not quite that simple, though. In the US, planning was fairly well underway for the development of the Joint Surveillance System to replace the Permanent radars. In Canada things were not proceeding so smoothly, despite the Trudeau government's official emphasis on sovereignty. Not surprisingly given the skepticism of the MOT about the military's role in air traffic control, planning for radar integration was going nowhere. Meanwhile, the longstanding electronic backbone of air defence in Canada the CADIN/Pinetree radar line, the oldest of whose stations was over twenty years old, was costly to maintain and operate when compared to a modern, highly automated radar system. Its remaining twenty-four stations required no fewer than 6,000 personnel to operate it. New radars would need only about a tenth. But installing them would be expensive for the Department of National Defence, too, especially if no agreement could be reached with MOT on cost sharing. The USAF had originally built most of the line and was still paying forty-five percent of the operating costs. But it was unlikely that it could be persuaded to pay for an update, because aside from its coastal radars, the Pinetree Line was no longer needed for the scaled-down anti-bomber defence. If Canada wanted civil-military radars for sovereignty purposes, it would have to pay for them itself.

Ottawa faced a similar dilemma with the Distant Early Warning Line. In McNamara's day, it was envisaged that the line would be replaced by US AWACS in constant flight or possibly by one over-the-horizon backscatter radar installation, if the technology could be made to work pointed north. However, in the wake of cutbacks there would be nowhere enough aircraft for the AWACS option and by the mid-1970s scientific tests had ruled out north-ward-pointing OTH-B. US air defence officials began to consider having built what they called an Enhanced Distant Early Warning Line, which, like the existing one, would be a chain of radar stations. The Americans also began to let their Canadian colleagues know that they expected Canada to help pay for the costs.

Thus, as John Anderson, who was at the time the assistant deputy minister of national defence for policy, later recalled, "[t]he situation, as it appeared to National Defence Headquarters in the early weeks of 1976, was not comfortable. It seemed possible that the defense budget would have to pay the full cost of replacing the CADIN/Pinetree Line, that the resulting expenditure would not be seen by the American government as an effective contribution to the modernization of the North American air defense system, and that the Canadian government would be pressed as well to make a sizable financial contribution to replacement of the DEW Line."[42] Ottawa therefore proposed to Washington that a bilateral group be formed to consider not only how the continent's air defence should be modernized, but how the costs should be shared. This came down to the question of how much the US should be expected to pay for the improvements located in Canada. Such a group was formed and began meeting in 1976, and continued to meet into 1977 and 1978 with little coming out of its discussions. Jimmy Carter took office as president in January 1977. As Anderson, who was Canadian co-chairman of the cost sharing group also later remembered, for the Carter administration, "North

American air defence modernization was even less of a priority than it had been for the Ford administration."[43] This was evident scarcely a month after the Carter administration took power when it deferred funding the for the purchase of F-15s intended to replace in 1980 ADCOM's six squadrons of aging F-106s, as well as six Air National Guard squadrons of the same aircraft.

The Canadian government kept plugging, though, and suggested that the two defence departments commission and split the costs of an air defence study. The result in 1979 was the Joint US–Canada Air Defence Study (JUSCADS). Not surprisingly, it categorized the weaknesses and deficiencies in the North America air defences. In addition to aging equipment, it also pointed out that "the current locations of surveillance radars, aircraft identification, and interceptor operating areas do not cover some potential bomber penetration routes and do not reflect the evolution of civil air traffic patterns."[44] A map accompanying the declassified excerpts from the report showed that the group was especially concerned about a great gap in radar coverage in the Davis Strait area that had arisen largely as a result of the US having had closed the eastward extensions of the DEW Line.

The report underlined as well the new dilemma for air defence planning posed by emerging technologies. It might be possible to replace ground-based radars with space-based radars or infra-red sensors. That meant, according to the JUSCADS report, the two governments needed to decide either to proceed soon with modernization based on conventional technology or to stretch out the life of the existing air defences while investing heavily in the rapid development of space-based air defence technologies.

According to Anderson, JUSCADS advanced Canada's interests by making sure that US planners kept them in mind.[45] Little would be done, though, until attitudes in Washington towards continental air defense changed.

Those attitudes did change, leading "the US – in the waning days of the Carter Administration – to take a new, critical look at its atrophying air defense capabilities."[46] In the background, the fading of *détente* with the Soviet Union, especially after its invasion of Afghanistan played a role. More immediately, the Soviets were equipping their bombers with air-launched cruise missiles, and there were indications that they were developing a new generation of strategic bombers as well as longer range air-launched cruise missiles. They were also adding Backfire bombers to their inventory which, because they were capable of reaching the US on one-way flights, or refuelled, some analysts saw as a growing intercontinental threat.

Most importantly, the USAF began to argue at the end of the decade that these enhancements in Soviet bomber capabilities and the deterioration in North American air defences were creating a new threat, that of a precursor or decapitation strike. Ever since the Soviets had acquired a significant number of ballistic missiles, US planners had largely assumed that the Soviets would use the bombers *after* having struck first with the ballistic missiles, some of which would be targeted against the North American air defences. That had led Schlesinger to conclude in 1974 that thick air defences were not worth the effort. They could only blunt a portion of the strike and they probably would be destroyed first anyway. As an official of the Department of External Affairs had put it later in 1974 after having been briefed in Washington on US air defence plans, "[t]he Americans have recently adopted the philosophy that for the period ahead there is virtually no scenario in which a first strike against North America by Soviet bombers would make any sense."[47]

By the end of the 1970s, the Americans could see just such a scenario. Soviet bombers and cruise missiles, undetected by NORAD, could strike at key decision-making centres including the National Command Authority (the president, the secretary of defense and their successors) and military command and control facilities. The strike would be timed so that nuclear warheads carried by the bombers and cruise missiles would detonate on target at the same moment that NORAD detected Soviet ballistic missile launches, thereby depriving the US of the maximum warning time before missile impact. Such a precursor raid could leave US strategic forces, in the words of a Canadian Senate Committee that later studied the issue, "decapitated, confused, unable to obtain orders and incapable of retaliating."[48]

Reflecting the new concern in Washington for continental air defences, the US Congress directed the defense department in 1979 to prepare a plan for their improvement. In response, the USAF developed what it called the Air Defense Master Plan. Both NORAD and the Canadian Department of National Defence cooperated closely in its preparation. The plan was based not on space-based technology, but the conventional kind, and took as its point of departure the need to deal with a precursor strike. "While considered unlikely, the precursor bomber strike was nonetheless used for planning purposes, because it was large enough, given the assumption of surprise, to be a significant threat. Equally, such a strike was small enough so that a reasonable defensive system against it might be considered 'affordable.'"[49] The Air Defense Master Plan was submitted for approval in January 1981 and became the basis for improvements in North American air defence that will be discussed in the next chapter.

In the meantime, there were improvements in Canadian air defence efforts. Canadian Forces personnel began in 1979 to fly on board US AWACS flights in North America, out of bases in Oklahoma and Arkansas. Canadians could serve in most air duty positions on these NORAD-related flights. The next year the Canadian government signed a contract with McDonnell Douglas for a fleet of CF-18A Hornet fighter aircraft, thereby guaranteeing that the Canadian air force could continue in the active air defence of Canada. Although the service life of the CF-101 Voodoos had been extended in 1972 as a result of a "swap" with the USAF whereby Canada received aircraft with fewer flight hours, they were aging and expensive to maintain. There were thirty six still in service, in three squadrons; a training squadron had a number, as well. The Hornets were to replace not only the Voodoos, but also the CF-104s flown by Canadian Forces Europe. In fact, as the Senate committee noted, the decision to buy new aircraft "was prompted by pressure from NATO and not by a strong belief on the part of the government or the country at large that Canada should do more in NORAD."[50]

Especially with the air defence of Canada in mind, the air force was clearly hoping to be equipped with the F-15 and had been disappointed when the Trudeau government had in 1975 turned down an offer to acquire it on advantageous terms. Thereafter, because of its price, it was knocked out of the competition leading up to the 1980 contract.[51] After the Hornet purchase was announced, there were charges that it was not well suited to NORAD roles because it was too slow (especially when compared to the F-15), and its radar range was limited. It also lacked a second seat for a navigator/weapons systems operator which many Canadian air defence pilots found important for North American operations at night and in bad weather, and to deal with the heavy electronic counter-measures carried by Soviet bombers. On the other hand, it did have two engines, considered a must for northern operations as a safety feature.[52] Brigadier-General Paul Manson, head of the new fighter project office (and another future chief of the defence staff) argued, however, that "[i]n the North American sovereignty and air defence mission the CF-18 performs very well, by virtue of its excellent climb characteristics, acceleration, radar, radius of action and fire control system." He went on to admit, though, that the Hornet's "maximum speed of about Mach 1.8 could limit its effectiveness in identifying high speed unknowns."[53]

NORAD AND ADCOM; TRUDEAU AND COSMOS 954

In the late 1970s North America's active strategic defences were at a nadir. The once vast continental air defence forces had been reduced to shadows of themselves. While a robust missile defence had once been envisaged, only one site had ever been built and it had been dismantled. Under Congressional pressure to reduce overhead management costs, the USAF considered whether the two commands devoted to strategic defence, NORAD and ADCOM, were still needed. The USAF chief of staff, General David Jones, is reputed upon visiting Colorado Springs in 1977 to have "expressed concern about the number of people sitting around waiting for something to happen." He established at USAF headquarters a small study group with the task of looking at how to do away with both NORAD and ADCOM. It soon realized that "[b]ecause of the political implications of NORAD, with Canadian involvement, eliminating that organization was not a tenable option. The group concluded that the service should keep NORAD, but look at the ADCOM functions and organization very closely."[54]

The group revived the plan the USAF had considered and rejected a few years before to close ADCOM, which would involve sending its assets to two other USAF commands. Its air defence forces would go to Tactical Air Command (TAC) and its missile warning and space surveillance assets (such as the BMEWS radars) to SAC. TAC was charged with maintaining battlefield-level (tactical) forces, overwhelmingly for use abroad. It already owned the AWACS aircraft that might be called upon for North American air defence. Since it also had fighter aircraft, ADCOM's interceptors could be folded readily into its responsibility. The study group made the powerful argument that such a transfer would allow Colorado Springs to concentrate on what had clearly become its main mission: assessment and warning of attack. As it put it, "by unburdening CINCNORAD/CINCAD of the duties and responsibilities inherent in a day-to-day management of a USAF major command, this proposal would permit more concentrated time and attention on the critical operational aspects of his strategic missions."[55]

The fit of the space surveillance and missile warning assets into SAC was rougher. Many USAF officers believed that their service's growing space operations needed a distinctive organizational home and thought that it should be built upon ADCOM. The USAF had always kept the offence and defence apart. SAC, under the new plan, would now have responsibility for some systems that were key to the defence.

It would not, however, have responsibility for attack warning and assessment. That would remain with NORAD, which would rely in part on data provided by SAC. NORAD would also retain responsibility for operational control over continental air defences, to be provided by TAC as well as by the Canadian air force, of course.

However, NORAD's relationship to the US command structure and budgeting process would probably be weakened. From the beginning it had been closely associated with the USAF command, first ADC and later ADCOM, that itself "owned" most US strategic defences and was responsible for their development. For neither of the new owners, TAC and SAC, was strategic defence the first priority. With this concern in mind the air staff planners proposed to give NORAD and ADCOM special responsibilities for strategic defence planning and guidance. This was not enough for General Daniel James, CINCNORAD/CINCAD who reacted absolutely furiously to the proposals. He wrote Jones that he had "strong objections to the approach, logic, appropriateness, rational, adequacy, and accuracy" of the air staff's proposals, and called them, "inaccurate" "superficial" and "biased." He argued that "a perceived de-emphasis in US air defence priority would signal the wrong intention to both our enemies and our allies," and "[i]f national defense is a valid priority, a strong air defense organization is required."[56]

Naturally enough, James singled out one ally, Canada, also telling Jones: "I am convinced that the Canadians will not tolerate any significant dependence on SAC for attack warning." At the same time, NORAD headquarters tried to enlist the Canadian government in the fight. Major General K.C. Lett, in the traditionally Canadian position of the command's director of operations, sent a message to Ottawa contending that the proposals were in violation of the NORAD agreement, as well as "underhanded, devious, full of half truths."[57]

It does not appear that NORAD found any strong support in Ottawa in the fight to retain ADCOM. James and Lett's argumentation with respect to Canada was weak; the secretary of the air force was on much sounder ground when he wrote Secretary of Defense Harold Brown that ADCOM could be eliminated "without disturbing ... our international agreements regarding Canada."[58] To the extent there was a Canadian sensitivity about SAC it was a touchiness about any perception of being too closely involved with the delivery of strategic nuclear weapons. But this sensitivity had never precluded NORAD's task of providing warning to SAC and Ottawa really could not expect to object to NORAD's being provided data by it. Closing ADCOM did not violate the NORAD agreement, for under its terms both countries retained the right to organize as they saw fit the forces they placed under NORAD's operational control.

NORAD's objections notwithstanding, the command structure changes took effect in late 1979. To work with NORAD, the US continued to need a twin command at Colorado Springs with which it could operationally command US aerospace defence forces for its national purposes. Confusingly, the name "Aerospace Defense Command" and its "ADCOM" acronym were both retained in 1979 for the twin. Prior to the change, ADCOM was a USAF "major" command with its own aerospace defence forces that had also been designated a "specified" command by the US Chiefs. After October 1979, only the specified command remained – essentially a headquarters organization only, just like its twin, NORAD.

NORAD's role in space surveillance and its anachronistic name as an air defence command were embarrassingly brought home for Trudeau, and vividly emphasized for Canadians when a Russian maritime surveillance satellite, COSMOS 954 fell out of orbit and crashed into the Northwest Territories near Baker Lake, on 24 January 1978. Canadian and US officials were also confronted with a problem for Canada caused by the relationship between NORAD on the one hand, and ADCOM and US intelligence operations on the other.

Power for the radars onboard the COSMOS 954 was provided by a nuclear reactor. Normally, the reactor would be jettisoned and then boosted into a higher orbit at the end of the satellite's useful life, with the rest of its parts burning up on re-entry. However, the US Defense Space and Missile Activity Center (DEFSMAC) informed Canadian intelligence officials at the Department of National Defence in early November 1977 that the satellite's power supply had not been jettisoned, apparently because of malfunction, and that it was expected to re-enter in April. If the reactor did not burn up on re-entry there was the possibility of a health hazard from radioactive matter being dispersed over a small area. Canadian territory was under the satellite's orbital path. On 11 January 1978 DEFSMAC told the department that the satellite's orbit was decaying much more rapidly than expected; re-entry was predicted for the 23 January. A week later the US Embassy in Ottawa informed the Department of External Affairs of the coming re-entry and offered help if satellite debris landed in Canada.

DEFSMAC had been formed after the Cuban missile crisis to evaluate foreign missile activity and threats. It was among the most secret of US intelligence organizations, a joint project of the National Security Agency and Defense Intelligence Agency. As a former director of the latter agency put it, "You didn't want NORAD fooling around in technologies that they didn't understand or trying to evaluate a bunch of raw data, so DEFSMAC was put in."[59]

NORAD's space surveillance system (SPADATS) was also monitoring the satellite's orbital decay. In December 1977 Trudeau visited NORAD (the only visit by a Canadian prime minister in NORAD's fifty-year history) and was told about it. On 20 January NORAD predicted re-entry on the 23rd, with probable impact near Sept-Isles, Quebec. In Ottawa, the chief of the defence staff, minister of national defence, clerk of the Privy Council and regional directors of Emergency Planning Canada were briefed; a note was sent to the prime minister and the RCMP was informed. However, information was not disseminated any further; in particular, provincial emergency authorities were not provided with information, nor were officials of several federal departments whose resources could be of use in dealing with radioactive debris. Ottawa was responding to US security concerns. A Canadian interdepartmental study later explained why: "From the time this satellite was launched, the US intelligence agencies had a continuing interest in it for numerous reasons and information pertaining to the COSMOS was highly classified. This is normal as the US would not want their intelligence capabilities to be known to the USSR."[60]

Re-entry on the 24th began at 06:53 over the Queen Charlotte Islands, with the reactor core hitting the Baker Lake area a few minutes later. President Carter called Trudeau at 07:10 to tell him what had just occurred. At about the same time Carter's national security advisor, Zbigniew Brzezinski, called his counterpart in Ottawa, Ivan Head. Not until 07:30 did NORAD directly inform the Department of National Defence what had occurred. NORAD may not have been the first to inform the department whose own report seems to indicate that the Pentagon and the US Department of Energy contacted it earlier, shortly after re-entry. Over the next eighty-four days, National Defence led an interdepartmental and Canada–US effort dubbed "Operation Morninglight" to find and collect the satellite's radioactive debris.[61]

Trudeau held a press conference about COSMOS 954 on 26 January, during the course of which he said, in essence, that he was grateful to President Carter for having called him, and for the US defence department for having provided information, because under the NORAD arrangements the US was under no obligation to share space-related information. An alert reporter politely suggested to the prime minister that he was "confused;" NORAD did indeed have responsibilities for monitoring satellites. Trudeau would not budge, though. He responded:

No, that is not the case. NORAD stands for North American Air Defence – NORAD, and that is what it is. It is an air defence agreement essentially against bombers and to a lesser extent against ballistic missiles but insofar as they are entering our air space, the air space of North America. That is the NORAD agreement. It is an agreement to put together our knowledge and to have a joint command to protect ourselves in air defence. The space activities don't come under NORAD, they come under NASA. They are monitored and operated to a large degree from the same place in Colorado Springs, but there is something else.

...

[The Americans] gave us more information earlier than they had to. They did use the NORAD site and they did indeed use the NORAD channels and gold phones and everything else to get the information through, but this is through the accident that space operations happen to be located in the same place as the NORAD operations.[62]

General James. E. Hill, CINCNORAD, arrived in Canada a few days later. It must have been with a certain amount of glee that the Canadian press got him to confirm at his own press conference in Ottawa that, as one reporter put it, NORAD "has been for some time in the business of tracking satellite traffic" and that NORAD had informed the prime minister about COSMOS 954 during his visit to NORAD a few months before.[63]

And it is easy to think of Trudeau as having been hoist on his own petard: after all, his own government had refused to change NORAD's name to include "aerospace." Still, Trudeau was in part misled by the circumstances at the time of re-entry. NORAD had not been able to act as a bi-national aerospace command fully responsive to the security interests of both countries. In particular, it did not contact either him or other senior officials in Ottawa immediately that morning. Only US officials, including the president, had been informed immediately, apparently because the Soviet satellite was of particular interest to and monitored by US intelligence agencies, including DEFSMAC. The Canadian interdepartmental study later concluded that senior Canadian officials had not been informed because of the division of responsibilities between NORAD and ADCOM: "when COSMOS 954 re-entered the atmosphere it was detected by a satellite early warning system that does not belong to NORAD but to the Aerospace Defence Command which is the US national portion of NORAD. This is why the information was passed on the National Security Agency net directly to the President."[64]

This explanation is not particularly convincing, though, at least not in itself. NORAD relied on all sorts of assets belonging to ADCOM, including satellite warning systems. A decision had to have been made to not pass on the information from ADCOM to NORAD (and on to Ottawa) in this case or in such cases. ADCOM had no doubt been directed to provide the information to DEFSMAC, which then passed it along on the National Security Agency network. DEFSMAC may have relied on other sources, too.

Michael Pitfield, the clerk of the Privy Council, was particularly miffed. He wrote the deputy ministers at National Defence and External Affairs in July 1978 that "[t]he re-entry of this satellite revealed a serious flaw in NORAD's agreement in that intelligence gathered by US national agencies is not necessarily available to Canada through NORAD even if it is related to our security and available in Colorado Springs." He called for a formal review with the US government of the terms of the NORAD accord; provisions for such a review were to be found in the accord itself.[65] C.R. Nixon, the deputy minister of national defence, assured Pitfield that there had been several discussions between Canadian and US defence officials, including those involving CINCNORAD about the matter. "On all of these occasions the US side has tacitly acknowledged its failure to provide timely information to Canada on a matter affecting the security of this country."[66] K. Goldschlag at external affairs told Pitfield: "The fact that there was this significant delay in the transmission of US technical intelligence through the NORAD system has serious implications ... recognized in the United States as it is here." He added, "I can assure you that we intend to satisfy ourselves that everything possible has been done to ensure that in the future, regardless of its source, all information related to our security and available at NORAD headquarters is fully shared."[67]

National Defence and External Affairs were both opposed to invoking the provision in the NORAD agreement for the review of its terms. Renewal negotiations with the Americans were less than a year off, Pitfield was told; that was the time to take it up.

THE 1980 AND 1981 RENEWALS: NORTH AMERICAN *AEROSPACE* DEFENCE COMMAND

After having dragged its heels for over ten years on recognizing in the agreement NORAD's roles beyond air defence, Ottawa found itself in the new position, as renewal negotiations got underway in 1979, of wanting the accord to emphasize certain aspects of space cooperation. The door had been opened by Pitfield's mandate to make sure NORAD would pass on to Ottawa space-related information. While the Department of National Defence had long supported putting more space policy into the agreement, it also had a new argument to make. As the JUSCADS study had just emphasized, some future air defence systems, in which Canada could have a strong interest, would probably be space-based.

When the US side presented the first of its negotiating points, a name change for NORAD, this time the Canadian side was receptive. Officials of the Department of External Affairs argued that the political climate in Canada for such a change was now different. In the debates of the past, "aerospace" had been associated by Canadians largely with missile defence, with which Canada wanted no part. Now, however, it meant something else: "NORAD's space vehicle tracking and re-entry prediction functions are public knowledge as a result of COSMOS 954, SKYLAB and the re-entry of other space debris. The renaming of NORAD, with a greater emphasis on the space identification role, should, in both public and practical terms, help encourage awareness and interest in Canada–USA cooperation in space generally."[68] Canadian officials probably also came to the conclusion that when a name confuses the prime minister, it is time to change it.

The second change the US side wanted was to "acknowledge NORAD's expanded responsibilities for aerospace surveillance and warning."[69] This was the opportunity for the Canadian side to take up the issue of NORAD passing on to Ottawa all information Colorado Springs had affecting Canadian security.

The US negotiators preferred a five-year renewal and also revived the proposal, first made by CINCNORAD prior to the 1973 renewal, that the "ABM clause" be removed. Except to meet the demands of "Gordon and company" back in 1968, the clause never made much sense, inasmuch as the NORAD agreement could not commit either country to participate in any new weapons system. Moreover, if missile defence was all but dead after the 1972 ABM Treaty, it had been buried when the US dismantled its sole missile defence site in 1976.

Or so it appeared at the time. While the 1979 negotiations were just getting underway, Ronald Reagan, the former governor of California who had made a run at the Republican nomination for president in 1976, visited NORAD where, as a private citizen, he toured Cheyenne Mountain and met with General Hill. They talked about how NORAD had no way to defend the United States against missile attack. A former aide, Martin Anderson, who accompanied him, later wrote about what Reagan said during the flight home to Los Angeles:

> He couldn't believe the United States had no defense against Soviet missiles. He slowly shook his head and said, "We have spent all that money and have all that equipment and there is nothing we can do to prevent a nuclear missile from hitting us." Towards the end of the flight he reflected on the terrible dilemma that would face a US president if, for whatever reason, nuclear missiles were fired at the United States and concluded, "We should have some way of defending ourselves against nuclear missiles."[70]

The Trudeau government was defeated at the polls in May 1979 and the minority Clark government assumed responsibility for the negotiations. When Trudeau and the Liberals were returned to power (and Michael Pitfield, who had been discharged by Clark, returned to his office in the Langevin Bloc) in the unexpected election of February 1980, expiry of the NORAD agreement was but ninety days away. The new Trudeau government, proclaiming that it wanted to give a House of Commons committee the opportunity to study renewal, and perhaps recalling the big trouble the new Diefenbaker government had gotten into in 1957 when it reached a decision about NORAD too quickly, obtained Washington's agreement to renew the accord for just one year and just as it was.

In 1980, Carter signed Presidential Directive 59, modifying US nuclear strategy. It mandated increased flexibility in nuclear targeting and placed greater targeting emphasis on Soviet military targets (as opposed to cities), command, communications, control and intelligence (C3I) structures, and war-supporting industries. It also emphasized improvements in the command and control of US nuclear forces during the course of a protracted nuclear conflict. This would include NORAD. In fact, it was during a visit to NORAD and SAC that Brzezinski, the driving force behind PD-59, became convinced "of the acute weakness of our C3I and of the urgent need to correct that deficiency, in the context of a broader review of our basic doctrinal assumptions."[71]

When reports began to appear in the newspapers that the Carter administration had adopted a new strategy that was radically different, the Secretary of Defense, Harold Brown, sought to reassure. PD-59 was, he said in an August 1980 public address, "*not* a new departure. The US has never had a doctrine based simply and solely on reflexive, massive attacks on Soviet cities. Instead, we have always planned both more selectively (options limiting urban-industrial damage) and more comprehensively (a range of military). He also emphasized that "[t]he fundamental premises of our countervailing strategy are a natural evolution of the conceptual foundations built over the course of generations, by, for example, Secretaries McNamara and Schlesinger, to name only two of my predecessors who have been most identified with development of our nuclear doctrine."[72]

While not a new departure, PD-59 also was not "stable mutual deterrence" as Canadians thought of it. The House of Commons Standing Committee on External Affairs and National Defence in its December 1980 report recommending NORAD paid no attention at all to this point in its final report, just as it had ignored the "Schlesinger Doctrine" six years earlier.

The US negotiators seem to have been more alert to the relationship between US strategy and NORAD. In the final text of the 1981 renewal, the reference to "enhancement of mutual deterrence" that had been inserted in 1975 was gone.[73] That expression must have been jarring to US defence officials who were struggling, with the waning of *détente*, to reinforce the deterrence of a resurgent Soviet Union.

Also gone was the useless and unnecessary "ABM clause." As well, NORAD was, at last, renamed the North American Aerospace Defence Command. The agreement was given a five-year term, and was updated to reflect more fully NORAD's responsibilities beyond air defence for space surveillance and for what the agreement termed "warning and characterization of aerospace attack."

In the wake of the COSMOS 954 incident, the two governments pledged in the renewed accord to "seek ways to enhance cooperation in accordance with mutually agreed arrangements in the surveillance of space and in the exchange of information on space events relevant to North American defence." The Canadian and US negotiators had to work hard to find that language, for in this sensitive area the US side wanted the agreement to convey "the clear and unmistakable implication that not everything is possible and there are thus limitations on the extent of our cooperation."[74] The renewal was signed at Ottawa in March 1981 in the presence of Trudeau and his visitor, the recently inaugurated President Reagan.

NOTES

[1] Bruce Thordarson, *Trudeau and Foreign Policy: A Study in Decision Making* (Toronto: Oxford University Press, 1972), 74.

[2] Statement by the prime minister, 3 April 1969, "A New Defence Policy for Canada," in Arthur E. Blanchette (ed.), *Canadian Foreign Policy: 1966-76: Selected Speeches and Documents* (NP: Gage Publishing, 1980), 46-48.

[3] Letter, vice chief of the defence staff to deputy chief of staff operations, NORAD, 24 September 1969. Department of National Defence, Directorate of History and Heritage, Raymont fonds, 874/47.

[4] Memorandum to Cabinet, "North American Defence Policy," 3 November 1969. Department of National Defence, Directorate of History and Heritage, Raymont fonds, 216/286.

[5] Ibid.

[6] R.M. Withers, "North American Defence Policy-PM's Letter to MIND 3 Nov 1969," 4 November 1969, Department of National Defence, Directorate of History and Heritage, Raymont fonds, 216/286.

[7] See note 4.

[8] Philipp Bobbitt, *Democracy and Deterrence: The History and Future of Nuclear Strategy* (New York: St. Martin's Press, 1988), 111.

[9] See note 4.

[10] Minister of National Defence, *Defence in the 70s*, August 1971, 20.

[11] Continental Air Defense Command, *Command History, 1972*. Copy in NORAD/ USNORTHCOM History Office.

[12] "Air Defence Policy Review," January 1973, attached to memorandum to minister of national defence "Air Defence Policy Review," 29 January 1973. Department of National Defence, Directorate of History and Heritage, Raymont fonds, 82/525.

[13] Ibid.

[14] Ibid.

[15] White paper, 4 (see note 10).

[16] White paper, 6 (see note 10).

[17] John Holmes, *Canada: A Middle-Aged Power* (Toronto: McClelland and Stewart, 1976), 213.

[18] Continental Air Defense Command, *Command History, 1972*, Command History Secretary, Joint Staff, Headquarters CONAD, 1 July 1973. Copy in NORAD/ USNORTHCOM History Office.

[19] Memorandum for the minister, "NORAD Agreement," 4 October 1972. Library and Archives Canada, R219-0-2-E, Files of the Department of External Affairs , 27-14-NORAD-3 pt. 2.

[20] US Congress, House, Committee on Armed Services, "Cuban Incident at New Orleans." Hearings before the ... Investigating Subcommittee, 3 January 1972, 92nd Cong, 1st Session 1972, 1-2.

[21] 4 October 1972, Memorandum for the minister (see note 19).

[22] "Exchange of Notes between Canada and the United States of America," *Canada Treaty Series* 1973, No. 2.

[23] Scott D. Sagan, "Nuclear Alerts and Crisis Management," *International Security* 9, No. 4 (Spring 1985), 128.

[24] Standing Committee on External Affairs and National Defence, *Minutes and Proceedings*. 18 March 1975, 7:13.

[25] Quoted in David R. Angell, "NORAD and Binational Nuclear Alert: Consultation and Decision Making in the Integrated Command," *Defence Analysis* 4. No 2, 137.

[26] *Minutes and Proceedings* (see note 24).

[27] The relevant command history sheds no light on this. While it discusses the alert, making it clear it was a CONAD action, it makes no mention of either a kerfuffle with the Canadians in Cheyenne Mountain or the arrangements subsequently made. Excerpts, *History of CONAD and Aerospace Defense Command, 1 Jan 1973-30 June 1974*. Copy in NORAD/USNORTHCOM History Office.

[28] Quoted in David N. Spires, *North American Air/Aerospace Defense, 1972–1983*, NORAD Special Historical Study, March 1992, Chapter 1.

[29] Quoted in ibid., Chapter 1.

[30] SM-356-75 to CINCs et al., 27 June 1975, quoted in *The History of the Unified Command Plan, 1946–1993*, Joint History Office, Office of the Chairman of the Joint Chiefs of Staff, February 1995, 46.

[31] Letter, Aird to Trudeau, 23 October 1972. Library and Archives Canada, R219-0-2-E, Files of the Department of External Affairs, 27-14-NORAD-3 pt. 2.

[32] Continental Air Defense Command, *Command History 1972*, 1 July 1973. Copy in NORAD/USNORTHCOM History Office.

[33] Secretary of Defense James R. Schlesinger, *Annual Defense Department Report, FY* 1976 2 (February 1975), 4.

[34] Quoted in Bobbit, 90 (see note 8).

[35] This paragraph is based on Lawrence Freedman, *The Evolution of Nuclear Strategy*, Third Edition (Houndsmills: Palgrave Macmillan, 2003), 360-65.

[36] Extract official report of Standing Committee on External Affairs and National Defence, 22 April 1975 attached to Memorandum to the Cabinet, "Renewal of NORAD Agreement," 28 April 1975. Library and Archives Canada, R219-0-2-E, Files of the Department of External Affairs, 27-14-NORAD-3 pt. 3.

[37] Defence Relations Division, "North American Air Defence," 5 November 1974. Library and Archives Canada, R219-0-2-E, Files of the Department of External Affairs files, 27-14-NORAD-3 pt. 3.

[38] "Trudeau Press Conference, Canadian Embassy, Washington," 5 December 1974. Library and Archives Canada, R219-0-2-E, Files of the Department of External Affairs 27-14-NORAD-3 Vol. 3.

[39] Memorandum to Cabinet, "Renewal of NORAD Agreement," 19 February 1975. Library and Archives Canada, R219-0-2-E Files of the Department of External Affairs, 27-14-NORAD-3 pt. 3.

[40] "Exchange of Notes between the Government of Canada and the Government of the United States of America ..." *Canada Treaty Series* 1975, No. 16.

[41] Ibid.

[42] John Anderson, "Canada and the Modernization of North American Air Defense," in David G. Haglund and Joel J. Sokolsky (eds.), *The US–Canada Security*

Relationship: The Politics, Strategy and Technology of Defense (Boulder, CO: Westview Press, 1989), 173.

[43] Ibid., 174.

[44] Cited in Senate, Special Committee on National Defence, *Canada's Territorial Air Defence,* January 1985, 11.

[45] Anderson, 175 (see note 42).

[46] Edgar Ulsamer, "Air Defense Master Plan," *Air Force Magazine,* October 1981, 80.

[47] Memo, Defence Relations Division, "North American Air Defence," 5 November 1975. Library and Archives Canada, R219-0-2-E, Files of the Department of External Affairs files, 27-14-NORAD-3 pt. 3.

[48] *Canada's Territorial Air Defence,* 24 (see note 44).

[49] John Hamre, "Continental Air Defence, United States Security Policy, and Canada–United States Defence Relations," in R.B. Byers, et al., *Aerospace Defence: Canada's Future Role?* Wellesley Papers 9/1985 (Toronto: Canadian Institute of International Affairs, 1985), 22.

[50] *Canada's Territorial Air Defence,* 10 (see note 44).

[51] Frank L. Boyd, Jr., "The Politics of Canadian Defence Procurement: The New Fighter Aircraft Decision," in David G. Haglund (ed.), *Canada's Defence Industrial Base: The Political Economy of Preparedness and Procurement* (Kingston: Ronald P. Frye and Co., 1988).

[52] Captain John Haazen, "The CF-18 and the Defence of North America," *Canadian Defence Quarterly* 10, No. 2 (Autumn 1980), 22-29.

[53] Brigidier-General P.D. Manson, "The CF-18: Canada's New Fighter Aircraft," *Canadian Defence Quarterly* 10, No. 1 (Summer 1980), 19.

[54] Earl S. Van Inwegen III, "The Air Force Develops and Operational Organization for Space," in *The US Air Force In Space: 1945 to the Twenty-first Century* (Proceedings, Air Force Historical Foundation Symposium, Andrews AFB, MD, 21-22 September 1995), (Washington: USAF History and Museums Program, 1998), 136.

[55] Quoted in Spires, Chapter V (see note 28).

[56] Quoted in "General's Quiet Protest and his Early Sacking," *Washington Post,* 23 November 1977.

[57] Quoted in ibid.

[58] Quoted in ibid.

[59] Lieutenant General Daniel O. Graham, quoted in James Bamford, *Body of Secrets* (New York: Doubleday, 2001), 502.

[60] "The Re-entry of COSMOS 954: Review of Procedures," 6 June 1978. Library and Archives Canada, R219-0-2-E, Files of the Department of External Affairs, 27-14-NORAD Vol. 1.

[61] Department of National Defence, "Operation Morninglight: Department of National Defence Final Report," 25 May 1979. Copy in library, Canadian Forces College, Toronto.

[62] Cable, US Defence attaché Ottawa to CINCNORAD, 26 January 1978, "Prime Minister Trudeau's Views on COSMOS 954 Matter." Copy in NORAD/USNORTHCOM History Office.

[63] "Excerpts from CINCNORAD press briefing, Ottawa," 31 January 1978. Copy in NORAD/USNORTHOM History Office.

[64] "Review of Procedures" (see note 60).

[65] Letter, Pitfield to A.E. Gotlieb, 6 July 1978. Library and Archives Canada, R219-0-2-E, Files of the Department of External Affairs, 27-14-NORAD Vol. 1.

[66] Letter, Nixon to Pitfield, 21 July 1978. Library and Archives Canada, R219-0-2-E, Files of the Department of External Affairs, 27-14-NORAD Vol. 1.

[67] Letter Goldschlag to Pitfield, 4 August 1978. Library and Archives Canada, R219-0-2-E, Files of the Department of External Affairs, 27-14-NORAD Vol. 1.

[68] Defence Relations Division, "NORAD Agreement Renewal – Issues for Consideration," 16 November 1979. Library and Archives Canada, R219-0-2-E, Files of the Department of External Affairs, 27-14-NORAD Vol. 1.

[69] NORAD DCS/Plans, Policy Programs and Requirements, "Talking Paper on Status of the NORAD Agreement," 1980. Copy NORAD/USNORTHCOM History Office.

[70] Martin Anderson, *Revolution* (New York: Harcourt Brace Jovanovich, 1988), 80-83.

[71] Zbniew Brzezinski, *Power and Principle: Memoirs of the National Security Adviser, 1977–1981* (New York: Farr, Straus, Giroux, 1983), 457.

[72] Quoted in Bobbitt, 92 (see note 8).

[73] "Exchange of Notes between the Government of Canada and the Government of the United States of America constituting an Agreement concerning the Organization and Operation of the North American Aerospace Defence Command (NORAD)," *Canada Treaty Series* 1981, No. 32.

[74] Cable 9543, US Embassy Ottawa to State Department, 3 March 1981, "President's Visit: NORAD Agreement." Freedom of Information Request.

CHAPTER FOUR

FROM STAR WARS TO THE WAR ON DRUGS, 1981–1991

THE BEST DEFENCE

Within a few days of the signing ceremony held in Ottawa for the 1981 NORAD renewal, General James V. Hartinger told a US Senate committee in Washington that "[m]y key mission as CINCNORAD is to support our country's flexible targeting strategy with unambiguous, reliable missile warning and precise attack assessment information – in a pre-, trans-, and post-attack environment."[1] The communications, command, control, and information (C3I) systems upon which NORAD relied, however, were still too vulnerable to perform this mission adequately in a protracted nuclear war, as US strategic policy now required. Most of NORAD's sensors, including the DEW Line, the BMEWS and other ballistic missile warning radars, the communications systems, and the NORAD Combat Operations Centre itself in Cheyenne Mountain would be destroyed early in a nuclear exchange, almost certainly in the first Soviet missile strike. So would the ground stations that communicated with the DSP missile detection satellites.

The USAF's response during the late Carter administration had been to propose a set of C3I improvements that would decrease not just NORAD's vulnerability but those of US strategic nuclear forces in general. These were adopted by the new Reagan administration in the broad strategic force modernization program it developed during its first year in office. The strategic C3I systems that were used in peacetime would be hardened and they would be backed up by other systems, many of which would be space-based, that would be activated and deployed only after the start of a nuclear war. In NORAD's specific case the wartime system would rely upon the DSP satellites; an airborne backup NORAD headquarters would communicate with them via survivable mobile ground terminals that could be fairly quickly deployed to replace the ones that Soviet strikes had destroyed.[2]

The new administration also moved to implement the USAF's Air Defense Master Plan, designed to provide protection against a Soviet precursor or decapitation bomber strike. The aging F-106 interceptors that were deployed for continental air defence would be replaced with F-15s, to be used for both air defence and as carriers for a new anti-satellite weapon still under development. The AWACS fleet would be expanded. Modernizing the continent's air defence radars, another element of the master plan, meant continuing the negotiations with Canada; here, too the administration immediately took steps. The new secretary of defense, Caspar Weinberger, accompanied the president to Ottawa during his March 1981 trip where Weinburger and the minister of national defence, Gilles Lamontagne discussed the air defence modernization plan and issued a public statement pledging progress.

But progress was thereafter slow. This was partially due to unresolved Canadian concerns about funding, management, radar locations, and special facilities in the north which needed to be addressed and which will be discussed below. Additional factors, "many of them extraneous to the subject matter of the negotiations," as John Anderson put it, also slowed things down. Among them, the US side grew preoccupied with other defence priorities, while on the Canadian side there was a change first of defence ministers and then in 1984 a change of government, twice.[3]

At one point there was also hesitation in the Pentagon about the kind of air defence modernization that was on the table. In the wake of the JUSCADS study, some US defence officials were not fully convinced that investing in new ground-based air defence radars, as called for in the master plan, made sense when space-based systems seemed to be not far off. This, too, led to delays. To meet such concerns the Pentagon established in December 1982 a study, called Strategic Defense Architecture 2000, to project the threat from Soviet bombers and cruise missiles out to the year 2000 and to suggest an air defence that might then be available to counter it. NORAD and Canadian air defence officials cooperated in the study.

The Reagan administration largely adopted the declaratory nuclear strategy of the Carter administration. Reagan, early in his presidency, signed National Security Directive 13, which confirmed the major points of PD-59; it was followed in early 1982 by a "Defense Guidance" issued by Weinburger, which more fully set out the new administration's approach. "Lying at the heart of this guidance was the old 'coercive strategy': hurt the enemy and make him quit by threatening to hurt him more with a durable reserve force held securely at bay."[4]

The public statements of the Regan administration officials on US strategic nuclear policy did not, in essence, differ much either from those of their predecessors in the late Carter administration. Nonetheless, in keeping with the new president's determination to strengthen the West's defences and where necessary confront the Soviet Union, their tone was much more forceful and many people were shocked by it: "What *was* shocking and new about many of the statements made by Reagan officials on nuclear war was their baldness, the nonchalant innocence with which they were frequently uttered."[5] There was still more shock when the *Washington Post* and *New York Times* published leaked excerpts from the secret Weinberger guidance. While the Carter administration had talked of relying on limited options in a protracted war to "countervail," Weinburger used a sterner term: "Should deterrence fail and strategic nuclear war with the USSR occur, the United States must prevail and be able to force the Soviet Union to seek earliest termination of hostilities on terms favorable to the United States." When challenged on this point, Weinburger replied, "You show me a secretary of defense who's planning not to prevail, and I'll show you a secretary of defense who ought to be impeached."[6]

Canadians began to notice and some were shocked, too. Professor Douglas Ross of the University of British Columbia seems to have been the first Canadian analyst to proclaim forcefully that US nuclear strategy was not what Canadians had long thought it to be and that this had implications for NORAD, whose key mission was also not quite what Canadians had long thought it to be. As Ross put it in a piece published by the Canadian Institute of International Affairs in April 1982: "If one values *mutual* deterrence – that is the capacity of *both* superpowers to 'ride out' any nuclear assault on their homeland confident of their capacity for retaliation no matter how long they delay a response – NORAD's potentially complementary role in the articulation and execution of first-strike threats is not reassuring" (original emphasis). Ross chided both the press and parliamentarians, especially those on the committee that had studied NORAD renewal, for not having paid attention to the strategic pronouncements of Carter officials, adding, "[f]ew members of our political elite are disposed to familiarize themselves with the current trends in thought about the unthinkable. The mind-numbing tedium of the constitutional debate may have had something to do with this state of affairs."[7]

Ross was only the first. Over the next several years in Canada, as well as in the US and other free societies around the world, the wisdom of the Reagan administration's nuclear policies became the subject of heavy debate. Did they shore up deterrence with their emphasis on sophisticated nuclear operations intended to allow the US to respond appropriately to a range of contingencies in a protracted war? Or did they make it much too likely that nuclear war would be unleashed? Canadians, who unlike Americans did not actually bear the responsibility of trying to deploy strategic nuclear weapons credibly to deter Soviet attacks not just on North America but on allies abroad, worried. They were affected, too, by the rise in the US (partially aided by clandestine KGB funding) of a strong "nuclear freeze" movement which, in reaction to the Reagan rhetoric and strategic modernization program, sought to lock US and Soviet nuclear arsenals in place.

Other Canadian analysts joined Ross in examining the implications of the changes in US nuclear strategy for NORAD. The debate had no chance of making any real, immediate impact on Canadian participation in NORAD, though, simply because it had gotten underway just a few months after the 1981 renewal. The next one, in 1986, was a long way off.

In the meantime – driven in good part by Canadian "peace" groups, whose numbers, like the "freeze" groups in the US grew in the early 1980s as the Cold War turned markedly cooler – the Canadian nuclear debate soon focused for the moment on a bilateral defence issue that was not part of Canada's NORAD commitments. Word leaked out in early 1982 that Washington had asked Ottawa for permission to test air-launched cruise missiles (ALCMs) unarmed over northern Canada. ALCMs are released from bombers. They carry small jet engines and wings that allow them to fly like airplanes. During flight their on-board guidance system periodically compares surface characteristics with profiles stored in their computers and corrects the track. This means that they are highly accurate. As the Department of National Defence explained, Washington had put in its request because "[u]nique among Western allies, including the United States, Canada has the combination of space, terrain and weather and test facilities suitable for operational testing of the air-launched cruise missile over representative terrain and realistic route lengths."[8]

Canadian opponents of testing often charged that ALCMs were "first-strike" weapons, meaning they could be used to disarm the Soviets. After all, the USAF was arguing that NORAD's air defences needed to be modernized to prevent Soviet bombers and cruise missiles from "decapitating" US strategic forces; if that was a real threat, couldn't US ALCMs be used for the same purpose against the Soviet Union? They could, but only if there were no air defence and the Soviets had an extensive air defence system. On the other hand, the peace groups and other opponents correctly observed that after an initial US missile strike on the Soviet Union that included attacks on its air defences, ALCMs could be of use, because of their accuracy, in sophisticated nuclear attacks during a protracted war in keeping with the US approach to targeting.

Despite this opposition, Trudeau steadfastly shepherded the ALCM testing agreement through his divided cabinet. After it had been approved, he defended it with tough words in a May 1983 open letter that appeared in newspapers across the country. "It is hardly fair to rely on the Americans to protect the West but to refuse to lend them a hand when the going gets rough," he wrote. "In that sense, the anti-Americanism of some Canadians verges on hypocrisy. They're eager to take refuge under the American umbrella but don't want to help build it."[9] This firm support from the father of "stable mutual deterrence" is surprising, all the more so since he had just spoken out in favour of "suffocation" as an approach to arms control. The historians J.L. Granatstein and Robert Bothwell concluded in their study of Trudeau's foreign policy that "[a]gainst his every instinct, Trudeau had supported cruise testing, knowing that his willingness to do so might win him some credit with Ronald Reagan that could have its effect on other issues. At the very least, the anger at the decision in Canada would let him tell the American leader that he had done his bit for Western defence and had the scars to prove it."[10] Trudeau was able to weather that anger partly because the ALCMs would only be briefly tested in Canada; this was quite unlike the decisions facing Diefenbaker and Pearson over whether nuclear weapons should be deployed indefinitely in Canada for potential use by the Canadian military in NORAD.

Reagan, for his part, came to the conclusion in 1983 that his administration had been talking too tough about its nuclear strategy. Beginning with a speech late in the year to the Japanese parliament, he adopted the mantra, "a nuclear war can never be won and must never be fought," that he would use again and again. Much more fundamentally, though, he sought a way to escape from nuclear weapons altogether. His horror at the all but complete vulnerability of the US to nuclear attack had only increased since he had assumed responsibility as president for nuclear deterrence. There was also in the US a network of advocates for strategic defence that had access to Reagan and encouraged him to act on his unease. At the end of a 23 March 1983 address to the nation on the importance of his defence modernization program, he did. He asked: "What if free people could live secure in the knowledge that their security did not rest upon the threat of instant US retaliation to deter a Soviet attack, that we could intercept and destroy strategic ballistic missiles before they reached our own soil or that of our allies?" And he announced a new initiative that, he said, could lead to not just a defence of the United States but also the abandonment of nuclear deterrence itself:

> I clearly recognize that defensive systems have limitations and raise certain problems and ambiguities. If paired with offensive systems, they can be viewed as fostering an aggressive policy, and no one wants that. But with these considerations firmly in mind, I call upon the scientific community in our country, those who gave us nuclear weapons, to turn their great talents now to the cause of mankind and world peace, to give us the means of rendering these nuclear weapons impotent and obsolete.

> Tonight, consistent with our obligations of the ABM treaty and recognizing the need for closer consultation with our allies, I'm taking an important first step. I am directing a comprehensive and intensive effort to define a long-term research and development program to begin to achieve our ultimate goal of eliminating the threat

posed by strategic nuclear missiles. This could pave the way for arms control meas-ures to eliminate the weapons themselves. We seek neither military superiority nor political advantage. Our only purpose – one all people share – is to search for ways to reduce the danger of nuclear war.[11]

Right after the speech there was a flurry of comment generally consisting of "ridicule from its opponents and righteous praise from its advocates."[12] Thereafter, the initiative all but disappeared for months. When the president had finished speaking it was still not clear exactly how what he had announced could or should be pursued. The administration immediately commissioned two special studies that took several months. The first concluded that new technologies were becoming available that might indeed provide the basis with which a powerful new defence against ballistic missiles might be built. The other one said that such technologies could be employed to enhance de-terrence and strategic stability.

Upon receiving the two reports, the administration moved to turn the presi-dential vision into a program. The Strategic Defense Initiative (SDI) was created in January 1984, and embodied within the Pentagon in a Strategic Defense Initiative Organization (SDIO). Critics soon started called SDI "Star Wars," alluding to what they saw as technological fantasy. The SDIO's man-date at its creation was to spend about US $26 billion over five to seven years on advanced missile defence technologies and to put the US in the early 1990s in a position to decide whether to deploy. It began to examine exotic technologies, such as laser beams, particle beams, space-based, chemically-launched projectiles, and space-based electromagnetic rail guns, as well as advanced versions of ground-based interceptors.

The second report's conclusions about how missile defences could strengthen deterrence and strategic stability were at odds with the president's emphasis on making "nuclear weapons impotent and obsolete." This contra-diction, as well as all the other uncertainties that quickly arose about how a robust missile defence system might be introduced and how it would func-tion, really did not have to be resolved at the time, though. SDI was neither a deployment program nor a plan for one; it was a broad research program alone.

AIR DEFENCE MODERNIZATION AND SDI

Reagan's March 1983 address did not go unnoticed in Canada, where there was also a brief flurry of reaction. Certainly there was no enthusiasm. It would be hard to imagine a defence development in the US more likely to elicit an unenthusiastic Canadian reaction. But there was at the time neither much interest nor deep controversy, especially because the speech was made when the unexpected drama pitting Trudeau against the cruise missile protestors was near centre stage in Canada. When SDI emerged as a formal research program a bit less than a year later and began to draw serious and sustained attention in both the US and Canada, Trudeau was back from a quixotic international "peace mission" and heading out of office. After the summer 1984 prime ministership of John Turner, the Progressive Conservatives, under Brian Mulroney, won the September election.

Mulroney wanted much better ties with the US. "Good relations, super relations, with the United States will be the cornerstone of our foreign policy," is how he once put it on the campaign trail. As he took office, on the defence agenda with the US was not the hypothetical possibility, a decade or more in the future, of lasers or particle beams knocking out incoming ballistic missiles, but the immediate task of completing the negotiations that had been underway for several years over the modernization of North American air defences. The Conservatives turned right away to this; the outcome was a North American Air Defence Modernization Agreement signed at Mulroney and Reagan's March 1985 "Shamrock Summit" in Quebec City.[13] (See Map 7. Note: aside from the OTH-B stations this map does not show radar stations in the US.)

Anticipating opposition attacks, the Conservatives defended the modernization at home largely on the grounds of sovereignty. As Erik Nielsen, the minister of national defence, told the House of Commons: "By this agreement, Canadian sovereignty has been enhanced, including sovereignty over Canadian territory, sovereignty over Canadian defences, sovereignty over Canada's North and sovereignty over our own airspace."[14]

Nielsen certainly had a good point, to the extent "sovereignty" simply meant getting the American military out of Canada and handing its tasks over to Canadians. The centrepiece of the accord was the North Warning System that would replace the DEW Line and provide coverage against low-flying aircraft and cruise missiles that the DEW Line lacked. The name had been changed at the behest of the Americans, reportedly because it seemed easier to secure Congressional funding if the word "distant" were dropped. Unlike the DEW Line, for which the Americans had paid all the construction and operating costs, the Americans would pay only 60 per cent of the construction and operating costs for the new system's stations in Canada. Nonetheless, they would be built and operated by Canada. This meant that the American presence on the ground in the high Canadian Arctic, long a sensitive point, would come to an end.

That had not been Washington's intent at the beginning of the negotiations. "Simply put, US officials wished to supervise the operations and maintenance function of the North Warning System, as they had with the DEW Line since the mid-1950s."[15] But in the autumn of 1984, Washington surprised the Canadian side, saying "you can manage the program."[16]

In fact, with the replacement of the DEW Line by the North Warning System, the Canadianization of peacetime air defence in Canada would be complete. Or, as the Department of National Defence concluded in 1986, NORAD resources on Canadian soil had been "successively nationalized."[17] The USAF's Newfoundland interceptor squadrons, the only such squadrons it had ever stationed in Canada, were long gone. The air defence boundaries had been redrawn and the trans-boundary air defence regions eliminated, leaving Canadian airspace to be controlled entirely out of North Bay. In 1984, with the replacement of the Voodoos by the CF-18s, the last nuclear air defence weapons in Canada returned to the US, as did the American forces that had been responsible for their custody. The Americans were also gone from the Pinetree radars across southern Canada; now they too were going to be shut down.

On the other hand, to the extent that "sovereignty" meant being able to use Canadian air defence forces to support the enforcement of Canadian regulations in the case of non-compliant civilian aircraft within Canada, the closing of the Pinetree radars meant its marked decrease. The US was unwilling to continue paying for these radar stations, inasmuch as they were no longer necessary for air defence purposes. Despite the fine pledges in the 1981 NORAD Agreement, the Departments of National Defence and Transport had been unable to create a joint civilian-military traffic control system that would replace the Pinetree system. General Paul Manson, at the time chief of air doctrine and operations, had to admit in 1984 to a Senate committee that if MOT traffic controllers picked up an aircraft within Canada that they could not identify, it would not make much sense for them to turn to the air force for help. As he went on to explain, "[t]he Department of Transport radar system is a system that has been established for the control of compliant air traffic, and by 'compliant' I mean, of course, those aircraft which file flight plans and which have certain electronic equipment which allows them to be identified by radar on the ground ... By and large, therefore, it would not be of great value to the air defence system."[18]

Canada would be left with only coastal air defence radars and some additional coverage around the main air defence bases at Cold Lake and Bagotville. There was no coverage within most of the country and along most of the border with the US. It was with a certain amount of envy that Manson seemed to describe the US Joint Surveillance System ringing the entire country, including the border with Canada: "I believe their motivation, is that no nation can really declare that it has full control and full jurisdiction over its own air space unless it has the capability of controlling and identifying air traffic within that zone. The Americans, I know, feel very strongly about this and they dedicate a lot of money and resources to the JSS system."[19] Still, the JSS system was pretty much limited to the periphery of the continental US.

Making sure that there would even be Canadian coastal air defence radar coverage had been an important goal of the Canadian side in the negotiations leading up to the 1985 agreement. The original USAF Air Defense Master Plan had envisaged a purely east–west North Warning Line terminating in Greenland, with peacetime radar coverage off the Canadian coasts to be provided solely by the long-range OTH-B stations. The Canadians argued that the new and not fully tested OTH-B technology should not be completely relied upon there, especially for interceptor control. The US agreed that the North Warning System should not terminate in Greenland but turn down Baffin Island and the Labrador coasts, and that coastal radars be built in Atlantic Canada, as well as in British Columbia and the Alaska panhandle. The geographic capabilities of the 1985 modernization were later well summarized in the comments of an official of the Department of External Affairs that "NORAD does not provide a means of knowing what is going on *in* our airspace but rather what may be *entering* our airspace" (original emphasis).[20]

The North Warning System would itself be vulnerable to attack and its detection and tracking capabilities were limited. It was therefore conceived of as a "peacetime surveillance system designed to give reasonable assurance that a precursor or surprise attack is ruled out."[21] The air defence planners had assumed that in peacetime and with no international crisis underway, a Soviet surprise attack coming as a complete "bolt from the blue" was so unlikely that a less than leakproof air defence detection perimeter constituted an acceptable risk. The extent of the North Warning System's capability to detect low-flying cruise missiles passing over it was open to some question. It was also located to the south of several release points for the most advanced Soviet air-launched cruise missiles; that is, the missile's long range would allow bombers, from points to the north of where they would be detected by North Warning System radar, to launch cruise missiles toward some targets in Canada and the northern United States. Soviet sea-launched cruise missiles could similarly be launched from some locations in the Canadian Arctic. While the North Warning System's capabilities against bombers would be greater, both bombers and cruise missiles would pass quickly through its radar envelope into the great radar "hole" to the south.

To compensate for the weaknesses of the peacetime system, the 1985 agreement also included provisions whereby in a crisis and wartime the warning and engagement zones could be pushed north. Map 8 shows this as envisaged in 1990. Five forward operating locations (FOLs) were to be built on the basis of "minimum essential upgrades" at Inuvik, Yellowknife, Rankin Inlet, Iqaluit (all at the time in the Northwest Territories) and Kuujjuaq in northern

Quebec, to permit emergency deployment of CF-18s and USAF F-15s. In addition to small airfields, each FOL was to include alert hangers and storage for ammunition, fuel and air-to-air missiles. Each was to be capable of supporting operations of a maximum of six fighter aircraft with personnel for up to 30 days. FOL costs were to be split between the two countries. No armed forces personnel of either country were to be permanently stationed at the FOLs, nor aircraft permanently located there. Map 8 also shows the roles Goose Bay and Comox would play on the east and west costs.

From the FOLs, the fighter aircraft could attempt immediately to intercept bombers or cruise missiles detected by the North Warning System just to the north, or optimally, in a crisis they could be operated forward well to the north of the North Warning system, in conjunction with USAF AWACS aircraft. NORAD had wanted Canada to buy several of its own AWACS. That must have been an attractive idea to Ottawa, for Canadian AWACS could have provided coverage in the ground radar "hole" in the centre of the country. But the costs were too high. Instead, Ottawa and NORAD wanted the USAF to "dedicate" several AWACS for North American defence, meaning that they could be counted on to be available. But the USAF was not prepared to go that far, since the aircraft might be needed elsewhere. Several AWACS were only to be "designated" for NORAD; they could also be used outside North America. To partially compensate for this, the 1985 agreement also provided for construction of dispersed operating bases (DOBs) in Canada, out of which the few AWACS available could more effectively operate in an emergency. One was to be at Bagotville, the other at CFB Edmonton, thus not far from Cold Lake.

Finally, the ability of fighter aircraft to operate northward could be enhanced through in-flight refuelling. Arrangements were made to be able to refuel CF-18s either from the small number of Canadian aircraft capable of being outfitted as tankers, or from American tankers. The air defence planners hoped that as a result of the 1985 modernization, operations could be undertaken as far forward as the North Pole.

Moving the air defence engagement zone far to the north was an improvement that had been suggested since the 1950s when there was still a thick air defence based on defence in depth. The 1985 plan was for a thin forward defence with all but no defence in depth. No one believed that the North Warning System and the OTH-B radars, the eight AWACS that probably would be available (fewer than had been planned for, just a couple of years earlier) and the limited number of US and Canadian fighter aircraft would be sufficient to detect, much less destroy, a very high percentage of approaching bombers and cruise missiles, even if most of the AWACS and all available fighters were aloft and operating. But that was not the intent. It was more of a trip-wire system, intended particularly to deter Soviet precursor attacks. The forward air defence operations would introduce a useful element of randomness, in that the Soviets would not know precisely where AWACS and associated fighters were. The Soviets could not be certain, therefore, that their bombers and cruise missiles would go entirely undetected and could therefore also not be certain that the cruise missiles essential for a successful decapitation strike would penetrate undetected to target.

The establishment of the FOLS for fighter aircraft and DOBs in the Canadian north had also been a major goal of the Canadian negotiators, and one reason the discussions between Washington and Ottawa over the modernization agreement had taken so long. As Paul Barton in the Defence Relations Division of the Department of External Affairs noted while the negotiations were still underway in late 1984, the US was emphasizing the funding of the North Warning System radars "because they would trigger the US deterrent. Attack assessment would be provided through a computerized probability, called an algorithm." Therefore, for the Americans, "[f]orward basing in Canada of interceptors and AWACS has low priority because it is the radar-based strategic warning which engages deterrence and the radars alone would dissuade Soviet planners from an over-the-pole first strike option." This dependence on radars and an algorithm made the Canadian side nervous. "In Canada's view, an attack assessment based solely on radar warning, intelligence reports and on algorithm is destabilizing because of the built-in ambiguity. Northern forward-basing within the NWS zone of coverage would permit on-the-spot attack assessment by AWACS and interceptors plus damage limitation if the intrusion proved genuine and hostile."[22]

Even before Mulroney and Nielsen had returned to Ottawa with the final version of the modernization agreement in hand, a fairly fierce debate had broken out over it in the country, especially in the House of Commons. When Michael Slack looked back at 1985 for the *Canadian Annual Review of Politics and Public Affairs* he concluded that "[i]n many respects reminiscent of the heated air defence debates of the late 1950s and early 1960s, the 1985 variant was plagued by a surfeit of partisan politics, by widespread ignorance of technical issues, and by an embarrassing series of imprecise and/or misinterpreted musings by senior American officials. The result was one of the most confused, muddled and contradictory debates in the history of Canadian defence policy."[23]

In response to Nielsen's claim that the accord would bolster Canadian sovereignty, the official opposition tried to give the charge of northern territorial sell-out to the Americans at least a good try. Jean Chrétien, then the Liberal official spokesman for foreign affairs, asked darkly: "Why will there be series of airstrips built everywhere in the North while under the DEW Line system, we did not need these airstrips. Is it for skidoo races? Is it for fishing trips?" A day later he offered the answer. The Mulroney government, he charged, had decided to "give Canadian territory to the Americans for operational purposes, namely "a sophisticated series of military bases in the Canadian north."[24] The government responded in exasperation that the airstrips were just that, not bases and would be used primarily by Canadian aircraft.

The opposition also tried to identify links between air defence modernization and the pursuit by the US of limited nuclear options in a protracted war. The main thrust of its attack, though, was that the elements of the modernization agreement were somehow part and parcel of SDI. With the battle over the cruise missile testing having been lost, Canadian peace groups refocused on SDI. They were far from alone in being against it. The "'defence is a dangerous thing' argument" was still dominant in Canada. Both the Liberal and New Democratic Parties opposed SDI. They tried to make the case that Mulroney, in search of a better relationship with the US, had become a pushover for Reagan, not just on defence, but on acid rain and trade as well. Together, the Liberals and NDP supported a resolution in the Commons, in the wake of the Quebec City summit, condemning the government for "its failure to make specific that Canada would not participate in any way in the 'star wars' project of the US."[25]

The Conservatives had offered SDI research cautious, almost grudging approval, in a January 1985 statement by Joe Clark, the secretary of state for external affairs, which called it "only prudent." Clark certainly offered no support for Reagan's vision of a world where nuclear weapons had been rendered "impotent and obsolete." Nor did he for a moment suggest that the Canadian government believed that the time had come seriously to consider the strategic desirability of eventually deploying a missile defence system to protect North America better or to bolster deterrence. Rather, he said, missile defence research by the US had been necessitated by "significant Soviet advances in ballistic missile defence research in recent years and deployment of an actual ballistic missile defence system [around Moscow]." The West would have to "keep abreast of such projects." To make it clear that the Conservatives were only endorsing research and research alone, Clark added that actual deployment of missile defences and any transgression of the ABM Treaty "could have serious implications for arms control and would therefore warrant close and careful attention by all concerned." Canada, therefore welcomed Reagan's pledge "that the USA would not proceed beyond research without discussion and negotiation."[26]

Charges about the relationship between the 1985 air defence modernization agreement and SDI were at times wild and irresponsible. *The Globe and Mail* called in an editorial for the government to "come clean on whether the new DEW Line is to be designed as a Star Wars accessory."[27] The NDP charged that "you cannot have a ground radar tracking system for star wars in Canada that is distinct from the updated NWS."[28] Again and again the Tories responded that the North Warning System could detect only bombers and cruise missiles, not ballistic missiles, that SDI was only a research program that might or might not yield results, which in turn might or might not lead to the actual deployment of new defences against ballistic missiles, and that in any event the Canadian government supported the ABM Treaty.

For the second time in history, the US State Department was prompted to take the unusual step of weighing into a Canadian defence debate via a press release from its embassy in Ottawa. This time, unlike 1963, the Americans took the side of the Canadian prime minister. SDI was solely a research program, the State Department's March 1985 release said. The government of the United States "clearly and categorically" denied that the North Warning System was part of SDI.[29]

Worried that the charges might still convince a public that could not fully grasp the difference between various existing, proposed and utterly hypothetical systems, and between cruise missiles and ballistic missiles, the frustrated Tories also sometimes overreacted; Clark claimed at one point early in the debate that "there is absolutely no relationship between the North Warning System and the Strategic Defense Initiative."[30] That went too far. If SDI ever bore fruit and new missile defences ever were deployed, they would take their place, along with the North Warning System and other air defence elements as part of the continent's coordinated defences – whether or not Canada participated in missile defence.

Nonetheless, it is easy to sympathize with Clark in the face of the recklessness of some of the opposition charges. The Reagan administration did not make things easy for the Tories, either. At the Quebec City summit the president, perhaps to the unspoken dismay of his host, delivered a televised address to the Canadian people in which he dwelt on his cherished SDI program. He said, no doubt from the heart, that "the possibility of developing and sharing with you the technology that could provide a security shield, and someday eliminate the threat of nuclear attack, is for us the most hopeful possibility of the nuclear age."[31]

It got still tougher for the Tories. The summit was scarcely over when Weinburger surprised NATO members, including Canada, with an invitation to participate in SDI research. After letting a parliamentary committee hold hearings on the matter and commissioning a confidential report by a senior public servant, Mulroney announced in September 1985 that Canada's "own policies and priorities do not warrant a government-to-government effort in support of SDI research." Nonetheless, he said, Canadian private companies and institutions would be free to do so.[32] After all, Ottawa still found such research "only prudent."

The Mulroney government's polite "no" to official governmental participation "was treated in fact as a victory of sorts by the anti-SDI forces across the country and thus that element of the population leaning towards militant rejectionism was mollified."[33] Mulroney himself saw it somewhat differently. He chortled that he had pulled the rug "right out from under" the feet of his critics.[34]

US SPACE COMMAND AND THE 1986 RENEWAL

In mid-1985, the Mulroney government, after the messy debate over the North American Air Defence Modernization Agreement, and grappling with whether to accept the US government's invitation to participate in SDI research, could not have welcomed the need to reach still another decision about North American aerospace defence. This occurred when Washington asked it to agree to CINCNORAD's being given another hat as commander-in-chief of the about-to-be-created US Space Command (USSPACECOM).

Beyond reliance on the DSP satellites for missile launch detection, space-based operations by the US military had grown enormously in recent years. As Paul B. Stares of the Brookings Institution summarized the situation the mid-1980s:

> The role of satellites ... is changing in a fundamental way. They are becoming more and more useful for enhancing the war-fighting effectiveness of armed forces. Virtually every type of military operation, from small conventional conflicts to strategic nuclear war, is now likely to involve satellites. Reconnaissance satellites, for instance, are increasingly being located to locate, track and target forces such as naval ships. Communications satellites, by being able to receive and rapidly distribute vital information, can improve in radical ways the command and control of military forces and thus their combat performance. And navigation satellites now make it possible to guide the "dumbest" munitions to their targets with nearly perfect precision. In military terms, satellites have become true "force multipliers."[35]

The US military was also developing a new anti-satellite capability. It had had none ever since the Johnson Island ASAT weapons were taken out of service in the early 1970s. A new anti-satellite weapon could be useful in a protracted nuclear war to deny the Soviets follow-on surveillance of the US after their initial attack on it. President Reagan announced in October 1981, also as part of the strategic modernization package, that the US anti-satellite program based on the F-15 interceptor would be speeded up. As envisaged, a specially equipped F-15 could pull up in flight and fire the ASAT rocket it carried into satellite operating heights where it would destroy the target kinetically. The aircraft could fly to where it was advantageous to intercept an adversary's satellite, according to its orbital path. This led to suspicions in some quarters in Canada that the FOLs in Northern Canada were partially intended to host F-15s for this purpose; there was no hard evidence for this, though. The first test of this F-15 system was conducted in 1983 and the first actual interception of a disused US satellite occurred in 1985.

Given this growing importance of space operations, the USAF began to have strong second thoughts in the early 1980s about having dissolved ADCOM as an air force command and having transferred its space responsibilities and assets to SAC, where they were not a priority. These doubts were shared within SAC itself. As its commander-in-chief put it in late 1981: "What we have to do is figure out how to walk the cat back."[36] As a result, those space responsibilities and assets were transferred back to Colorado Springs in 1982 to a new Air Force Space Command. Hartinger was triple-hatted, with command over NORAD, ADCOM (the vestigial "specified" command) and Air Force Space Command.

The official USAF press release announcing the establishing of its Space Command ended with the statement that "[i]t is the Air Force's hope and belief that Space Command will develop quickly into a unified command."[37] Hartinger and his staff proceeded to draw up plans for such a unified command, based upon Air Force Space Command as its central component. "As such," according to an official USAF history, "the Air Force would take the lead in coordinating all American military space operations, and he would serve as commander of both the unified and major commands, as well as NORAD."[38] The other US services, with their own growing interest in space, could hardly be enthusiastic about an air force-dominated unified command having responsibility over their space operations. This was especially the case with the US Navy, which established its own Space Command in 1983.

The president's March 1983 address on strategic defence provided Hartinger with the key opening. A month after the address, the Joint Chiefs of Staff requested suggestions as to how the president's initiative could best be supported by the military. Hartinger responded with a proposal for a unified space command. Presumably he argued that such a command, in addition to other responsibilities, could provide operational planning for missile defence, and then could stand ready and experienced to take operational command over any new missile defence system that might be decided upon early in the 1990s.

The other services remained cool to the idea of a unified space command. Upon White House intervention, though, the Chiefs agreed in November 1983 to recommend its creation. After working on defining its role and missions, the Chiefs then turned in mid-1984 to its relationship to NORAD. They agreed that the new command would replace ADCOM (the vestigial, specified command) which would be dissolved, in that it would take over ADCOM's responsibilities for providing NORAD with information on missile launches and trajectories and on what was occurring in space. This was the information that NORAD relied upon, in addition to the information it received from the air defences in Canada and the US, to execute its responsibilities for warning of and assessing an attack on the continent. For this purpose, the new unified space command would be, in JCS parlance, a "supporting command" to NORAD.

General Robert T. Herres, who succeeded Hartinger as CINCNORAD/ CINCAD/CINCAFSPACECOM in 1984, argued that when the command restructuring took place CINCNORAD should be double-hatted as USCINCSPACE. He was supported in this by the chairman of the JCS as well as the USAF and army Chiefs. He later explained why he wanted a close relationship between the two commands: "My position was you cannot separate the air breathing defense missions from the missile and space defense missions if you truly want the best possible structure for strategic aerospace defence in the United States."[39] Still, as will be discussed below, a close relationship between the two commands did not mean for Herres that they could not be kept quite distinct from one another.

The chief of naval operations and the commandant of the Marine Corps opposed the double-hatting. The duties of USCINCSPACE and CINCNORAD, they argued, "were different and expanding." Also, by standing apart, USCINCSPACE and CINCNORAD would provide "the proper military focus and singleness of purpose as well as send the political signals consistent with presidential guidance."[40] The navy no doubt was concerned that too close a link to NORAD, with its continuing air defence responsibilities, would only further strengthen USAF dominance over the space command.

The issue went back to the White House where President Reagan decided that General Herres would be both CINCNORAD and USCINCSPACE for at least the first year after the command restructuring began to go into effect in September 1985. If Canada did not object, that is. Although strictly speaking Canadian permission was not needed, US officials took pains in 1985 to obtain it. Officials at both National Defence and External Affairs were fairly eager to give it.

Canada had no military space program. This was, according to John Kirton, the result of "a deliberate civilianization, commercialization and internationalization of the Canadian space program as the Liberal government of Pierre Trudeau terminated the military-sponsored projects of the previous period, abolished the Defence Research Board, and deprived the Canadian military of the funds needed to invest in significant space projects. Thus, in just over two decades, a space program that had begun, flourished, and acquired world leadership as a scientifically, militarily and nationally-based activity was transformed into a languishing, commercially-oriented, internationally-dependent civilian enterprise."[41] Canadian officials saw in USSPACECOM's impending creation the opportunity to help rectify this by securing access to US military space technology, not only for the Canadian military but for Canadian industry.

This would require more than just acceptance of the CINC's double-hatting. Barton wrote in 1985 that "[t]here is a danger that unless Canada is prepared to contribute meaningfully in terms of money and role and effort we will be excluded from all but the peripheral areas of 'high technology.' This might mean that Canada could have a lesser voice in continental defence and would be less likely to enjoy the industrial benefits that involvement in space development is likely to bring." Technology for air defence was particularly important for Canada. Barton also noted that "[w]ithin the next 20 years, the North American air defence surveillance systems currently slated for modernization will, in all likelihood, be replaced by space-based systems. If we do not ensure our participation now, we will be in great danger of having to rely entirely on the USA to supply us with information on what is happening within the confines of out own airspace."[42]

The secretary of state for external affairs had his doubts about USSPACECOM, however. Clark responded negatively to his department's May 1985 recommendation that Canada not object to the double-hatting of CINCNORAD as USCINCSPACE. He told US Secretary of State George Shultz that he was concerned that the new space command "not be organized in such a way to compromise decisions Canada might wish to take regarding its role in NORAD."[43] Only after further discussions did Canadian acquiescence come later in the year. The two countries had by 1985 a long track record of running twin commands with a single commander at Colorado Springs, having in the past kept under the operational command of the US "twin" activities such as the Safeguard missile defence, and the Johnson Island ASAT system in which Canada took no direct part. If Clark was worried about SDI or the F-15 ASAT system, the US was able to assure him that there was no need to place either under NORAD.

Nonetheless, in at least one respect USSPACECOM was a departure from the past. NORAD's two earlier twins, CONAD and ADCOM, had been air defence and aerospace defence commands. The new twin, as a space command, had no responsibility for traditional air defence. But the US still needed a way to exercise out of Colorado Springs, when necessary, national control over its air defence forces in the continental US and Alaska, the way it had done so through CONAD and ADCOM. This led to another command change, for which the US also politely asked Canadian acquiescence. CINCNORAD was to be given still another hat (a fourth), as "Commander, US Element NORAD" (USELEMNORAD) through which he could exercise such operational command over US air defences. US Element NORAD would have no separate staff. In an echo of the original relationship between CONAD and

NORAD, the staff of the US element would completely consist of US officers on the NORAD staff. Nielsen, when asked at an October 1985 meeting by Weinburger to give his approval to this change demurred, probably out of caution and puzzlement with the arcaneness of it all. When Weinburger nudged him, writing a month later, "I had the impression I had answered all of your questions," Nielsen arranged for Canada's agreement to be given.[44]

After the Mulroney government's SDI decision, the attention of Canadian peace groups and other critics shifted to the 1986 NORAD renewal. This time, they would be alert to the issue of NORAD's role in existing US strategy that had first arisen just after the 1981 renewal. They had also begun to charge that NORAD could turn out to be the Trojan horse that eventually brought missile defence to Canada, especially through its relationship to USSPACECOM or perhaps through Strategic Defense Architecture 2000, Phase II. The removal in 1981 of the ABM clause from the NORAD agreement now looked quite suspicious to them. Without it, was Canada not vulnerable to being dragged into SDI? They also still worried about the 1985 air defence modernization. Putting interceptors at FOLs in the north, they said, could be destabilizing, threaten Canadian sovereignty, and be part of the US plans for ASAT.

The custom was well established that NORAD renewal would be referred to the Standing Committee on External Affairs and National Defence of the House of Commons. The committee had held fairly quiet hearings on renewals and had dutifully filed reports which drew little attention. With the critics worked up and itching to testify as the 1986 renewal approached, the Mulroney government made arrangements for the committee to hear them and anyone else who deserved to be listened to. The committee then conducted by far the most extensive parliamentary review ever held on the joint command, listening to briefings and conducting hearings that took it to sixteen towns and military bases across the country. Witnesses ranged from peace groups, to supporters of the military, to academics, to Canadian government officials, to CINCNORAD, who testified at a packed hearing in Ottawa. The committee also traveled to Washington, where it met with State Department and Pentagon officials, and Colorado Springs, where it again met CINCNORAD. All in all, the committee reported when done, it had held "35 open meetings, was given 13 sets of briefings, collected 1,407 pages of evidence at public hearings, heard from 126 officials, individuals and groups and logged 38,000 air kilometers between August 1 and December 13, 1985."[45]

There was little chance that just about any Canadian government, much less the Mulroney Conservatives, would withdraw in 1986 from the accord. NORAD was just too much of a fixture of Canada–US relations. Strikingly, very few of the NORAD critics who appeared before the committee called for such a step, the most prominent exceptions being the representatives of Project

Ploughshares, the Canadian Council of Churches and the Canadian Conference of Catholic Bishops. NORAD's role in warning of an attack was not controversial. Most of the critics suggested caution and urged that conditions be placed on Canada's future involvement. These included keeping the number of air defence interceptors to a minimum, keeping ASAT-capable F-15 aircraft out of Canadian air space, and formally rejecting SDI. The most frequently suggested condition, though, was the reinsertion into the agreement of the "ABM clause."

The committee's final report was also the longest and most extensive ever on NORAD. Written at the behest of its Progressive Conservative majority, it rejected not only all these suggestions but completely dismissed the criticisms upon which they were based. The majority pronounced itself "unconvinced that US strategy has changed to the extent that it no longer relies on offensive retaliation and MAD as the basis for deterrence." As for SDI research, the committee agreed with the Mulroney government as to its prudence and it rejected the idea that NORAD could drag Canada into SDI: "NORAD is the here and now; for the foreseeable future SDI will be nothing more than a research program." There was no reason to expect any new missile defence deployments by the US before 1991, when the NORAD accord would again come up for renewal. There was, the committee said, "nothing ominous" about USSPACECOM. Strategic Defense Architecture 2000 Phase II was a sensible planning exercise in which the Canadian military should be involved. The 1985 air defence agreement was "entirely justifiable given the advance stage of obsolescence of the existing system and actual or expected improvements in the capabilities of the Soviet bombers and cruise missiles." As for the FOLs, "most Committee members fail to understand the concerns voiced by many disarmament group representatives." There would be only limited, random deployments of interceptors there, under Canadian control, and they had absolutely nothing to do with the ASAT F-15s.[46]

"Thus," concluded William Winegard, the committee's chairman, "there seems to be no good reason *not* to renew NORAD until 1991. The combined command for North American aerospace defence remains clearly in the interest of both this country and its neighbour to the south" (original emphasis). The committee did attempt to make a gesture of sorts on the issue of the "ABM clause." It did not believe that the clause was necessary, because "ballistic missile defence and NORAD are separate issues" and did not recommend its reinsertion. But it did suggest "in the hope it will allay public concern" that Washington and Ottawa issue a joint declaration at the time of NORAD renewal, pledging their support for the ABM Treaty, deterrence and strategic stability, and arms control.[47]

That was just as well, for the US side had no interest in putting the legally useless but provocative clause back into the agreement. In November 1985,

Shultz proposed to Clark straight renewal of the NORAD agreement, with no changes that would raise any controversial issues. Reinsertion of the ABM clause, he pointedly emphasized, would be "unhelpful."[48] On that basis the agreement was renewed in March 1986, during a visit Mulroney made to Washington. The text that had been extensively revised in 1981 remained in force. There was no joint declaration of the kind the Commons committee had recommended, although both the prime minister and the president emphasized in separate statements that the renewed accord was fully consistent with the ABM Treaty. That did not stop NDP leader Ed Broadbent from immediately claiming once again that without the clause "we could find ourselves willy-nilly forced into Star Wars through NORAD." The Liberals agreed with him.[49]

CANADIANS IN AND OUT: ADI AND AEROSPACE DEFENCE PLANNING

If SDI research ever led to a robust ballistic missile defence, North America's vitiated air defences would have had to be thoroughly reconstituted. The technology for that would have been needed, too. With this in mind, President Reagan issued in July 1985 National Security Decision Directive 178 which instructed that an air defence research program be undertaken "to allow for possible future deployment decisions for defense against low observable air-breathing threats to occur in the same time frame as possible deployment decisions on ballistic missile defense under the program."[50] Pursuant to that directive, the USAF announced the establishment of an Air Defense Initiative (ADI) in 1986. ADI gathered under its wing a number of research projects already underway. It was officially described as "separate from but complementary to SDI;" there were a number of areas of overlapping research between the two programs.[51]

Yet whatever happened with SDI and ballistic missile defence, it seemed at the time of ADI's creation that, at the least, its new air defence technologies were still eventually going to be needed just to replace the somewhat make-shift 1985 air defence modernization arrangements. The capabilities of the North Warning and OTH-B radars against existing Soviet cruise missiles remained questionable. The impending arrival of Soviet supersonic cruise missiles, under development, would further complicate the problem. Still more worrisome was the potential development by the Soviets, over the next decade or so, of "stealthy" bombers and cruise missiles, reopening the possibility of a no-warning "decapitation" attack. These are the "low observable air-breathing threats" that the president's decision directive referred to.

Given the weaknesses in these radars, ADI's self-described "number one priority" was "the development of wide area surveillance systems that can detect carriers at long ranges and track them with sufficient accuracy to allow engagement systems to be deployed."[52] It assumed responsibility for Pentagon programs investigating space-based infrared sensors and space-based radar. Originally, infrared air defence sensors, which would detect the heat emitted by bombers and cruise missiles, seemed to have had the inside track and an experimental satellite was scheduled to be carried into orbit by a US space shuttle. But the program suffered a major setback when US space shuttles were grounded in the wake of the January 1986 *Challenger* catastrophe. Thereafter, priority shifted to the exploration of space-based radar. USAF officials hoped to be able to launch a prototype radar satellite by 1993, followed, perhaps in the late-1990s, by a space-based radar constellation of anywhere from three to fifteen satellites that could provide very early warning of the approach of Soviet bombers, conceivably as soon as they left their home bases and staging areas in and near the Soviet Union.

As conceived by ADI, the space-based radars would hand off surveillance and tracking responsibilities to other advanced sensors, although these might well operate alone if space-based radar was not found feasible and affordable. An advanced airborne detection system based on phased-array radar technology that could be used as a successor to AWACS radar was also an ADI research project. To engage attacking bombers and cruise missiles at very-long, long, and shorter ranges, a host of weapons systems was under research or development, including new air-to-air and surface-to-air missiles. By the 1990s the USAF might be able to deploy for North American air defence the supersonic Advanced Tactical Fighter that, independent of ADI, it had under development, and by the turn of the century the National Aerospace Plane, that would permit intercepts at very long distances and at hypersonic speeds.

The final element of the ADI research program was devoted to battle management and command control and communications (BM/C3) systems, in order to tie together the possible surveillance and engagement systems. The US, it was expected, would be able to choose which level of air defence it wanted to deploy, ranging from the ability just to warn of attack by advanced Soviet bombers and cruise missiles to a heavy air defence complementary to a heavy missile defence.

Upon its establishment, ADI came in for criticism in Canada, especially because of its origins as a program complementary to SDI and because of the overlap between some SDI and ADI research. Obviously ADI's very name was a liability in Canada, too. This posed a problem for Ottawa. In recognition of Canada's strong interest in access to advanced air defence technology, the 1985 modernization agreement included a pledge by the two governments to cooperate on relevant research. A bilateral Aerospace Defense Advanced Technologies Working Group (ADATS) was formed shortly after the agreement was signed to oversee coordination of these efforts, including those related to space-based radar and infrared sensing. As a study on ADI undertaken for the Canadian Centre for Arms Control and Disarmament pointed out, "[a]s much of the US air defence research and development now wears the ADI label, Canadian participation in follow-on air defence technological development through the ADAT Working Group is of necessity connected to ADI; distancing Canada from what is seen as a natural evolution of ongoing modernization efforts would deprive Canada of input into decisions which could affect Canadian territory and airspace."[53]

The Mulroney government decided to tough the criticism out. Air defence technology was just too important. While Canada remained out of SDI, it would get into ADI and just accept the overlap. The government's 1987 defence white paper included the one-sentence confirmation that Canada planned "to participate in research on future air defence systems in conjunction with the United States Air Defense Initiative."[54] Canadian officials became members of the ADI coordinating committee and its operations requirements panel, and served as technical evaluators to preliminary ADI research and development proposals. Several Canadian officers were sent on ADI-related postings to the US and a couple of Canadian companies were designated as subcontractors for ADI-sponsored projects.

Ottawa backed up its interest with some cash. A Canadian space-based radar research program was set in motion in December 1986 with an initial budget of $47 million. Officials of the Department of National Defence said at one point that "given the political decision to do it and the funding," Canada would have the capability to deploy four to ten radar satellites by the mid-1990s, except for the capability to launch them into orbit.[55] In reality there was no way, though, that the funding would ever be there for a purely Canadian system, inasmuch as each satellite was expected to cost between half a billion and a billion dollars. So it only made sense to cooperate with the US; the $47 million was earnest money. "Certainly $50 million buys them a seat at the table," Herres said.[56]

On the other hand, the Canadian air force found itself in the late 1980s, to its frustration, without a seat at the table when the US military considered its plans for the broader aerospace defence of the continent. Discussions involving Canadians were being limited to air defence. This was not only a break with the past. It was also out of keeping with the NORAD agreement, which since 1981 had described aerospace defence as a joint interest and responsibility.

In part, the Canadians had been shut out because of the new command structure at Colorado Springs. As mentioned above, USSPACECOM was the first "twin" to NORAD that was neither an air defence nor aerospace defence command. Its mandate extended across the range of US military space operations. ADCOM had been a "component" command of NORAD; USSPACECOM was not. Herres called this "very important, but a very subtle change."[57] Herres was responsible for another important change. While he supported "dual-hatting" for himself as CINC, in June 1985 he issued guidance to put an end to the extensive dual-hatting of US officers at Colorado Springs that went back to the 1950s and also to establish separate staffs for NORAD and USSPACECOM. As he explained to the Joint Chiefs of Staff, "faithful to the missions of each organization" his guidance "ensures that each command maintains its own identity."[58] In large part, Herres' motivation was to assure the other US services, especially the Navy, that USSPACECOM would not be too dominated by the USAF.

The joint strategic defence planning staff was placed within USSPACECOM, not NORAD, creating a bureaucratic barrier for Canadians. When they wanted to, the Americans at Colorado Springs had long been able to get around such bureaucratic and legal barriers and to bring the Canadians in. But in the late 1980s Americans at USSPACECOM did not want to, or they were explicitly forbidden to when it came to aerospace defence planning. Frustrated Canadians began to enquire why they were shut out not just in Colorado Springs but also in other fora.

The answer came in spring 1989. As the Department of External Affairs recorded somewhat later, "it was made clear by USA officials at joint Military Coordinating Cttee Mtg in April that this exclusion and other restrictions in recent years on CDN access to USA info which we deem relevant to our combined North American efforts, were a direct result of CDA's 1985 policy against official CDN participation in SDI."[59] Canadian officials were attempting to convince the US to restore Canadian access. The US was also irritated that Ottawa publicly adhered to the so-called "narrow interpretation" of the ABM Treaty that ruled out the testing and development of space-based or airborne elements of a missile defence system.

Together, Canadian and US air force officials began in 1989 to formulate a "Combined Policy Statement on the Aerospace Defence of North America" that would include a sort-of-Canadian endorsement of missile defence and so, they hoped, smooth the way to make Canada once again an acceptable partner for aerospace defence planning. The draft statement said that technology eventually might make it possible to defend against ballistic missile and space attacks. If that occurred and if the decisions were made to deploy such defences they would be, according to the draft statement, included in the North American aerospace defence system; in the meantime, the US and Canada would cooperate in planning for their possible deployment.[60]

With the 1991 NORAD renewal approaching, officials discussed taking the wording originally formulated for the draft statement and using it instead in what they called a "forward-looking clause" that would be inserted into the new NORAD agreement. Meanwhile, the two air forces turned up the heat on Ottawa with respect to missile defence. Bill McKnight, the minister of national defence, was told by his department in March 1990 that not only was Canada being kept out aerospace defence planning because of its stance on missile defence, but NORAD's core function of integrated warning and attack assessment might itself now be in jeopardy. In particular, McKnight was informed that DCINCNORAD, Lieutenant-General Robert W. Morton, had warned that the warning and assessment function might be transferred from NORAD to USSPACECOM, leaving NORAD solely as an air defence command and shutting Canada out of involvement in space systems.[61]

The attempts to place the "forward-looking clause" in the 1991 NORAD agreement came to an end in the summer of 1990 when the USAF insisted that only explicit Canadian endorsement of SDI and of the "broad" interpretation of the ABM Treaty would do, yet at the same time promised that Canadian access to strategic defence planning could be informally worked out between the air forces. The Cold War was ending and the US was rethinking missile defence. Everyone was happy, except Derek Burney, the Canadian ambassador in Washington. He cabled Ottawa in July 1990 that he was miffed at "too much service-to-service micromanagement" of important Canada–US defence issues. "A recent example was the air force-to-air force negotiation of the quote USA/CDA joint statement on aerospace defence unquote in which USAF tried to get us to sign on unconditionally to the SDI program without the authority of the office of the secretary of defence (which recently asked us whether govt of CDA really wanted to pursue such a politically sensitive course)."[62] Partridge, Slemon, and Foulkes would have nodded in recognition.

DRUGS AND THE 1991 RENEWAL

In September 1988 the US Congress conscripted a largely reluctant military into the war on drugs. Its *Fiscal Year 1989 National Defense Authorization Act* designated the defense department as the lead agency for detecting and monitoring the smuggling of illegal drugs into the country. In response, the department gave in January 1989 the CINCs of four US commands responsibilities for implementing the act. At the same time it gave General John L. Piotrowski, in his capacity as commander, USELEMNORAD, responsibility for using US air defence assets to detect and monitor suspected airborne drug traffic entering the country, in coordination with other US agencies. While the Pentagon had acted correctly in tasking not the bi-national NORAD but USELEMNORAD for this national operation, Piotrowski found the situation awkward. As commander of the national element he had only a truncated headquarters staff. Inasmuch as the drug trade also affected Canada, he suggested that the US State Department approach Ottawa for permission to make counter-drug operations a NORAD responsibility, thereby involving both the Canadians at Colorado Springs and Canadian air defences.[63]

The Mulroney government readily agreed in February 1989. There were to be no new Canadian radars or aircraft acquired specifically for NORAD's counter-drug operations. However, NORAD anticipated that the 1985 air defence modernization program would make the radar barrier in Canada "much more difficult to penetrate by airborne drug traffickers."[64] Moreover, the real focus of operations was not northward but southward, and on cocaine, largely produced in South America, which reached the US across the Mexican border or through the Caribbean. Along that border the US had placed radars mounted on tethered dirigible balloons with which to detect low-flying smugglers, and it also deployed a relocatable version of OTH-B looking southward into the Caribbean. Still, as Fraser Holman, a former director of NORAD combat operations noted, "[d]irect flights to locations farther north on either east or west coast, including those to Canada, are much rarer but not unknown. Since there is no network of islands to support their staging or navigation, it takes a more sophisticated smuggler to attempt this routing."[65]

Once counter-drug operations got underway, NORAD strongly emphasized in public that there was an important limitation to the command's role. As Piotrowski put it in a speech to the Council on Foreign Relations in New York: "Let me stress that this detection and monitoring mission does not, I repeat, does not include interdicting suspected drug-smuggling aircraft."[66] That was the job of law enforcement agencies. The intent was decidedly not to have NORAD's fighter interceptors shoot down suspected smugglers.

The first cooperative Canadian–US drug interdiction operation in which NORAD was involved occurred on 12 March 1989. NORAD's detection and monitoring went well. But the interdiction by US customs supported by the US Army did not. Canadian sovereignty was violated, leading to a flurry of bad publicity in Canada for the new arrangements. The incident began when US air defence radar detected off the south coast of Florida and followed a small turboprop aircraft that had not filed a flight plan. Two USAF interceptors pursued it into Canadian airspace over Nova Scotia, whereupon it landed at a Sorel, Quebec airstrip. According to press reports, armed US customs agents then landed at the airstrip, where they arrested the smugglers and forced the manager to lie face down in the parking lot while they searched for drugs. The manager's son, fearing that his father was being kidnapped, called the Quebec provincial police and then went to his father's aid. When they arrived they found the US customs officials reading the suspects their rights under the US constitution, while a US Army helicopter landed. Only then did the RCMP arrive to supervise. No doubt the chief of the defence staff, General Paul Manson, agreed with the assessment Piotrowski sent him of the incident that said the two countries needed to develop better guidelines for such operations.[67]

Strategic bombers fly at speeds greater than 180 knots (nautical miles per hour). As a result, NORAD had automatically classified as not a threat and then ignored the radar tracks of slower aircraft approaching the continent (except in the US southeast and in western Polar regions), making no effort to correlate them with flight plans that had been filed. With the onset in of counter-drug operations, that had to change, because smugglers could rely on slow-flying aircraft. This required new procedures and the retraining of operators at NORAD facilities as well as at the FAA in the US and the MOT in Canada, where flight plans were filed. McKnight announced in 1990 that all aircraft approaching Canada's coasts would have to file a flight plan; previously that had only been required of aircraft flying at speeds over 180 knots.

While new, NORAD's counter-drug operations still clearly fell under various provisions of the existing NORAD agreement. Washington and Ottawa decided to spell it out in the 1991 renewal, though, by including the sentence, "With respect to our common interest in maintaining effective surveillance and control of North American airspace, our two governments understand that such control includes the surveillance and monitoring of aircraft suspected of smuggling illegal drugs into North America."[68]

That was the only change. Otherwise the 1981 text stayed in force. Quite unlike 1986, this time NORAD renewal went through quietly and without controversy. The fear of an east–west clash and nuclear war that had so dominated the 1986 renewal was gone. In the few weeks before the 30 April 1991 exchange of diplomatic notes between Ottawa and Washington that constituted renewal, Germany had been reunited and the Warsaw Pact had been dissolved, while the Soviet Union tottered. It was hard to absorb it all. Yet the Soviet strategic nuclear arsenal capable of striking North America was still in place. For the moment, and as the astonishing and wonderful changes in the world continued to roll on, doing nothing new really was the most sensible thing to do about NORAD.

NOTES

[1] Quoted in Robert Frank Futrell, *Ideas, Concepts, Doctrine: Basic Thinking in the United States Air Force, 1961–1984,* Vol II (Maxwell Air Force Base, Alabama: Air University Press, 1989), 446.

[2] Jeffrey Richelson, "PD-59, NSDD-13 and the Reagan Strategic Modernization Program," *Journal of Strategic Studies* 6, No. 1 (March 1983), 125-45.

[3] John Anderson, "Canada and the Modernization of North American Air Defense," in David G. Haglund and Joel J. Sokolsky (eds.), *The US–Canada Security Relationship: The Politics, Strategy and Technology of Defense* (Boulder, CO: Westview Press, 1989), 180.

[4] Fred Kaplan, *The Wizards of Armageddon* (New York: Simon and Shuster, 1983), 387.

[5] Ibid., 389.

[6] Both quoted in Lawrence Freedman, *The Evolution of Nuclear Strategy,* Third Edition (Houndsmills: Palgrave Macmillan, 2003), 388.

[7] Douglas A. Ross, "American Nuclear Revisionism, Canadian Strategic Interests, and the Renewal of NORAD," *Behind the Headlines* 29, No. 6 (1982), 16, 13-14.

[8] Department of National Defence, "Cruise Missile Testing in Canada: Background Notes." ND. 1983.

[9] *The Globe and Mail*, 10 May 1983.

[10] J.L. Granatstein and Robert Bothwell, *Pirouette: Pierre Trudeau and Canadian Foreign* Policy (Toronto: University of Toronto Press, 1990), 363-64.

[11] Address to the Nation on Defense and National Security, 23 March 1983. *Public Papers of the President: Ronald Reagan*, Reagan Presidential Library, available online.

[12] Daniel Wirls, *Buildup: The Politics of Defense in the Reagan Era* (Ithaca: Cornell University Press, 1992), 154.

[13] "Exchange of Notes and Memorandum of Understanding on the Modernization of the North American Air Defence System," 18 March 1985.

[14] House of Commons, *Debates*, 13 March 1985, 2976-77.

[15] Christopher Kirkey, "Negotiating the 1985 North American Air Defence Modernization Agreement," *International Journal of Canadian Studies* (Fall 1998), 164.

[16] Quoted in Ibid., 164.

[17] Confidential source.

[18] General Paul Manson, in Senate, *Proceedings of the Special Committee of the Senate on National Defence*, 17 April 1984, 9:8.

[19] Ibid., 9:19.

[20] Ian McLean, director, US General Relations Division, comments on memo, "Status Report to SSEA Re NORAD Renewal," 30 November 1990. Files of the Department of Foreign Affairs and International Trade, 27-14-NORAD-3.

[21] David Cox, *Trends in Continental Defence: A Canadian Perspective* (Ottawa: Canadian Institute for International Peace and Security, 1986), 36.

[22] P. Barton, "Canadian Concerns Regarding North American Air Defence Responsibility—sharing with the USA," 15 November 1984. Files of the Department of Foreign Affairs and International Trade, 27-14-NORAD Vol. 13, 82-04-01–89-04-30.

[23] Michael Slack, "NORAD," in R.B. Byers (ed.), *Canadian Annual Review of Politics and Public Affairs* (Toronto: University of Toronto Press, 1988), 236.

[24] House of Commons, *Debates,* 19 March 1985, 3163; 20 March 1985, 3200-1.

[25] Ibid., 19 March 1985, 3193-94.

[26] Ibid., 21 January 1985, 1502.

[27] "Doubts About the DEW Line," *The Globe and Mail*, 29 January 1985.

[28] House of Commons, *Debates*, 5 February 1985, 2014.

[29] Press release, US Embassy Ottawa, 7 March 1985.

[30] House of Commons, *Debates*, 6 March 1985, 2777.

[31] Presidential address, Quebec City, 18 March 1985, *Weekly Compilation of Presidential Documents*, 25 March 1985, 322.

[32] Prime Minister's statement, 7 September 1985. Text, Prime Minister's Office, Ottawa.

[33] Douglas Ross, "Canadian–American Relations and the Strategic Defense Initiative: A Case Study in the Management of Strategic Doctrinal Incompatibilities," paper presented for the 1987 Pearson-Dickey Conference, Montebello, Quebec, 4-6 November 1987, 25.

[34] House of Commons, *Debates*, 10 September 1985, 6454.

[35] Paul B. Stares, *Space and National Security* (Washington: The Brookings Institution, 1987), 4.

[36] General Bennie David, quoted in Earl S. Van Inwegen III, "The Air Force Develops and Operational Organization for Space," in *The US Air Force in Space: 1945 to the Twenty-first Century* (Proceedings, Air Force Historical Foundation Symposium, Andrews AFB, MD, 21-22 September 1995) (Washington: USAF History and Museums Program, 1998), 141.

[37] Quoted in David N. Spires, *Beyond Horizons: A Half Century of Air Force Space Leadership* (NP: Air Force Space Command/Air University Press, 1998), 205.

[38] Ibid., 218.

[39] "Command Interview, General Robert T. Herres," 21 January 1987, Office of History, US Space Command. Copy in NORAD/USNORTHCOM History Office.

[40] *The History of the Unified Command Plan, 1946–1993*, Joint History Office, Office of the Chairman of the Joint Chiefs of Staff, February 1995, 97.

[41] John Kirton, "A Renewed Opportunity: The Role of Space in Canadian Security Policy," in David B. Dewitt and David Leyton-Brown (eds.), *Canada's International Security Policy* (Scarborough: Prentice Hall Canada, 1995), 115.

[42] P.E. Barton, "Background Paper on Inter-relationship between NORAD and USA Space Activities," 2 May 1984, Files of the Department of Foreign Affairs and International trade, 27-14-NORAD-1 Vol. 17.

[43] P.E. Barton, department memo to SSEA, 18 June 1985. Files of the Department of Foreign Affairs and International trade, 26-14-NORAD Vol. 13 82-04-01– 89-04-30.

[44] Confidential source.

[45] *NORAD 1986: Report of the Standing Committee on External Affairs and National Defence*, February 1986, xiii.

[46] Ibid., 75-77.

[47] Ibid., 78.

[48] Cable, EXOTT URR 1028, 5 November 1985, "Report on Shultz-Clark Breakfast." Files of the Department of Foreign Affairs and International Trade, 27-14-NORAD Vol. 13 82-04-01– 89-04-30.

[49] "PM Not Tough Enough at Summit, Opposition Says," *The Globe and Mail*, 20 March 1986.

[50] Quoted in unclassified briefing materials on the ADI, Headquarters, US Air Force, September 1987.

[51] Ibid.

[52] Ibid.

[53] Daniel Hayward, *The Air Defence Initiative*, Issue Brief No. 9 (Ottawa: Canadian Centre for Arms Control and Disarmament, 1988), 22.

[54] *Challenge and Commitment: A Defence Policy for Canada*, June 1987, 56-57.

[55] DND Director of Space Doctrine and Operations quoted in Sharon Hobson, "Canada's Space-based Radar Project," *Jane's Defence Weekly* 7, No. 6 (14 February 1987), 226.

[56] Quoted in *Military Space*, 14 September 1987, 4.

[57] Herres interview (see note 39).

[58] Letter, Herres to chairman, Joint Chiefs of Staff, July 1985, quoted in "Background Paper: NORAD & USSPACECOM Staff Relationships at Activation of USSAPCECOM September 1985," 20 November 1992. Copy in NORAD/USNORTHCOM History Office.

[59] Draft cable, EXTOT IDR to WSHDC, 22 December 1989. Files of the Department of Foreign Affairs and International Trade, 27-14-NORAD-3.860316-901130.

[60] Confidential source.

[61] Confidential source.

[62] Cable, Burney to department, 31 July 1990. Files of the Department of Foreign Affairs and International Trade, 27-14-NORAD-3 860316-901130.

[63] Based on Dixie Dysart, "'Committed to Make a Difference:' Canada's Role in the Inception of NORAD Counterdrug Operations," in *Canada in NORAD*, 7th Annual Air Force Historical Proceedings, Peterson AFB Colorado, 2001, Office of Air Force Heritage and History (Canada), 126-40.

[64] Quoted in Ibid., 129.

[65] D.F. Holman, *NORAD in the New Millennium* (Toronto: Irwin Publishing Ltd, 2000), Canadian Institute of International Affairs, Contemporary affairs series, No. 5, 84.

[66] "Remarks prepared for General John L. Piotrowski to the Council on Foreign Relations," 17 May 1989. Copy in NORAD/USNORTHCOM History Office.

[67] Dysart (see note 63) and Rick Dolphin, et al., Flight into Danger," *Maclean's*, 3 April 1989, 12-13.

[68] "Exchange of Notes between the Government of Canada and the Government of the United States of America," *Canada Treaty Series*, 1991, No. 19.

CHAPTER FIVE

A COMMAND IN SEARCH OF POST COLD WAR ROLES, 1991–2001

"A VERY UNCERTAIN FUTURE FOR NORAD"

After the 1991 renewal, NORAD launched a review, under the direction of its DCINC, Lieutenant-General Robert W. Morton, of how it should approach its own future. An external study commissioned as part of that review told the NORAD planners something they no doubt themselves already had concluded at the Cold War's end: "The major changes that have occurred in the strategic environment and the changes resulting from emerging Canadian and US policies and strategies indicate a very uncertain future for NORAD. It is possible that NORAD could be faced with a reduced mission, a reduced capability, or becoming non-viable as a command in the absence of a coherent and compelling strategy that fully takes into account the new strategic environment."[1]

NORAD's air defence capability was, in fact, significantly reduced during the early 1990s, especially in the Canadian north. The chances were small that the post-Soviet Russians would want, much less be able, to use their deteriorating long-range bomber fleet against North America in a precursor or decapitation strike. Therefore, as CINCNORAD General Charles A. Horner put in 1994, "there is essentially no military air threat against North America today."[2] As a result, the 1985 North American Air Defence Modernization program was never fully completed and was partially rolled back. The west coast OTH-B radar station was built, but was never turned on to be used operationally and went right into storage. The east coast station became operational, but was turned off and put into "warm storage" in 1994 and soon thereafter into "cold storage." While the North Warning System was completed and was declared operational in 1995, its unattended short-range radars that provided low-altitude coverage were turned off for increasingly long periods and put in "warm storage." Of the five Forward Operations planned for the Canadian north, out of which fighter aircraft would operate in an emergency, the one at Kuujjuaq was at first deferred and then cancelled. The others were completed but without the munitions storage facilities that had been planned. And of these four, only the ones at Inuvik and Iqaluit were used by NORAD at least once a year in the early 1990s for exercises. The ones at Rankin Inlet and Yellowknife were considered in storage. Another key element of the 1985 plan had been access to AWACS with which the fighters could operate out of the forward operating locations. In 1992 the USAF "realigned" AWACS usage, meaning that NORAD could not at all count on such aircraft being available.

NORAD's ability to readily mount a thin air defence engagement zone in the far north was gone, although the command hoped to be able to retain the capability to regenerate air defences in the unlikely event the Cold War started up again. The vestigial, standing air defences were to be concentrated close in on the Atlantic and Pacific coasts and along the US southern periphery where – looking outward – they could provide sovereign backup to the aviation traffic control authorities and law enforcement agencies. In Canada, air defence operations remained centred on Cold Lake and Bagotville with CF-18s also relying on Goose Bay, Labrador and Comox, BC as needed. In the continental US, the number of fighter alert sites was reduced, and the USAF proceeded during the 1990s to turn air defence operations there over to Air National Guard squadrons equipped with F-16s and F-15s and deployed at seven alert sites, two in Florida and one each in Texas, California, Oregon, Massachusetts and Virginia (see Map 9). The Pentagon considered in 1998 closing three of these sites and relying on a "four corners" deployment; NORAD successfully resisted this.

Air defence operations became more regionalized. The three NORAD regions (Canada, continental US, and Alaska) were equipped with different air defence battle management systems that had been developed independently and were not directly interoperable. Colorado Springs itself was without an automated, NORAD-wide air defence battle management system, although it was working on installing one. The continental US region was divided into three sectors; in Canada there were two, both of which were controlled out of North Bay; the headquarters for the Canadian NORAD Region (CANR) was located in Winnipeg. Closing the North Bay centre and moving its capabilities to Winnipeg made financial sense but politics stood in the way. In 1993 NORAD announced that it was adopting a "flexible alert" posture for its fighters. This was a break from the Cold War practice whereby many fighters were kept on 24-hour alert status across the continent. Henceforth, the sectoral air defence commanders were to have the authority to raise or lower alert levels locally as needed. This gave them, in the words of one US sectoral commander, the "freedom to scramble."[3] Two aircraft were usually kept on alert at each of the two Canadian and seven continental US sites, as well as at an Alaskan site, for a total of twenty. This meant that Canada devoted eight CF-18s to regular NORAD duty: four for alert, and four for backup.

Contrary to what had been expected at the time of the 1991 renewal of the NORAD agreement, NORAD's relatively high profile role in the war on drugs was short lived. To be sure, Canadians visiting Colorado Springs in 1992 were told that counter-drug operations constituted a third of NORAD operations.[4] But US counter-drug strategy shifted in 1993 away from interdiction of shipments in transit to interdiction within the countries of origin. In consequence, an intelligence unit at Colorado Springs linking NORAD to US drug enforcement agencies was closed and the command's counter-drug efforts fell off.

GLOBAL PROTECTION, WORLD-WIDE WARNING, AND THE 1996 RENEWAL

With Russia still in possession of nuclear-tipped ballistic missiles capable of striking North America, no one argued that the USAF's missile detection and tracking sensors could be turned off and NORAD's warning and assessment responsibilities ended. NORAD's review of its own future, completed in 1992, concluded that the command should attempt to acquire two new, additional missions: ballistic missile defence for North America and world-wide warning of ballistic missile attack. Horner championed both approaches enthusiastically. As he put it in early 1993:

As I see it, the future NORAD mission may well revolve around two basic responsibilities: theater aerospace control for North American and world-wide warning. The former would include surveillance and appropriate action to counter hostile activities, both active air defense and ballistic missile defense. World-wide warning is a logical extension of NORAD's present 'Integrated Tactical Warning and Attack Assessment' role. NORAD's procedures for detecting and characterizing missile launches would serve well to alert participants in a global protection system. In times of crisis or attack on North America, NORAD would, of course, provide warning to both nations just as we do today.[5]

There was nothing at all new to the CINC at Colorado Springs wanting to give missile defence to NORAD, and not the "twin" command. The problem was still with getting Ottawa to agree. Horner had good reason to be optimistic about this, though. In January 1991 the Bush administration redirected the SDI program away from systems to stop a massive Soviet missile attack and towards providing Global Protection Against Limited Strikes (GPALS) to the US, its forces overseas, and its friends and allies. As envisaged by the administration, GPALS was to have three main components. The first was a National Missile Defense (NMD) for the US itself, consisting of about a thousand interceptors located at five or six sites. The second was a set of theatre missile defences that could be deployed abroad. Finally, and spectacularly, there would be a global missile defence provided by a thousand or more lightweight, watermelon-size satellites that would fire "brilliant pebbles" at ballistic missiles launched from anywhere in the world.

The 1991 Persian Gulf War against Saddam Hussein lent strong impetus to the GPALS program. During the war, Iraq attacked coalition forces in the region and Israel with SCUD missiles, dramatically underlining the danger of ballistic missile proliferation. Even more dramatically, the war also provided a rough indication of how part of a GPALS system might work. DSP satellites under USSPACECOM's operational command that had been deployed to watch for Soviet missile launches were redirected during the war to look toward Iraq where they could detect Iraqi SCUD launches. This permitted USSPACECOM to provide warning and to cue the rudimentary missile defences that had been fashioned out of Patriot air defence weapons and deployed to protect Israel and the US-led coalition that was freeing Kuwait. The NORAD/USSPACECOM missile warning centre in Cheyenne Mountain was involved, apparently peripherally.[6] For the first time ever, hostile ballistic missiles were intercepted in trajectory. How effective the Patriot-based missile defences had in fact been was thereafter the subject of considerable debate.

In September 1991 President Bush called upon the Soviet Union to join with the US in deploying a GPALS system. Soviet President Gorbachev responded that he was willing to talk. Both Gorbachev and the Soviet Union were soon history; Boris Yeltsin, president of the newly sovereign Russian Federation, went even further in his response to the Bush administration, announcing in January 1992 that "[w]e are ready jointly to work out and subsequently to create and jointly operate a global system of defense in place of SDI." A few days later he proposed to the UN General Assembly the "creation of a global system for protection of the world community" which "could make use of high technologies developed in Russia's defence complex." At a June summit in Washington, the US and Russian presidents agreed that "their two nations should work together with allies and other interested states in developing a concept for such a system as part of an overall strategy regarding the proliferation of ballistic missiles and weapons of mass destruction."[7] During the course of 1992 Russian-American working groups met to try to flesh out the concept.

The Mulroney government made generally approving remarks about the Russian-American discussions over global protection and awaited developments. The new DCINC at NORAD, Lieutenant-General B.L. Smith, saw the opportunity to get Canada out of the doghouse at Colorado Springs, where it had been ever since Ottawa's 1985 decision not to participate in SDI research. He wrote Horner in September 1992 that since he had arrived at the command the month before, he had received "the impression that the prevailing view among the USSPACECOM and NORAD senior leadership is that Canada is rather negative towards the concept" of GPALS. That wasn't fair, he said, citing the prime minister's generally approving words in a letter Mulroney had written to Bush. Smith concluded that he was "relatively confident," that "after all is said and done, Canada will wish to participate in BMD within North America, and to do so only under the auspices of NORAD. I will certainly work towards that goal. In the meantime we should not support the impression that Canada is at all negative in its approach to this important issue."[8]

After such encouragement, NORAD issued in 1993 a draft "NORAD/ USSPACECOM Ballistic Missile Defense Concept of Operations." It assumed that NORAD – not USSPACECOM and certainly not another command – would in the first instance be responsible for the use of the missile defence of North America. In particular, CINCNORAD would exercise operational control over any ground-based interceptors deployed to protect North America; that is, he would decide at which incoming missiles to shoot. This meant that senior Canadians at Colorado Springs would exercise such authority in the CINC's absence. USSPACECOM would support NORAD's missile defence operations by detecting missile launches and tracking their trajectories, much as it already provided NORAD with such information for the binational command to undertake its warning and assessment responsibilities. USSPACECOM would also provide such information to other US theatre CINCs, as it had so visibly done during the Gulf War. As the "twin," USSPACECOM also would be given operational command over the defences, to exercise if NORAD could not fulfill operational control.[9]

The draft concept of operations was left unclassified, which gives a pretty good indication of how much more relaxed the political climate in Canada surrounding missile defence had become in the short period since the end of the Cold War. Such a document would have been incendiary during the late 1980s when NORAD was suspected in some Canadian quarters of being SDI's Trojan horse. Nonetheless, it was just a Colorado Springs notion of how missile defence would work. Washington and Ottawa would have to agree on any decision to assign missile defence to NORAD.

It may be that Horner took the initiative to develop the draft concept of operations document partially to emphasize to Washington the utility of NORAD as a strategic defence command, regardless of what happened to USSPACECOM. Once again, just as in 1974–75 and in 1977–79, a proposal had arisen to dissolve NORAD's twin command and transfer its space assets to a US command responsible for strategic forces. In the past, this had been the USAF's Strategic Air Command (SAC); as discussed in Chapter Three, it was to SAC that the space assets were transferred in 1979, only to be transferred back to Colorado Springs upon the establishment of Air Force Space Command and then USSPACECOM in 1985. SAC was dissolved in 1992, whereupon operational command over all US strategic nuclear forces was assumed by a newly created unified Strategic Command (USSTRATCOM).

While USSTRATCOM was still in the planning stages, the US Joint Chiefs of Staff had considered fragmenting USSPACECOM or subordinating it to USSTRATCOM. This took somewhat more concrete form in 1993 when the Pentagon, at the direction of both the chairman of the Joint Chiefs and the secretary of defense, conducted a formal review of the possibility of eliminating USSPACECOM and assigning its space responsibilities to the new USSTRATCOM.

NORAD was markedly indifferent to the future of its twin as the review got underway. The strategic defence of North America was distinguishable from US military space operations. As NORAD's deputy director for policy and programs put it in a letter to the Pentagon, "[t]he relationship between NORAD and USSPACECOM has been a close one since 1986 [sic], based on physical proximity, mission similarity and a dual-hatted CINC ... However, although the close relationship has been useful, it is hardly necessary for NORAD to accomplish its assigned objectives." USPACECOM played no role in air defence. While under the existing command arrangements USSPACECOM did provide data to NORAD for warning and assessment of missile attack, other US commands could do the job if necessary. Therefore "[w]ith or without USSPACECOM, NORAD's assigned responsibility for warning and characterization of attack can be discharged." The deputy director warned Washington, however, that any attempt, upon dissolution of USSPACECOM, to double-hat CINCNORAD as USCINCSTRAT would cause real problems with Ottawa because of "Canadian sensitivity about close association with a nuclear command."[10] Canadian defence officials expressed concern to Washington. Such a step was unlikely, though, given the longstanding principle of keeping the command responsible for warning of attack on North America apart from the command responsible for a strategic nuclear response.

USSPACECOM survived the 1993 review. While merging it into USSTRATCOM would have saved 100 to 300 staff positions, the review team was sharply divided over whether such a step would provide enough "'value-added' – that is, improving space support, operational effectiveness, efficiency and interoperability while maintaining joint Service expertise and a joint operational focus."[11]

GPALS did not survive 1993, though. The Clinton administration, which took office in January of that year, dismantled the program. Work on "brilliant pebbles" was halted. The administration also cut funds for the development of a National Missile Defense to a bare minimum, and directed that emphasis be placed on development of theatre missile defences for US forces abroad. To underline the break they were making with the Reagan past, the Democrats changed the name of the Strategic Defense Initiative Organization to the Ballistic Missile Defense Organization.

Later that year there was also a new government in Canada, when the Liberals under Jean Chrétien won the October election. With SDI having been proclaimed dead by Washington and with the chances that there would be even a limited missile defence for North America anytime soon having diminished greatly, the Liberals reversed the Mulroney government's 1985 decision that the Canadian government would stay completely out of the US missile defence research program. That policy change was announced in a 1994 defence white paper. The Liberals also decided it was safe to convey in couched language the message that Ottawa did not categorically rule out Canadian participation in the operation of any missile defence system that the US might eventually decide upon. As the white paper put it: "In the future, Canada's potential role in ballistic missile defence will not be determined in isolation, but in conjunction with the evolution of North American and possible NATO-wide aerospace defence arrangements. Canadian involvement in ballistic missile defence would also have to be cost-effective and affordable, make an unambiguous contribution to Canada's defence needs, and build on missions the Forces already perform such as surveillance and communications."[12]

The Republican takeover of the US Congress in November 1994 precipitated a change of direction by the Clinton administration on strategic defence. The Republicans, inspired by Reagan, remained firm supporters of national missile defences, convinced that American voters would approve of efforts to protect them against nuclear strikes. As promised in their campaign platform, the "Contract with America," the congressional Republicans adopted a bill mandating deployment of a national missile defence by 2003. The president vetoed the bill, but soon sought to co-opt the issue. In a February 1996 press conference, Secretary of Defense William J. Perry formally announced a "three-plus-three" missile defence program. According to this plan, a limited national missile defence system would be developed and tested for three years, starting in 1997, meaning that the decision whether to deploy would be taken in 2000. If the threat warranted deployment, the system could be in place by 2003. If the threat did not then warrant deployment, development would continue with the goal of being able to create a system that was more capable than the one that would have been deployed in 2003. At any point after 1999, when there would be a major test of the missile defence architecture, the US would remain able to deploy a national missile defence system within three years. Republicans grumbled that it was a ruse, that the Democrats had no intention of ever deploying, and that 'three-plus-never" would have been a better title.

World-wide warning of ballistic missile attack, the second mission upon which NORAD thought in 1992–1993 its future might be built, was conceptually distinct from GPALS. But the two were tightly linked politically. In early 1992, in response to Yeltsin's positive response to GPALS, US Secretary of State James Baker proposed to the Russians that in addition to discussing how to deploy missile defences jointly, the two countries begin such cooperation by "the sharing of early warning information on ballistic missile launches through a Joint Ballistic Missile Early Warning Center that would integrate and display early warning information from all participants."[13] At the June summit the two presidents put the proposal onto the agenda of the bilateral working groups.

Thereafter, NORAD sketched out the concept, that it sometimes called the "Global Warning Initiative," whereby it would provide integrated warning and assessment not just to the US and Canada, but to the proposed Joint Early Warning Center as well, which in turn would pass it on to participating countries. NORAD would receive data not just from the US sensors for which USSPACECOM was responsible, but also from the other countries. It is not clear how extensive a blueprint for the initiative NORAD ever developed.[14] Certainly the notion raises questions about precisely how the relationship would function between USSPACECOM, the source of much of the detection and tracking information; NORAD, the amalgamator and assessor of such information; and the Joint Early Warning Center, presumably a second amalgamator and second assessor of what it received not just from NORAD but also from Russian sources. USSPACECOM had the responsibility of warning US theatre commanders of missile attack, as it had during the Gulf War. It is easy to imagine an alternative model for global warning whereby USSPACECOM would have provided warning directly to the Joint Center, without NORAD's added assessment.

The Global Warning Initiative had some obvious attractions for the Canadian government. While NORAD would remain a bilateral command in which Canada had a privileged place, it would, if the initiative were implemented, support not just the strategic nuclear deterrent of the United States, but also a multilateral and potentially highly visible effort for international peace and security. Yet there was potentially a small embarrassment, as well. It was still the case that no sensor to detect or track ballistic missiles had ever either been located in Canada or operated by a unit of the Canadian Forces. All Canada had to contribute to the effort was its personnel at Colorado Springs and a few other US defence installations. During the 1990s, fifty or sixty "NORAD/ OUTCAN" personnel took up posts at various Air Force Space Command units responsible for missile warning and tracking and space surveillance. There were also several at USSPACECOM. The personnel slots had been freed up by the closing of radar stations in Canada. These Canadians provided a contribution to NORAD-related efforts and, after leaving their US space posts, expertise for the Canadian Forces in this area. Among their numbers, starting in the late 1990s, were navy and army personnel. NORAD service was no longer the bailiwick of the Canadian air force alone.

When the Clinton administration pulled the plug in 1993 on discussions with the Russians over GPALS, the steam went out of the proposal for the Joint Early Warning Center, as well.[15] Without it, NORAD's Global Warning Initiative ran out of steam, too.

As the May 1996 expiry date for the NORAD agreement approached, neither missile defence for North America nor global warning, the two new missions upon which Horner had thought much of the command's future might be built, had any prospect of being realized any time soon. Still, the American negotiators wanted some mention to be made in the new accord of missile defence, while their Canadian counterparts wanted the same for global warning. In the end, both were left out, when the accord – but not the command – was modernized in 1996.

The overall low priority which the Clinton administration placed on North American missile defence, and the much more relaxed position that the Chrétien government had taken on the subject since its 1994 defence white paper made it easy for Ottawa to agree, early on in the negotiations, to one of NORAD's two primary missions being specified in the new accord as simply "aerospace control for North America." This broad term amply covered, as Horner had pointed out several years before, both air defence and missile defence. To be sure, the 1996 agreement went on to stipulate that "it is understood that 'aerospace control' *currently* includes providing surveillance and control of the airspace of Canada and the United States" (emphasis added).[16]

And in the future? The US side proposed early on during the negotiations that missile defence be referred to as a possible future NORAD responsibility and as a form of aerospace control. Even though under the "three-plus-three" program the US simply could not deploy a missile defence before the agreement again expired in 2001, identifying it as a potential NORAD role was still a step a bit too far for the Canadians and the language never made it into the final agreement. Instead, the agreement stipulated that the expansion of the command's missions "should be examined and could evolve if both nations agree." There would be "full and meaningful consultations" on mission expansion or on other matters, whenever either government requested it.

NORAD's other primary mission, according to the 1996 accord, was to be "aerospace warning for North America." The Canadian side, for its part, had wanted the accord to refer specifically to the possibility of its expansion beyond

North America to global warning. Here the US side demurred. Such a step, too, would have to wait for those full and meaningful consultations. The Canadians also had hope during the negotiations of including a reference to potential Canadian involvement in ballistic missile research, now that Canadian policy had been changed. This also was left out.

The renewed accord included for the first time an environmental clause. This resulted from recent Canadian legislation requiring the federal government to take the environment into consideration when entering into international agreements. Attempts to negotiate some specific language about environmental protection bogged down to the point where they delayed renewal. Washington and Ottawa thereupon abandoned the attempt in favour of pledges in the agreement to be good to the environment and to send environmental matters related to NORAD operations to the largely moribund Canada–US Permanent Joint Board on Defence for the board's review, whence they were unlikely ever to reappear in public. The accord also included provisions regularizing the status of NORAD/OUTCAN personnel.

An overall Canadian goal in the renewal negotiations had been, in the words of a NORAD staff paper, "to provide the flexibility in the Agreement which would allow NORAD's mandate to evolve to encompass new aspects of the aerospace control and aerospace warning missions."[17] That had been admirably achieved in the 1996 text. But in reality such flexibility was of little use right away, for the US government was just not interested in immediately pursuing such new aspects of aerospace control and warning.

ASYMMETRY: SPACE SURVEILLANCE AND MISSILE DEFENCE

After the 1996 renewal, the Canadian military focused more actively on the relationship between NORAD and military space operations. It believed that NORAD could be useful in helping to obtain for Canada a range of badly-needed space capabilities. Yet at the same time, it worried that if Canada did not itself invest in a distinctive new contribution to NORAD's own space responsibilities, Canada's future in Colorado Springs could be called into question.

The experience with Operation Friction, Canada's military contribution to the Gulf War coalition, had shocked the Canadian Forces into the realization that among its deficiencies was "space support, a capability that Canada not only did not have but also few in its ranks understood. The quick-fix space support delivered for Operation Friction came from American sources and Canadian Forces depended on the United States completely."[18] The problem was not that Canada had no military satellites; few countries did. The Canadian military was inadequately set up to draw on available US military and other satellites. Over the next several years the Canadian military developed a space policy and equipped itself with a structure for implementing it. A Directorate of Space Development was created in National Defence Headquarters in 1995 and the deputy chief of the defence staff designated in 1997 as the departmental "space advocate."

In 1998 the deputy chief, Lieutenant-General R.R. Crabbe, acting in his new space advocacy role, disseminated within the Department of National Defence a list of military space capability requirements, along with his observation that "[s]pace Systems provide essential capability that arguably will mean the difference between mission success and failure in future operations." The list included communications, navigation, search and rescue, intelligence support, weather monitoring, and geomatics (mapping and charting) support, the surveillance from space of land, sea, and air, and warning of ballistic missile attack for Canadian Forces deployed abroad. The list also included space-based defence against ballistic missiles, with the important caveat that Canadian policy still limited involvement to research and consultation; and surveillance of space, which will be discussed below.[19] The department had concluded, Crabbe pointed out, that "[i]n light of the limited resources allocated to space in the CF Long Term Capital Plan, cooperative participation in US programs is considered a key component in the development of a modest space capability for the CF. Our partnership in NORAD will be leveraged, where practicable, to provide Canada a conduit into US space programs and ensure an equitable contribution to burden-sharing in the future."[20]

It is not clear whether the Canadian military ever had a well thought out strategy for trying to use NORAD as such a conduit. Certainly NORAD provided ready links to US space operations immediately related to its responsibilities for aerospace warning and control. NORAD/OUTCAN personnel were working in these areas. But how could it help in the other areas on the Canadian military's space capability wish list? At one point DCINCNORAD, Lieutenant-General L.W.F. Cuppens, indulged in the daydream that NORAD could be transformed into a sort of multilateral space-support command with a special place for Canada. "Through NORAD" he suggested, "Canada could be the nation that facilitates, tests and promotes the use of space in future coalition operations. In an era where there is the risk that the US military might so outdistance its allies through technology, especially space technology, Canada could 'lead the way' in ensuring that coalition operations remain achievable."[21]

A more realistic notion may have been that Canada could simply trade on its reputation as a longstanding NORAD partner. The ties between NORAD and USSPACECOM, especially the double-hatting of the CINC, could not hurt, either. The CINCs in the late 1990s were, in fact, prepared to go along. General Richard B. Myers, the CINC at the very end of the decade, promised "to energize the USSPACECOM staff" in support of enhanced military space cooperation between Canada and the United States.[22] Space cooperation between Ottawa and the Pentagon was spotty at best and NORAD provided a tangible link that otherwise would not be available. Still, inasmuch as USSPACECOM was at the time also pursuing cooperative partnerships with other "allied space faring nations" as it called them, it is fair to wonder about the extent to which the NORAD link was key to Canadian space aspirations. It was in the interest of the US that its allies and potential coalition partners have certain space capabilities, whether or not they were NORAD partners.

Since the closing of the last Canadian Baker-Nunn camera in 1992, Canada no longer made any direct contribution to NORAD's Space Surveillance Network (SSN), the successor to SPADATS, in which Canada had played a role almost from its beginning. Lest it remain a free rider and endanger thereby not only space cooperation with the US in general, but its place in Colorado Springs as well, the Canadian military began in 1998 to explore seriously how it could become a full partner in SSN. This could mean locating a new ground-based sensor in Canada or putting a new Canadian satellite into orbit with space surveillance capability. Because of the locations of the existing ground-based sensors in the US, adding a new one in Canada would be only of limited value. This made a Canadian satellite a technologically more attractive option. As a first step to getting into SSN, the Canadian military leased time at and posted officers to a space surveillance radar facility at the Lincoln Laboratories near Boston (which had been instrumental decades before in developing essential technology used for the DEW Line).

There were a number of advantages to making space surveillance a Canadian niche. It was manifestly compatible with existing international law. It revived an old Canadian specialty, and thus broke no new controversial ground; moreover, it was passive. It had useful non-military applications, including alerting commercial and other civilian users of space to potential collisions with active satellites and space debris, as well as providing warning of satellites, like Cosmos 954, falling out of orbit and striking the earth. Of course it also had had several military applications. One was to reduce the possibility that a satellite falling out of orbit would be misinterpreted as a missile attack. Crabbe pointed another application out, writing, "an often-overlooked component in planning for operations is the identification of a potential adversary's space resources. A theatre-level commander must know when such space assets threaten his classified operations in order to take appropriate action to minimize the effectiveness of that system."[23] In other words, space surveillance could let you know when the adversary's satellites were overhead.

Not the least of its advantages to the Canadian military, though, was that the US military, especially at NORAD, was prepared to view Canadian contributions to space surveillance as compensating for Canada's failure to participate directly in the development of missile defence. Upon the adoption of the three-plus-three program, NORAD was once again intently focused on missile defence as a pillar of its future. Official Canada–US collaborative research and consultation on missile defence, permitted since the 1994 white paper and conducted since 1997 within a framework agreement with the BMDO, turned out to be insignificant; the Department of National Defence estimated that it was spending only about a million dollars a year on it, mostly going to personnel costs. Even if Ottawa had been interested in spending much more it was almost certainly too late to carve out a direct Canadian contribution.

However, Canadian investment in space surveillance could constitute what was called an "asymmetrical contribution." As Cuppens outlined the idea, "this non-contentious approach by Canada would make a major contribution to further the future of the binational area of BMD (ballistic missile defence) without risking potential negative Canadian political and public opinions."[24] Both General Howell M. Estes, who was CINCNORAD from 1996 to 1998 and Myers, his successor, strongly supported the notion. Estes wrote the director of the Ballistic Missile Defense Organization: "This asymmetric approach parallels the success story of US–Canadian cooperation during the cold war years where Canada invested heavily in NORAD (defense) while avoiding direct contribution to the US nuclear forces (offense) to gain the benefit of protection by the US nuclear umbrella."[25]

Estes was hoping for more from Ottawa than just the asymmetrical contribution. "It has been my goal as CINCNORAD," he also wrote, "to evolve the US NMD program into a Ballistic Missile Defense of North America (BMD-NA) program for the US and Canada. I have personally worked long and hard during my tenure as both USCINCSPACE and CINCNORAD to get Canada formally involved in the BMD-NA program and policy development process as early as possible."[26]

Estes' goal was not to persuade Ottawa to endorse right away any North American missile defence deployment. That would have put it ahead of the Clinton administration, which was still counting off "three-plus-three." Moreover, Ottawa was paralyzed by anxiety over what might happen to the ABM Treaty. Even if the Canadian government wanted to recognize that the treaty was no longer relevant in the post-Cold War world, it would find it politically extremely difficult to do so. The treaty had become sacrosanct in Canadian thinking; every Canadian government since 1972 had firmly and frequently supported it. Such proclamations of allegiance had grown especially intense after the Reagan administration launched SDI. What would Ottawa do if the US eventually withdrew from the treaty – as provided for under its terms – to deploy missile defences? The Canadian government had every incentive to avoid answering that hypothetical question. And it might never have to give an answer, if the Clinton administration was able to negotiate an agreement with the Russians clarifying or amending the treaty to permit deployment – or if it did not deploy a missile defence at all.

Rather, Estes hoped that involving Canada in the development of missile defence, coupled with an informal, but continuing information program, would help the Canadian government eventually reach what he saw as the right decision. "Our task is to help inform and educate as many key leaders as possible in the interim and to ensure they are well prepared to make this critical deployment decision, if and when the time comes. As such, we must maintain a constant and consistent position at every opportunity for interaction."[27]

Estes did what he could in his contacts with civilian and military leaders in both countries to promote the conversion of NMD into BMD-NA. He welcomed senior Canadian officials to Colorado Springs for briefings and orientation visits at NORAD headquarters at which missile defence featured prominently on the agenda. He was also especially encouraged by an impending November 1997 meeting in Ottawa between John Hamre, the deputy secretary of defense, and his Canadian counterpart Louise Fréchette, the deputy minister of national defence. But at that session Hamre in effect undercut Estes, telling Fréchette, when asked by her, that he did not think the Clinton administration would make a deployment decision on BMD (much as the Congressional Republicans had suspected). He added that it might even be 10 years before a decision to deploy might be taken.[28]

That took the pressure off the Chrétien government to become involved in development. In the wake of the Hamre-Fréchette meeting, National Defence Headquarters in Ottawa complained to NORAD that it was not getting consistent signals from Colorado Springs and Washington, noting the "difference between Dr. Hamre's message of 'no sense of urgency' regarding BMD and NORAD's continual press to move forward." NORAD headquarters could only reply that "Dr. Hamre's remarks were consistent with the Administration's position on this issue. However, as the command tasked to defend North America against aerospace threats, NORAD must be ready when the threat emerges."[29] In the meantime, NORAD also did what it could to engage Canadians in BMD activities, if only peripherally. In 1998 it arranged for a Canadian Forces officer to be appointed liaison at the BMDO in Washington and for senior officials from the Departments of National Defence and Foreign Affairs to participate in a missile defence simulation, the first of several at the Joint National Test Facility located just outside Colorado Springs at Falcon Air Force Base.

During 1998 the chances increased substantially that a missile defence would be deployed by the US, if not under the Clinton administration then under its successor. Both North Korea and Iran caught the US intelligence community off guard with tests that showed progress in missile development programs. A special bipartisan Commission to Assess the Ballistic Missile Threat to the United States, headed by former Secretary of Defense Donald Rumsfeld, reported in the summer that "[c]oncerted efforts by a number of overtly or potentially hostile nations to acquire ballistic missiles with biological or nuclear payloads pose a growing threat to the United States." That threat was "broader, more mature and evolving more rapidly than has been reported in estimates and reports by the Intelligence Community."[30]

In January 1999 Secretary of Defense William Cohen, invoking both recent North Korean missile tests and the Rumsfeld report, announced that in the Clinton's administration's view, the potential ballistic missile threat to the US posed by countries such as North Korea, Iraq and Iran warranted a missile national defence. Spending on development was to be increased. That still did not mean that there necessarily would be deployment; still ahead were tests of the technology and a presidential decision in 2000.

At the same time, Clinton wrote Yelstin to put him on notice that an NMD decision was pending and to seek renegotiation of the ABM Treaty. That spring both the US Senate and House of Representatives voted to endorse missile defence. The majorities were large: 97 to 3 in the Senate and 317 to 105 in the House. In the words of a critic of NMD, these congressional votes "exploded like thunderclaps across the American national security landscape."[31] The Russians were not impressed. While they originally seemed receptive to the argument that NMD was to be directed not against them but against "rogue" states, their tone then turned toughly negative. "There can be no compromise on this issue," said the first deputy chief of the Russian general staff in autumn.[32] They also looked for support in the international community, introducing in the UN General Assembly a resolution calling for the preservation and strengthening of the ABM Treaty through "strict compliance." The resolution was adopted by a vote of 80 in favour and 4 against (the US, Israel, Micronesia, and Albania) with 68 abstentions, among them Canada. Among the majority was none other than North Korea whose representative declared that his government viewed the ABM Treaty as a "pillar of stability."[33]

This deepening disagreement between Washington and Moscow raised the spectre of what a gathering at Merrickville, Ontario, of Canadian officials and defence academics, summoned together in late 1998 by the Department of National Defence to think about missile defence, had called "the worst nightmare for Canada," namely "a deployed NMD system that the Russians argue is non-compliant. Canada would be faced with the choice of either having its policy held hostage by Moscow, or rejecting its longstanding support of the ABM Treaty in favour of its strategic relationship with Washington."[34]

SUDDEN RENEWAL, 2000–2001

There was a related nightmare for the Canadians at NORAD. They worried that if Ottawa opted for the treaty and out of NMD, NORAD itself would be in danger. To be sure, if Canada opted out of NMD, it could easily be placed under the operational command of USSPACECOM only (or whatever "twin" NORAD was paired with), just as the Safeguard missile defence system had been placed in 1974 not under NORAD, but under the US "twin" that then existed. At the same time, no element of the Safeguard system was located on Canadian soil or operated by the Canadian Forces. That had been good enough for Ottawa, even though the Canadians at NORAD during the mid-1970s had still been closely involved with Safeguard, especially by providing warning of attack that would be used to help cue it.

No element of the proposed NMD needed to be put in Canada, either. The interceptors would be located in the US (sites in Alaska and California were eventually chosen) and the existing missile detection sensors, none of which were in Canada, would be used. Roughly the same relationship could be created between NORAD and USSPACECOM with respect to NMD as had once existed between the "twins" when Safeguard was operational. But as the Canadians at NORAD worried, that might no longer be good enough for Canada. Ever since the Mulroney government's decision to stay out of SDI, critics had warned about Trojan Horses dragging the country willy-nilly into missile defence and would be quick to try to identify them. Providing through NORAD warning for NMD might itself be just too close an association for the Canadian government to want to try to explain and to sell at home. In that case, USSPACECOM could take over NORAD's responsibility for warning of and assessing a missile attack. There would be a heavy cost to such a step: NORAD would lose thereby a core responsibility. Continuing its existence would make little sense, except perhaps as a minor air defence command.

NORAD had also begun to think and worry about how it was going fit into the new US interest in what was being called "homeland defense." In November 1998, the command conducted a study exercise once again to consider its future. As the DCINC, Lieutenant-General George Macdonald reported to Myers, the study exercise had revealed "a lack of clarity about who specifically is or should be in charge of overall defense of North America. Without such clarity, it is obviously difficult for NORAD to know its precise role."[35]

Especially since the 1993 attempted bombing of the World Trade Center in New York and the 1995 Oklahoma City bombing had demonstrated that the US was not invulnerable to terrorist attack, there had been talk, both in and outside the Pentagon, about how the US should defend itself at home. The 1995 Sarin attack in the Tokyo subway had shown how terrorists could use a weapon of mass destruction on a civilian populace. As at least a first step in equipping itself organizationally at the unified command level for homeland defence, the US military gave Joint Forces Command at Norfolk, Virginia, responsibility, starting in 1999, for aiding civilian agencies in the event of an attack with such weapons. If Joint Forces Command were to evolve into a true homeland defence command, the air sovereignty operations for which NORAD was responsible would fit logically into its responsibilities. Canadian attentions could wind up divided between a US homeland defence command at Norfolk and USSPACECOM at Colorado Springs. NORAD would, in effect, be pulled apart.

On the other hand, NORAD itself had begun to explore how it could undertake new homeland defence responsibilities, such as protecting against an enemy's concerted attack on computer systems and space infrastructure in North America. USSPACECOM was given formal responsibility in this area, also starting in 1999. It could be extended into a NORAD role; the study exercise said that "NORAD has the potential as cyber defense umbrella for North America."[36] It was also conceivable that not Norfolk, but Colorado Springs, could wind up as the location of a homeland defence command. If USSPACECOM were ever dissolved and its assets transferred to USSTRATCOM, as had been proposed in 1993, that would leave Colorado Springs with a homeland defence emphasis. Nonetheless, as Macdonald also reported to Myers, during the study exercise "two separate groups came to disparate viewpoints regarding whether NORAD should be the principal CINC to deal with defense of North America. While consensus was not reached, and the multiple difficulties of NORAD taking on such a role were recognized, it was by no mean clear that the logic is any more compelling that some other (US) CINC is a better choice for the mission than would be NORAD."[37]

When the discussions between Washington and Ottawa over renewing the NORAD agreement began to get underway, NORAD headquarters suggested that they include the possible expansion of the command's responsibilities to include protection of cyber-systems and space infrastructure, as well the "asymmetrical contribution" from Canada in space surveillance, and NORAD's role in Canada–US space cooperation. NORAD also hoped that the two governments would consider renewal for ten years, instead of the five that had become the norm.[38]

All these suggestions were swept away by concerns over the potential impact of the outcome of "three-plus-three" on NORAD renewal in Canada. President Clinton was scheduled to make the decision in summer 2000 whether to begin NMD deployment. Presidential elections would follow in November, and the NORAD agreement would expire in May 2001. If Clinton decided to deploy without Russian consent, or if a newly elected president promised to do so, in Canada the renewal would be caught up in the issue. Therefore, as early as 1998 Ottawa and Washington decided, as they put it, to "deconflict" or "insulate" the renewal by completing it well in advance of the Clinton decision and the US elections.[39] Originally they considered a two-year renewal; this later became the usual five.

Accordingly, the minister of foreign affairs, Lloyd Axworthy, and the secretary of state, Madeleine Albright, signed a renewal in June 2000. It extended the 1996 agreement for another five years, starting from its May 2001 expiration. The broad and flexible language of the 1996 agreement categorizing NORAD's roles as "aerospace warning for North America" and "aerospace control for North America" was left unchanged.[40]

In August 2000, Cohen recommended to the president that he authorize the start of NMD deployment, which would entail construction of a radar site in Alaska, even though agreement had not been reached with the Russians. The next month Clinton announced during a speech at Georgetown University that he had rejected that advice. But in February 2001 the new president, George W. Bush, reiterating a point he had made on the campaign trail, said in his first address to Congress that "[t]o protect our own people, our allies and friends, we must develop and we must deploy effective missile defenses."[41]

NOTES

[1] ANSER, "White Paper on NORAD Defense Policy and Strategy Review," 23 October 1991. Copy in NORAD/USNORTHCOM History Office.

[2] "The most frequent question I'm asked about NORAD is, 'What's the threat?' I have responded publicly that there is essentially no military air threat against North America today." Letter, Horner to commander, Canadian Forces Fighter Group, 7 March 1994. Copy in NORAD/NORTHCOM History Office.

[3] Quoted in Rebecca Grant, *The First 600 Days of Combat: The US Air Force in the Global War on Terrorism* (Washington: IRIS Press, 2004), 14.

[4] *Defence News*, 13-19 April 1992, 42.

[5] Horner statement of 22 February 1993 excerpted in letter, HQ/NORAD/J5X deputy director for policy and programs to deputy director, strategic defense policy, OASD/ISP, 26 February 1993, Copy in NORAD/USNORTHCOM History Office.

[6] For details see USSPACECOM, *United States Space Command, Operations Dessert Shield and Desert Storm: Assessment,* January 1992. Copy available online in Jeffrey T. Richelson, "Electronic Briefing Book: Operation Desert Storm: Ten Years After," January 2001. The National Security Archive, George Washington University.

[7] All quotations in this paragraph were originally cited in US, Department of Defense, Strategic Defense Initiative Organization, *1993 Report to the Congress on the Strategic Defense Initiative*, January 1993.

[8] Memo, Smith to CINCNORAD, 10 September 1992. Copy in NORAD/USNORTHCOM History Office.

[9] "NORAD/USSPACECOM Ballistic Missile Defense Concept of Operations," draft 13 August 1993. Copy in NORAD/NORTHCOM History Office.

[10] Letter, 26 February 1993 (see note 5).

[11] *The History of the Unified Command Plan, 1946–1993*, Joint History Office, Office of the Chairman of the Joint Chiefs of Staff, February 1995, 111.

[12] Department of National Defence, *1994 Defence White Paper,* 25.

[13] Quoted in *1993 Report* (see note 7).

[14] David L. Bashow, at the time executive officer to the DCINC provides a schematic in his article, "NORAD: Past, Present and Future," *Forum* 80, No. 8, 77-80.

[15] Clinton and Yeltsin revived the notion in 2000, whereupon it again went nowhere.

[16] "Exchange of Notes between the Government of Canada and the Government of the United States of America constituting an Agreement to Extend the NORAD Agreement for a further five-year period," 28 March 1996 with effect from 12 May 1996, *Canada Treaty Series* 1996, No. 36.

[17] "Point Paper on the NORAD Agreement Renewal," 13 July 1995, Copy in NORAD/USNORTHCOM History Office.

[18] Andrew B. Godefroy, "From Alliance to Dependence: Canadian American Defence Cooperation through Space," MA thesis Royal Military College of Canada, April 1999, 90.

[19] R.R. Crabbe, deputy chief of staff, Memo for distribution, "A Canadian Military Strategy: The Way Ahead for DND and the Canadian Forces," 24 April 1998. Copy courtesy DND Directorate of Space Operations.

[20] The quotation, in ibid., is from the Defence Policy Guidance 1998.

[21] L.W.F. Cuppens, DCINCNORAD, Memo for distribution, "Whither CF Involvement in Space," 20 March 1998. Copy in NORAD/USNORTHCOM History Office.

[22] Memo Richard B. Myers, CINCNORAD/USCINCSPACE 17 December 1998, to DCINC and others, "Canadian Space Initiatives." Copy in NORAD/USNORTHCOM History Office.

[23] See note 19.

[24] Cable, HQ NORAD to DEPSECDEF, 25 Feb 1998, "BMD Discussions with CDS." Copy in NORAD/USNORTHCOM History Office.

[25] Letter, General Howell M. Estes CINCNORAD to Lieutenant-General Lester L. Lyles, director, BMDO, 1 June 1998, Copy in NORAD/NORTHCOM history office.

[26] Ibid.

[27] Ibid.

[28] NORAD NJ5PX, "Report on DepSecDef (Dr. Hamre) and Deputy Minister of Defence (Ms Frechette) Meeting in Ottawa, 14 November 97" 19 November 1997. Copy in NORAD/USNORTHCOM History Office. Hamre's "ten years" comment is reported in "Briefing Note for the Chief of the Defence Staff: Ballistic Missile Defence for North America" 4 November 1998. Department of National Defence Access to Information Request 1999 0904.

[29] Ibid.

[30] United States, Commission to Assess the Ballistic Missile Threat to the United States, "Executive Summary of the Report," 15 July 1998.

[31] John Isaacs, "Missile Defense: It's Back," *Bulletin of the Atomic Scientists* (May-June 1999), 26.

[32] Quoted in Michael R. Gordon, "Russians Firmly Reject Plan to Reopen ABM Treaty," *New York Times*, 21 October 1999, A3.

[33] United Nations, General Assembly, Press Release GA/9675, 1 December 1999.

[34] James Fergusson, "Forum Report: Canada and Ballistic Missile Defence, 26-27 November 1998," Centre for Defence and Security Studies, University of Manitoba, N.D.

[35] Memo, DCINC to CINCNORAD, 1 December 1998, "NORAD Pathway Event." Copy in NORAD/USNORTHCOM History Office.

[36] Ibid.

[37] Ibid.

[38] "Point Paper on NORAD Agreement Renewal," 22 October 1998. Copy in NORAD/USNORTHCOM History Office.

[39] "Deconflict": in ibid. "Insulate": "Briefing Note for the Minister of National Defence, 'NORAD Renewal,'" 7 September 1999, Department of National Defence Access to Information request 1999 01341.

[40] "Exchange of Notes," *Canada Treaty Series* 2000, No. 11.

[41] Address of the President to the Joint Session of Congress, 27 February 2001. White House Press Release.

CHAPTER SIX

HOMELAND DEFENCE, 2001–2006

9/11 AND OPERATION NOBLE EAGLE

Having been created over forty years earlier to watch for, warn of, and defend against an external air attack on North America, when an attack eventually came on the terrible morning of 9/11 not from without but from within, NORAD was blind to it, offered no swift warning, and was unable to defend against it. The US National Commission on Terrorist Attacks upon the United States (the "9/11 Commission") was critical in its report of the command:

> America's homeland defenders faced outward. NORAD itself was barely able to retain any alert bases. Its planning scenarios occasionally considered the danger of hijacked aircraft being guided to American targets, but only aircraft that were coming from overseas. We recognize that a costly change in NORAD's defense posture to deal with the danger of suicide hijackers, before such a threat had ever actually been realized, would have been a tough sell. But NORAD did not canvass available intelligence and try to make the case.[1]

One of the 9/11 commissioners, Richard Ben-Veniste, was even more direct. During public hearings he indignantly asked the commander of the Continental US NORAD Region: "given the awareness of the terrorists' use of planes as weapons, how is it that NORAD was still focusing outward protecting the United States against attacks from the Soviet Union or elsewhere, and was not better prepared to defend against the hijacking scenarios of a commercial jet laden with fuel used as a weapon to target citizens of the United States?"[2]

NORAD was far from alone in coming in for such criticism. Across the entire US government there had been, the 9/11 commission concluded, failures in imagination, policies, capabilities, and management that had made the terrorist attacks possible. The first, the failures in imagination, had been the most crippling, and they had affected NORAD, too.

NORAD officials were the first to acknowledge this. "You hate to admit it, but we hadn't thought about this," said General Myers, the former CINCNORAD who just after the attacks had become the chairman of the US Joint Chiefs of Staff.[3] His point was echoed by Lieutenant-General Ken Pennie who had become DCINCNORAD just before them. "We have been doing this job for 43 years," he said, "and nobody anticipated what happened on the 11th of September."[4]

The existing protocol in the US between NORAD and the FAA for dealing with a hijacking rested on the assumption that it would be traditional in nature; the hijackers would make demands and the plane probably would be diverted at their insistence to a distant airport. It was also assumed that the aircraft usually would remain readily visible by leaving its transponder on, thereby not attempting to disappear from radar view. While NORAD might be called upon to provide a fighter escort, it was not contemplated that there would be a need to shoot such a hijacked aircraft down. There would also be plenty of time to respond to the emergency, which meant that the protocol provided for word of the hijacking to be passed from the traffic controllers first confronted with it, up the FAA chain of command to its Washington headquarters, which would contact the Pentagon, which in turn would transmit orders down through the NORAD chain of command. Thus, as the 9/11 commission concluded, "[o]n the morning of 9/11 the existing protocol was unsuited in every respect for what was about to happen."[5]

It was not completely followed, though. When air traffic controllers in Boston realized that the American Airlines 11 flight headed from Boston to Los Angeles was hijacked, in addition to notifying FAA authorities as required, they also directly contacted the headquarters of NORAD's Northeast Air Defense Sector (NEADS) at Rome, New York. NEADS scrambled two F-15 aircraft from Otis Air Force Base in Massachusetts. But with the airliner's transponder having been turned off, NEADS was still trying to find it on its radars when it crashed into the World Trade Center. NEADS was not alerted by New York traffic controllers about hijacked United Airlines flight 175, also headed from Boston to Los Angeles, until it already had become the second aircraft to strike the twin towers. NEADS scrambled jets out of Langley, Viriginia in response to an FAA report of hijacked American Airlines aircraft headed to Washington. The FAA was mistaken, and only in the course of the conversation over this phantom hijacking did NEADS learn of another aircraft, American Airlines 77 from Washington to Los Angeles, just before it struck the Pentagon. Moreover, the scrambled Langley jets had been improperly positioned to provide immediate protection to Washington. Finally, NEADS was not informed at all about United Airlines 93, underway from Newark to San Francisco, until it had crashed into a Pennsylvania field, apparently thanks to the heroism of it passengers. In short, again according to the 9/11 commission, the immediate responses to the hijackings were "improvised by civilians who had never handled a hijacked aircraft that attempted to disappear, and by a military unprepared for the transformation of commercial aircraft into weapons of mass destruction. As it turned out, the NEADS air defenders had nine minutes' notice on the first hijacked plane, no advance notice on the second, no advance notice on the third and no advance notice on the fourth."[6]

The scrambling of the fighter aircraft out of Virginia and Massachusetts was, in effect, the first step towards the reconfiguration of North American air defences from a system oriented to threats from outside North America to one dealing with threats *both* approaching *and* arising inside the continent. Moments after the hijacked planes crashed, NORAD rushed to deal with the possibility that more attacks with hijacked civilian aircraft might be imminent, while not long thereafter the governments of the United States and Canada temporarily halted all civil aviation inside the continent.

After 15 September, NORAD's air defence operations against terrorism were dubbed Operation Noble Eagle (ONE) and began to take on a permanent character.[7] As a USAF-sponsored study put it: "Of all the unusual things about Operation Noble Eagle, one that stands out is that it started as a tactical response and then slowly acquired a strategy to guide it."[8]

The second step was to put many more fighter aircraft on alert and into the air on combat air patrol. Air defence commanders at all levels immediately grasped the importance of this, as did pilots who swiftly reported for duty; they were given full encouragement by NORAD headquarters. Major-General Eric A. Findley of the Canadian Forces, NORAD's director of combat operations, was in command there at the time, an air defence exercise, "Vigilant Guardian" having coincidentally been underway. "Generate, generate, generate," Findley ordered. [9] Within eighteen hours of the attacks, over three hundred fighter aircraft were on duty from twenty-six locations. The Air National Guard fighters normally responsible for air defence in the US were joined by aircraft from the USAF and the US Navy.

The Canadian air force increased the number of CF-18s on NORAD duty from the usual four to twelve; these aircraft were deployed not only at Bagotville and Cold Lake but also at Comox, Goose Bay, and Trenton. While Canadian air defence plans had long included deployment as needed to the coastal bases of Comox and Goose Bay, the deployment to Trenton to offer a measure of additional protection and reassurance to southern Canada was unusual. It is not clear whether these twelve Canadian aircraft and five alert bases are included in the overall figure of 300 aircraft and twenty-six bases noted above.

Right from 11 September, "the core of the strategy guidance was to protect New York and Washington."[10] So was protecting the US president from air attack on the ground and in the air, which had never before been a NORAD mission. Over the next six months, fighter operations in both the US and Canada were reduced as ONE became more focused. In the US, in addition to the emphasis on protecting New York, Washington, and the president, fighters on ground alert were positioned to be able to reach what were defined as critical assets within twenty minutes. Fighters also flew random combat air patrols.

CF-18s were kept in Trenton for a few months after 9/11. The government of Canada developed meanwhile a list of "vital points" such as metropolitan areas, nuclear facilities and critical infrastructure. Ottawa did not publicly release the list, and neither it nor NORAD provided an estimation of how much day-to-day protection the points on the list could be provided by the Canadian NORAD Region (CANR), relying on its own fighters at Cold Lake and Bagotville, as well as on US ones located nearby. Presumably much would depend on how much advance warning from intelligence sources CANR received that an aircraft was, or might be, in the hands of terrorists.

Starting with the February 2002 Salt Lake City Olympics, a permanent and recurring ONE mission became providing enhanced air defence at special events. Most of these were in the US, such as the 2004 Democratic and Republican Conventions and the 2005 presidential inauguration. But they also included Canadian airspace, notably over Kananaskis, Alberta, while the G-8 summit met there in 2002, and over Windsor when the 2006 Superbowl was held in neighbouring Detroit. At Kananaskis the Canadian army made its first return to active North American air defence since the 1950s, deploying air defence equipment that had been bought to protect Canadian bases in Germany. NORAD officials anticipated providing ONE coverage at the Vancouver Olympics in 2010.

After the attacks, the air defenders suddenly and urgently needed to have radar coverage within the North American periphery, especially over the interior of the United States, which was not covered by the JSS radars. To establish quick coverage, USAF AWACS aircraft, often carrying Canadian crew members, were deployed on NORAD duty. Several mobile military radars were placed where badly needed. Five AWACS belonging to NATO were also sent from Germany in October and began to operate out of an air base in Oklahoma. It was the first time in NATO's history that alliance military assets had been deployed in the defence of the United States. This deployment followed in the wake of NATO having invoked, also for the first time in its history, Article 5 of its charter, the North Atlantic Treaty, which provided that an attack on one member was to be considered an attack on all the others as well. The NATO AWACS remained until May 2002. While John Diefenbaker obviously would have been horrified by the terrorist attacks, he nonetheless was from October 2001 to May 2002 doing whatever the opposite is of spinning in one's grave because of this prominent link between NATO and NORAD.

A more permanent solution for the Continental US NORAD Region (CONR) was found in linking interior radars belonging to the FAA into the NORAD system. In CANR there was a good deal of secondary radar coverage, capable of detecting and tracking aircraft with transponders. But it remained the case that ever since the closing of the Pinetree Line, there was only spotty coverage by the primary radar which could track aircraft themselves with their transponders turned off (see Map 10). After 9/11 there was considerable worry at CANR that this dearth of primary coverage left the country especially vulnerable to a similar attack. A terrorist aircraft approaching, say Toronto, that had turned off its transponder might not be detected until it was too late. Similar to the radar holes, there were also places within the country in which communications with CF-18 interceptors would fall out. To partly deal with the surveillance gaps, the Canadian air force developed a program called "Ground-based Urban Detection" (GUARD) to deploy new radars around population centres. In 2006 an air force spokesman called GUARD "mainly a post-September 11 project" that would deal with the "capability deficiency associated with our air surveillance and communications capability inside the country."[11] The air force hoped that GUARD could begin in 2008, with full operational capability in 2011. Even if GUARD were deployed, it would still leave large areas of the country without primary radar coverage.

Another essential element in dealing with the new terrorist air threat was establishing provisions whereby senior authorities could be swiftly given the opportunity to consider, and if need be order, in time the destruction of hijacked planes. The US and Canada handled this quite differently. CINCNORAD had longstanding and broad, although not unlimited, authority to order the destruction of military aircraft, i.e. strategic bombers, approaching the continent. As discussed in Chapter Two, Ottawa had balked in 1964-65 at giving him the right to use nuclear air defence weapons over Canada to destroy a single aircraft. When it came to hijacked civilian planes, he had no such authority in either Canada or the US. On the assumption that hijackings would be traditional, both governments had reserved the authority to themselves.

On the morning of 11 September, Vice President Cheney hurriedly authorized the engagement of aircraft that looked like they were committing a hostile act over New York or Washington. According to some accounts he was acting on his own behalf; others hold that he was passing on authority he had received by telephone from President Bush. Shortly thereafter, Secretary of Defense Donald R. Rumsfeld instituted more permanent arrangements for US airspace. It is clear that authority to attack hijacked aircraft was delegated to US military commanders located both inside and outside of Colorado Springs. But the US military and NORAD declined to provide much further detail. The contours can be gleaned from two statements, one by Rumsfeld at a 27 September 2001 press conference and the other by Major General Craig McKinley, at the time CONR commander, in his 23 May 2003 testimony before the 9/11 commission. In response to a question about whether "mid-level generals" had been given the authority, Rumsfeld said, in part, that "the chain of command is from the president to the Secretary of Defense and then to a – generally a

CINC, a combatant commander somewhere in the world. There are times when the situation is sufficiently immediate that the authority is delegated below the CINC for periods of time, but always, in case like this, always with the understanding that if time permits, it would be immediately brought up to the CINC, and then to me, and if time still permits, for me to go to the president."[12]

McKinley told the commission that "[s]ubsequent to 9/11, the president delegated to the Secretary of Defense, delegated to the combatant commander at NORAD and now United States Northern Command, has [sic] the authority to declare a hostile target ... And I, as the joint force air component commander, have delegated emergency in the very rare occasion." He added: "So the clearances now are in place. General Eberhart is in place in Colorado Springs or his designated representative."[13] There was no indication that DCINCNORAD or any other senior Canadian officer in command during the CINC's absence could act as such a designated representative. Given the enormity of destroying a civilian aircraft, it can be concluded that only an American could make this call for US airspace.

Matters were clearer in Canada. Ottawa did not delegate to CINCNORAD in 2001 or thereafter the authority to destroy hijacked civilian aircraft over Canada. Nor did the government delegate it to the commander CANR either, reserving the right to itself. Art Eggleton, the minister of national defence, told a parliamentary committee in October 2001 that "[i]f this was to happen in Canada, the decision would be made by the Canadian government acting through me in consultation with the prime minister. In the United States that same authority is being delegated to members of the general staff, as I understand it."[14] Officials at CANR were by no means confident that there would be enough time under certain hijacking circumstances for the two ministers to be reached to give such permission. An exercise conducted by CANR not long after 9/11 only increased this worry.

The emphasis on responding to air-breathing threats arising inside the continent certainly did not mean that NORAD had lost interest in guarding the periphery. Terrorist aircraft, such as hijacked airliners, could arrive from abroad. CANR had in this respect some specifically Canadian concerns. Aircraft flying westward from Europe on the North Atlantic Route entered Canadian airspace off the coast of Labrador whereupon, heading inland, they passed into the primary radar "hole" over much of the country. The same was true for aircraft inbound from Asia on the Polar Air Route after they passed through the coverage of the North Warning System.

Cruise missiles launched from vessels off North America's long Atlantic and Pacific coasts had been a growing concern at NORAD since the mid 1990s. Such missiles could be equipped with a conventional explosive, or a chemical, biological, or nuclear warhead and a GPS-based guidance system. They would be relatively cheap to build or even to buy as "off-the-shelf" items.

Unmanned aerial vehicles, such as reconnaissance and target drones, might also be converted into cruise missiles. While such weapons would be launched from sea towards NORAD's coastal radar perimeter, they could be too small and fly too low to be detected and tracked easily. This led NORAD officials to joke sometimes that the command's capabilities included being able to detect and track, but not engage incoming ballistic missiles, while at the same time being able to engage, but not detect and track incoming cruise missiles. If there were advance warning of approaching vessels carrying cruise missiles, which might be provided by US and Canadian maritime forces, the air defenders might be able to deploy AWACS on time to detect and track them, enabling fighters to engage them.

A full-scale continental defence against cruise missiles would be tremendously expensive. NORAD was reconciled to less. Its commander, Admiral Timothy J. Keating, told a US Congressional committee in 2006 that the command had approved a concept of operations for a "Deployable Homeland Air and Cruise Missile Defense" that would provide for putting "highly responsible, scalable integrated air defense packages" at chosen locales.[15]

"PART OF" MISSILE DEFENCE

If the Bush administration had any doubts about proceeding with missile defence without the acquiescence of the Russian government, they were no doubt swept away by 9/11. Negotiations with Russia to amend the ABM treaty in order to allow limited deployment went nowhere. In December 2001 the administration officially informed Moscow that the US was withdrawing from the treaty, as provided for under its terms. The withdrawal would take effect six months later, leaving Washington free to develop, test, and deploy missile defences. The sky did not fall, and the earth kept turning. President Putin reacted calmly, saying that the move did not threaten his country's security. As a study undertaken within the Canadian Department of National Defence put it, "[t]he withdrawal of the US from the ABM Treaty was initially viewed with concern by many members of the international community. It was feared that such a move would dramatically destabilize arms control and disarmament norms. This however has not been the case."[16]

In December 2002, President Bush directed the defense department to field a rudimentary missile defense of the US by 2004. The term "National Missile Defense" was dropped in order to emphasize that the US hoped eventually to be able to provide missile defense not just for itself, but also for its forces overseas, its friends, and its allies.

It also hoped to develop the technology to attack ballistic missiles in the boost, mid-course, and terminal phase – a layered defence, in other words;

this might eventually include both ground- and space-based weapons. Opposition to Canadian participation in missile defence began to centre on "the weaponization of space"; this largely replaced the argument that a US defence would touch off a new arms race.

Space-based missile defences could only be years in the future, though. The very limited system that the president had approved for immediate deployment, designed to deal with missiles that might be acquired by countries like Iraq, Iran, or North Korea, involved placing no weapons in space – or in Canada, for that matter. Twenty ground-based interceptors would be divided between Fort Greeley, Alaska and Vandenberg Air Force Base, California. Plans also called for twenty sea-based interceptors to be put in place somewhat later. This initial system was dubbed "Ground-based Midcourse Defense" (GMD).

In the spirit of the "Trojan Horse" arguments of the 1980s, Canadian opponents said that if Canada were to be involved in GMD, it would be dragged into future space-based systems. But there was still good reason to think as Paul Cellucci, the US ambassador to Canada, did – that Ottawa would probably agree to participate in its operation. Cellucci wrote in a memoir of his time in Ottawa that in April 2003, he "felt upbeat about the prospects of Canada joining with us in missile defense. Cabinet was discussing the issue and several in Prime Minister Chrétien's government, including Defence Minister John McCallum, Deputy Prime Minister John Manley and Foreign Affairs Minister Bill Graham had all spoken publicly in favor of cooperating with the US on missile defence."[17] McCallum announced in May 2003 that that the Chrétien government had "decided to begin talks with the United States on Canadian participation in a missile defence system," adding only that the Canadian government remained opposed to any future weaponization of space.[18]

Chrétien was heading out of office. "But," Cellucci added, "I expected that even if Prime Minister Chrétien wouldn't support missile defense, his successor would."[19] Paul Martin had made vaguely positive noises about missile defence while still finance minister and a Liberal Party leadership candidate. Relations between Washington and Ottawa had soured, especially over the Iraq War. If Martin wanted to make improvements, signing on to missile defence would be one especially good way.

David Pratt, the minister of national defence in the brand new Martin government, proposed in a January 2004 letter to US Secretary of Defense Rumsfeld, released to the public, that formal negotiations be split into two parts. First, the two countries "should move on an expedited basis to amend the NORAD agreement to take into account NORAD's contribution to missile defence."[20] GMD was scheduled to begin becoming operational as early as later in the year. It was therefore imperative, if NORAD was to keep its central role in North American aerospace defence, to clear the way for Canadian NORAD personnel in Cheyenne Mountain to be able to support missile defence, regardless of whether Canada decided to participate directly in the operation of the system. At issue was NORAD's core function of ITW/AA, or missile warning and assessment. If the Canadians at NORAD could not be involved in providing warning and assessment to the missile defence, the US would be obliged to move ITW/AA out of NORAD. The command would be operationally gutted.

The splitting of the negotiations was the first indication that the Martin government might have trouble reaching a positive decision about direct Canadian participation. After all, if Canada were ready to participate directly, and in particular, if it were to agree to missile defence itself becoming a NORAD mission, the ITW/AA question would be reduced to a minor technical side issue. There was an election coming up in 2004 and Martin did not want to announce a decision before it. Nonetheless, a section of Pratt's letter to Rumsfeld that concerned the second part of the negotiations certainly seemed to signal that there eventually would be a "yes" decision to missile defence itself. "It is our intent," Pratt wrote, "to negotiate in the coming months a Missile Defence Framework Memorandum of Understanding (MOU) with the United States with the objective of including Canada as a participant in the current US missile defence program and expanding and enhancing information exchange."[21]

The ITW/AA issue was dealt with by an August 2004 exchange of diplomatic notes amending the NORAD agreement, the only time the agreement has ever been amended.[22] Under its terms, NORAD personnel could be involved in providing warning. Referring to the amendment, the Canadian ambassador in Washington, Frank McKenna, told reporters in February 2005 that it meant Canada was already part of the missile defence system. "We're part of it now," was how he put it. "There's no doubt looking back that the NORAD amendment has given, has created part – in fact, a great deal – of what the US means in terms of being able to get the input for the defensive weaponry."[23] McKenna's point was a good one. By agreeing to participate in providing warning, Canada was already involved in missile defence. Some Canadian peace groups would later castigate Ottawa for precisely this.

The Martin government never spelled out what other forms of Canadian participation it would have countenanced. In December 2004 press interviews Martin had outlined what participation would *not* involve, namely putting interceptors in Canada (which were going to Alaska and California, anyway), weapons in space (which the US had not developed and were not part of GMD) or Canadian money directly into the missile the defence budget. No Canadian spending was also acceptable to the US, inasmuch as it had expected to pay for GMD itself. Moreover, the Canadian military was proceeding with its plan, as discussed in Chapter Five, to invest in an "asymmetrical contribution" to North American defence based on reviving Canada's role in space surveillance.

Canada could have contributed some senior military personnel to the operation of the missile defence system, probably in addition to the Canadians already serving in NORAD and NORAD/OUTCAN billets. In return, it would have had a say in setting the priorities for interception of incoming missiles. GMD was expected to be able to take out only a small number such missiles; directing more than one interceptor at an incoming missile would increase the chances of its being destroyed. That meant priorities would have to be set for defending North American targets. In the 1990s it had been the understanding that giving NORAD the missile defence mission meant that senior Canadians in Cheyenne Mountain could exercise the command's weapons release authority over the system. It is not clear whether Washington would have agreed to that in late 2004 and early 2005. In January 2003, the US altered its unified command plan to assign weapons release authority over GMD to US Northern Command (USNORTHCOM), while USTRATCOM was given responsibility for the operation of the system. That decision would have had to be altered if it had later been agreed upon to assign NORAD the mission.

Just two days after McKenna's "we're already part" interview appeared in the press, the Martin government announced that being involved through NORAD in providing warning and assessment was to be the full extent of Canadian involvement. Foreign Affairs Minister Pierre Pettigrew told the House of Commons that "[a]fter careful consideration of the issue of missile defence, we have decided that Canada will not participate in the US ballistic missile defence system at this time."[24] The curious wording led to clarifications by the government later in the day that the decision was final.

The US government had been informed somewhat earlier. The Bush administration had been angered in 2003 over the way the Chrétien government had communicated its decision not to join the coalition in Iraq. In this respect, the Martin government's 2005 decision looked to Washington like Iraq all over. Cellucci wrote:

> What added to the disappointment of the decision was the clumsy manner in which it was announced. Foreign Affairs Minister Pierre Pettigrew communicated the decision to Secretary of State Condi Rice at the NATO summit in Brussels. The timing and method of the announcement certainly were not well received in Washington. Just when the president was in Europe trying to show some unity with NATO allies after the rift that had opened over Iraq, our close ally and next-door neighbor chose that moment to signal its rejection of something that we considered to be crucial to our future security. Then there was the fact that the prime minister did not tell the president himself, although the two men were both at the NATO meeting and at several points were standing side by side. But not a word was said. All in all, it was an inept ending to a frustrating process.[25]

As soon as the decision was announced, the conventional wisdom concluded that it had been intended to secure badly needed votes for the Liberals in Quebec. The Martin government had won only a minority in the June 2004 federal election and was still wounded by the sponsorship scandal. Another election could not be far off and Quebec was the part of the country most consistently opposed to participation in missile defence. It certainly was difficult to believe that the government, having opened the discussions with Washington, had suddenly developed strategic scruples over some aspect of GMD or had encountered an unexpected and unmanageable obstacle during the course of negotiations with Washington. Pettigrew, when making his statement to the Commons, had the decency not to make any such claims to justify the decision, instead just offering the complete vagaries that Canada had to act in its own interests, and determine both its own priorities and where its investments would bring the greatest tangible result.

The Quebec political scientist Pierre Martin later convincingly argued that just attributing the decision to a hunt for Quebec voters would not do as a complete explanation. There was opposition in English Canada, too, that was expressed not just by the New Democratic Party but increasingly in the Liberal caucus in the Commons. To be sure, Professor Martin agreed, Quebec had cooled markedly towards the US: "What could explain this reversal? Part of the answer must lie with the radicalization of US foreign policy, but also with perceptions of a sharp turn to the right domestically and increasingly salient cultural differences between Americans and Canadians."[26] In other words, for many in Quebec, opposing missile defence was a way of renouncing George W. Bush and all his works. Despite this, the prime minister's hesitation to act could not be overlooked. In fact, here, according to Professor Martin, was the ultimate explanation. "How difficult would it have been to defend a cost free decision of no real global strategic consequence (Canada's decision, that is) in the name of maintaining good relations with the country's most important ally and economic partner, when about 90 per cent of all Canadians, including Quebecers, agree that it should be an important goal of Canada's foreign policy?"[27] Cellucci reached the same conclusion, writing that he "was convinced that with leadership from the prime minister, making the case that participation in missile defense was in Canada's security *and* sovereignty interests" the approval of the House of Commons could have been secured.[28]

After the August 2004 amendment of the NORAD agreement, the appropriate Canadians at Colorado Springs were given familiarization training and then direct necessary access to missile defence-related systems within the Cheyenne Mountain Operations Center. There they continued their longstanding NORAD ITW/AA role, now alongside and in support of the incipient US GMD operations.

There were complications to having the US exercise GMD command and control within a bi-national setting. The position of command director in Cheyenne Mountain was directly affected. The command director, a US or Canadian colonel or naval captain, functioned as the single conduit of high-priority to information to the commander. In the event of an attack, the director would pass on an overall battle picture to the commander and recommend courses of action for him to take. If the command director on duty were an American, he could exercise both ITW/AA and missile defence responsibilities. In other words, he could advise the commander both that North America be declared under attack and that the interceptors be released. With a Canadian command director on duty, the process, as some NORAD officials put it, would be "splintered." There would be "two paths of information for the same event." The Canadian director could advise that North America be declared under attack, but would defer to a US deputy command director to make the recommendation on interception. So with a Canadian command director on duty, the commander would "receive two concurrent calls ... one for ITW/AA attack assessments, one for missile defence weapons release authority."[29]

There was a second notable complication. If the commander were absent and NORAD's deputy commander or other senior Canadian were in command, that Canadian could confirm a recommendation that North America be declared under missile attack. But only an American general or admiral on duty could order, on behalf of USNORTHCOM, interception.

After the February 2005 decision the Canadians at NORAD began to wonder how many years this situation would last. It was not that the arrangements allowing them to support but not be directly involved in missile defence were unmanageable at the moment. Nor were the Canadians worried that an angry Washington would turn them right out of Cheyenne Mountain to spite Ottawa. Rather, it might become steadily more difficult for them to do the job if the US later deployed, as planned, more elements of a layered missile defence, of which Canada still wanted no direct part. James Fergusson, of the University of Manitoba, reflected these concerns when he argued, shortly after the Martin government said "no," that "[a]s future components of the layered system come on line and the components are integrated together into a single system, NORAD's ITW/AA for GMD becomes increasingly problematic with Canada on the outside of missile defence. At best, it becomes a redundant ITW/AA system, with its primary function to inform the Canadian National Command Authority of strategic attack and, in turn, the success or failure of intercepts."[30] At worst, the US might some day decide to bring NORAD's ITW/AA role to an end.

USNORTHCOM, CANADA COM – AND NORAD

Before the 9/11 attacks, it looked like one of the hallmarks of the Bush administration's defence policy would be requiring the US military to focus more on space, with implications for NORAD's twin, USSPACECOM. Until Rumsfeld left to take office for the second time as secretary of defense, he had been chairman of the Commission to Assess United States National Space Management and Organization, a bipartisan entity with members appointed by the previous secretary and both parties in Congress. In January 2001, the commission reported that "the US Government – in particular, the Department of Defense and the Intelligence Community – is not yet arranged or focused to meet the national security space needs of the 21st century. Our growing dependence on space, our vulnerabilities in space and the burgeoning opportunities from space simply are not reflected in the present institutional arrangements." Among its many recommendations, it urged that CINCUSSPACE "continue to concentrate on space as it relates to warfare in the mediums of air, land and sea, as well as space. This, it went on to explain, would "leave less time for his other assigned duties."[31] As secretary of defense, Rumsfeld implemented in 2001 two specific changes to the CINC's position which the commission had recommended. One was designed to reduce those other duties: CINCNORAD/CINCUSSPACE would no longer wear a "third hat" as commander of the USAF Space Command. The other ended the practice, which had its roots in NORAD's origins as an air defence command, of appointing only USAF pilots to head the two commands. Henceforth, general or flag officers from any of the services would be eligible.

In Ottawa, the Department of National Defence thought it saw an advantage for Canada in the removal of the CINC's "third hat." Reminding its deputy minister that CINCNORAD and CINCUSSPACE were the same individual, the department told him that "[t]he appointment of a separate Commander USAFSPACE may insulate the CF and Canada from sensitive space-related issues such as the weaponization of space, space control, and the application of force from space." While Air Force Space Command worked on developing future US capabilities in these areas, there they would have "less visibility within NORAD."[32] Of course it was only reasonable to expect that if the US ever moved to the actual deployment of such weapons, they would then be placed under the operational command of USSPACECOM, where they would be eminently visible. USSPACECOM was soon swept away, though, in the 2002 US command reorganization undertaken to meet the new priority of homeland defence.

Not long after the 9/11 attacks, the planning staff at NORAD developed a proposal for a homeland defence command be built upon NORAD, undoubtedly with provisions for a "twin" command, "US Element," or similar structure that would allow unilateral action by the US. It made sense. After all, NORAD could be thought of as the original homeland defence command. More practically, as an outside study of command possibilities for homeland defense written about the same time observed, "NORAD possesses a wealth of organizational and military experience and a robust infrastructure for command, control, communications, computers and intelligence that could serve as the foundation for additional missions in homeland security."[33]

The relationship between NORAD and USSPACECOM potentially posed an obstacle to such a step; as that same study put it, "shifting all homeland security missions to CINC Space Command/CINCNORAD could result in an excessive span-of-control for the command's senior leadership, especially in time of crisis and conflict."[34] The Pentagon's response to this, quite a departure from the emphasis that it had been placing on space at the administration's behest, was to close USSPACECOM. In a repeat of the transfer that had occurred in 1979 upon the demise of ADCOM as a unified command, USSPACECOM's assets and responsibilities were handed over to USSTRATCOM, headquartered near Omaha. Air Force Space Command, on the other hand, remained both intact and headquartered in Colorado Springs.

Another potential obstacle was geographic. NORAD's headquarters were "far removed from America's political leadership as well as from the interagency players with whom a homeland security CINC would have to coordinate closely. Although NORAD has robust communications capabilities, this would not be a substitute for face-to-face operations."[35] Despite these strong arguments for putting the new command within or near the Capital Beltway, Colorado Springs still won out.

Yet it was not an expanded NORAD upon which the new homeland defence command was to be built. There would have been problems extending NORAD beyond aerospace defence. "As a command largely dominated, for good historical reasons, by air warriors, it would ... be difficult to quickly absorb and integrate a large influx of Army, Navy and Marine Corps forces to execute homeland security, which is clearly a grouping of joint missions."[36] Nonetheless, there are good indications that the US government, including Rumsfeld, was open to transforming NORAD into a homeland defence command linked to a US entity, and thus to include Canada. According to one account, the US defence department "contacted the Canadian Department of National Defence on this new approach to North American security" in April, emphasizing that a quick response was needed.[37]

Ottawa hesitated, not feeling the urgency Washington did, still reeling from the September attacks. Within the Canadian bureaucracy there was no consensus, while the ever-cautious Chrétien government was not prepared to step in. Therefore, the US acted without Canada and created a homeland defence command built not out of or with NORAD, but alongside it. The Pentagon made the announcement of USNORTHCOM's creation in April 2002. Its mission was to defend the US and provide military support to civilian authorities.[38] That October, the new command replaced USSPACECOM as the NORAD "twin." Like its predecessors, it shared with NORAD a commander, a headquarters and some staffs as well as the Cheyenne Mountain operations centre. USSTRATCOM would have a presence in the mountain, too, as USSPACECOM's successor.

Quite unlike NORAD's standing operational control over US and Canadian air defence forces, USNORTHCOM had almost no forces assigned to its standing operational command; they would be given it by the Pentagon on a case-to-case basis to deal with contingencies as they arose. The assumption was that there would be time to respond to, for example, the aftermath of a terrorist attack or a natural disaster or the approach at sea of a suspicious vessel. The standing operational command that USNORTHCOM *was* given over missile defence in 2003 was a significant exception. Like missile defence, the air defence of North America also required the ability to respond quickly; air defence remained a NORAD mission, as did ITW/AA. NORAD's responsibilities were, in fact, unchanged at USNORTHCOM's creation.

Especially right after the April announcement of USNORTHCOM's creation, there was plenty of talk in Canada about whether the Canadian government had turned down an invitation to be part of it or whether an invitation effectively was still on the table. In reality, joining USNORTHCOM was always out of the question, unlike transforming NORAD, which seemed possible in late 2001 and early 2002. "There has been no overt invitation to join NORTHCOM per se," Lieutenant-General George Macdonald, vice chief of the defence staff (and former DCINCNORAD) told a Senate committee in May. "NORTHCOM is a US unified command and it would be quite extraordinary for us to participate in that. That is not being discussed right now."[39] As it organized for better homeland defence, the US was always going to keep a structure in place for unilateral action, be it in the form of an "element" to a bilateral command or, as emerged, a US unified command.

Instead of expanding NORAD's responsibilities, the two governments established in December 2002 at Colorado Springs a temporary "Bi-national Planning Group" with the NORAD deputy commander at its head, to work on future arrangements affecting North American land and maritime defence cooperation, and joint responses to calamities such as natural disaster or terrorist attack. That led to plenty of speculation to the effect that while Ottawa had hesitated at first after 9/11 to expand NORAD's mandate, the Bi-national Planning Group would pave the way towards its future expansion. A good deal of this was directed toward the possibility of the command's eventually being given broad responsibility for guarding the sea approaches to the North American coasts, much as it long had had responsibility for guarding the air approaches. In reality, though, the Bi-national Planning Group focused on something more limited, namely "maritime awareness and warning" or "bi-national strategic level maritime situational awareness." The two governments, it observed, were not working closely enough to share and analyze information that could reveal potential maritime threats to the continent such as a suspicious vessel that might be carrying biological, chemical or even nuclear weapons, or cruise missiles.[40] Here NORAD might have a role. Its responsibility for warning could be expanded from just aerospace to include maritime warning.

The speculation about a new naval role was fuelled by confusing public comments made by US naval officials, including the chief of naval operations, about the need for a "maritime NORAD." They were not talking about NORAD itself, however, but invoking it as a sort of model for a series of regional maritime security arrangements with overseas US allies.[41]

The work of the Bi-national Planning Group was well underway when official word came from Ottawa in 2005 that Canada, too, would have a national homeland defence organization, to be called Canada Command. Wags immediately dubbed it "true NORTHCOM." The military initially used the abbreviation "CANCOM," but having decided that was too flip and insufficiently patriotic, it soon replaced the term with the somewhat awkward "Canada COM." The new command, headquartered in Ottawa, stood up in February 2006.

The creation of Canada COM was part of an overall restructuring of the Canadian military that the energetic chief of the defence staff (CDS), General Rick Hillier, saw as a step in what he called "Canadian Forces transformation." The concept of operations that Hillier issued in October 2005 for Canada COM and the other new Canadian command structures that were being created sought specifically not to disrupt NORAD command and control relations. It provided that the Canada COM commander would be "responsible to the CDS for the execution of all routine and contingency and operations within Canada and its approaches *less those operations under the direct command of the CDS or NORAD*" (emphasis added). To be sure, Canada COM was also enjoined by the chief to establish "effective liaison" with NORAD and USNORTHCOM.[42]

Nonetheless, the action team that Hillier had set up to propose a structure for Canada COM did not expect it to stay out of NORAD operations for long. The team predicted that Canada COM's relationship would change with "the cold war apparatus of NORAD," as well as with the up-and-coming USNORTHCOM. It emphasized that Canada COM would need to pay particular attention to developing ties with USNORTHCOM. This would be complicated by the fact that for the moment it was CANR headquarters at Winnipeg that still had the most important links to Colorado Springs and they were with NORAD, not USNORTHCOM. But, Hillier's team concluded, "[a]s CANCOM [sic] develops into the sole operational HQ responsible for the Canadian theatre of operations it will likely absorb CANR and its NORAD requirements and will thus become the sole operational connection with US military authorities. The evolution of a Canada Command will in turn lead to the development of close ties between it and USNORTHCOM." [43]

USNORTHCOM was more than willing to return any such interest. As a command with broad responsibilities for the defence of the US, it was natural for it to see Canada COM, with its similarly broad responsibilities for military operations in Canada and approaches, as its partner. USNORTHCOM was also formally charged under the US unified command plan with shaping defence relations with both Canada and Mexico. Here, too, Canada COM seemed to be its natural interlocutor. NORAD, by contrast, was only an aging aerospace defence command. Moreover, just as Canada COM was expected to find CANR an inconvenience, USNORTHCOM began to look at NORAD itself in much the same way. It chafed, in particular, at NORAD's retention of Noble Eagle responsibilities; some USNORTHCOM officials argued that such sensitive post 9/11 tasks as the protection of Washington and the president while he travelled belonged not in a bi-national command but in the national homeland defence command.

In 2005 and 2006, USNORTHCOM officials developed several different models for the structure of North American defence cooperation in the future. Four of these also made it for discussion purposes into the March 2006 final report of the Bi-national Planning Group. One involved keeping NORAD pretty much as it was while giving it the new responsibilities for maritime warning already under discussion. Another was based on a beefed-up NORAD, that the Bi-national Planning Group called a "North American Defence Command." Yet even under this model, USNORTHCOM and Canada COM would remain in place. The Bi-national Planning Group had to admit, too, that such a beefed-up NORAD ran "counter to the prevailing trends in Canada and the United States towards the strengthening of their national defense Commands."[44]

Strikingly, the final two models involved getting rid of NORAD as a full bi-national command reporting to the secretary of defence in Washington and the chief of the defence staff in Canada. In one, it would be replaced by a "Combined Joint Task Force" supporting both USNORTHCOM and Canada COM. This task force "could be based" on NORAD, although "the role of NORAD would be clearly diminished."[45] In the other, the command's place would be taken by a "Continental Joint Interagency Task Force," supporting not only Canada COM and USNORTHCOM, but also the lead civilian agency in each country for homeland security, Public Security and Emergency Preparedness Canada and the US Department of Homeland Security. It was an ironic outcome. The Bi-national Planning Group, which many had expected at its creation inevitably to champion NORAD's enhancement, had at the end of its existence turned into a vehicle for publicly considering not only a strengthened command but also its diminution or replacement.

"IN PERPETUITY": THE 2006 RENEWAL

As the Canadian side sat down to prepare to negotiate the 2006 renewal of the NORAD accord, it realized that for all the emphasis being placed on homeland defence since 9/11, the chances had become slim that NORAD's role would be much enhanced. A brief working paper on renewal written in the Department of National Defence in early 2005 summarized why this was the case:

- CDS has announced a new domestic command concept ... This new command, when linked with NORTHCOM, has the potential to reduce the flexibility of NORAD to expand.
- There is a growing sense in the US that the defence of the United States in particular, and North America in general, is a national concern whose responsibility rests with NORTHCOM. Few defence functions are viewed as requiring a bi-national command/control component.
- There is a strong view in the United States that enhancement of NORAD comes at the expense of NORTHCOM. Any enhanced cooperation is likely to be in the area of indications and warning, all execution resting at the national level.
- These factors, combined with the current view in OSD [office of the secretary of defense] of Canada as an unreliable partner for a variety of reasons, has re-duced the appetite in the United States for enhanced bi-national defence cooperation.[46]

The paper was written just before the Martin government took the Bush ad-ministration by surprise with its decision on missile defence, which could only further reduce the American appetite for cooperation.

When the agreement was renewed in May of the next year it left, as the negotiators had anticipated, NORAD's responsibilities largely, although not completely, unchanged.[47] The agreement added "maritime warning for North America" to the NORAD missions, the first time they were extended beyond the aerospace realm. It was a limited task. The renewal made explicitly clear that NORAD had not been given any responsibility for "maritime surveil-lance and control" – in other words, for almost all of the work of naval forces in protecting the continent. The US and Canadian navies were opposed to that, as was Admiral Thomas Keating, the NORAD/USNORTHCOM com-mander, and he had said so in public. Surveillance and control were to remain fully outside of NORAD and fully in national hands, although the two countries remained free to continue to coordinate bilaterally. To provide maritime warning, a new cell at NORAD was created after the renewal and given the responsibility for gathering existing information from where it could in the two countries, especially from the intelligence and naval establishments, concerning maritime threats to the continent, and then sifting and comparing it. As the 2006 agreement put it, NORAD's task here consisted of "processing, assessing and disseminating intelligence and information related to the respective maritime areas and internal waterways of, and the maritime approaches to, or attacks against North American utilizing mutual support arrangements with other commands and agencies responsible for maritime defense and security." Although skeptics abounded who contended that Colorado Springs was not the right place for this, the new mission could well enhance maritime homeland security efforts by adding the additional degree of analysis, synthesis and information sharing. Nevertheless, NORAD's new warning mission was a far cry from the earlier public speculation after 9/11 that the command might soon operationally control the forces that guard the sea approaches to the continent, much as it had controlled the defence of the air approaches for almost fifty years.

After adding maritime warning as a NORAD responsibility, the renewal rhetorically downgraded the prospects of another responsibility, namely missile defence. The 1996 accord, renewed in 2000/2001, had said that NORAD's aerospace control mission "currently" included air defense, against the day that Ottawa and Washington might expand it to missile defence. In the wake of the Martin government's 2005 decision, the 2006 renewal said that aerospace control was air defense, period.

Most of the renewal negotiations were conducted under the authority of the Martin government. They were completed after the Conservative government of Stephen Harper took office on 6 February 2006 and was immediately faced with the accord's 12 May expiration date. The new government opted not to go for a short renewal period as the Trudeau government had done under similar circumstances after unexpectedly returning to power in early 1980. Had the Conservatives done so, they would have been in the company of USNORTHCOM, which argued for a two-year renewal. Instead, the renewal was, for the first time, without expiration date. "In perpetuity" was how some officials informally described it. The Martin government had seized upon the idea as a way of demonstrating that it wanted an improved defence relationship – of sorts – with the US. The Conservatives kept the provision, probably also to demonstrate a commitment to binational defence cooperation.

"In perpetuity" did not mean, though that NORAD's future somehow had been guaranteed indefinitely, despite the challenges that had recently arisen to it within the militaries of both countries. The renewal provided for a review within four years, or even earlier if either government wanted it.

NOTES

[1] National Commission on Terrorist Attacks Upon the United States, *The 9/11 Commission Report*, Authorized Edition (New York: W.W. Norton, 2004), 346.

[2] National Commission on Terrorist Attacks Upon the United States, Public hearing, 23 May 2003, Panel 1: September 11, 2001: The Attacks and the Response. Available online.

[3] "Myers and September 11: 'We Hadn't Thought About This,'" *American Forces Information Service*, News Articles, 23 October 2001.

[4] *Toronto Star*, 23 October 2001, A10.

[5] 9/11 report, 18 (see note 1).

[6] 9/11 report, 31 (see note 1).

[7] Strictly speaking, Operation Noble Eagle was a broader US military undertaking. But inasmuch as at NORAD and within the Canadian military it was almost always used to refer to just NORAD's counter-terrorist air defence operations, the practice will be adopted here.

[8] Rebecca Grant, *The First 600 Days of Combat: The US Air Force in the Global War on Terrorism* (Washington: IRIS Press, 2004), 32

[9] Willian B. Scott, "Exercise Jump-Starts Response to Attacks," *Aviation Week and Space Technology*, 3 June 2002.

[10] Grant, 33 (see note 8).

[11] Sharon Hobson, "Canadian Air Force to install GUARD," *Jane's Defence Weekly*, 10 March 2006.

[12] US Department of Defense, News Transcript, "DOD News Briefing – Secretary Rumsfeld," 27 September 2001.

[13] 9/11 Commission Hearing, 23 May 2003 (see note 2).

[14] House of Commons, Standing Committee on National Defence and Veterans Affairs, *Minutes of Proceedings*, 4 October 2001.

[15] US Senate, Armed Services Committee, *Statement of Admiral Timothy J. Keating, USN.....before the Senate Armed Services Committee*, 14 March 2006.

[16] [Title redacted], Section, "ANALYSIS, Issue: Whether to begin negotiations with the United States on Canadian participation in the Ballistic Missile Defence System," 16 March 2003. Files of the assistant deputy minister of national defence (policy).

[17] Paul Cellucci, *Unquiet Diplomacy* (Toronto: Key Porter Books, 2005), 152.

[18] House of Commons, *Debates*, 29 May 2003, 11:15.

[19] Cellucci, 153 (see note 17).

[20] "Letter from Minister Pratt to Secretary Rumsfeld." 15 January 2006. Available online.

[21] Ibid.

[22] "Agreement amending the agreement of March 28, 1996, as extended and amended, regarding the organization and operation of the North American Aerospace Defense Command (NORAD)," 5 August 2004.

[23] Oliver Moore, "Canada 'already part of missile defence': McKenna," *Globe and Mail*, 22 February 2005.

[24] House of Commons, *Debates*, 24 February 2005, 12:00.

[25] Cellucci, 164 (see note 17).

[26] Pierre Martin, "All Quebec's Fault, Again? Quebec Public Opinion and Canada's Rejection of Missile Defence," *Policy Options* (May 2005), 43.

[27] Ibid., 44.

[28] Cellucci, 165 (see note 17).

[29] NORAD briefing materials, May 2006.

[30] James Fergusson, "Shall we Dance? The Missile Defence Decision, NORAD Renewal and the Future of Canada–US Defence Relations," *Canadian Military Journal* 6, No. 2 (Summer 2005), 20.

[31] *Report of the Commission to Assess United States National Security, Space Management and Organization*, 11 January 2001, 9, 33.

[32] Briefing Note to deputy minister: "DND/CF Implications of the Folllow-Up Policy Directives to the Report of the US Space Commission," 8 November 2001. DND Access to information request A200201059.

[33] Michael Dobbs," "Establishing a CINC for Homeland Security," *Journal of Homeland Security* (October 2001), n.p.

[34] Ibid.

[35] Ibid.

[36] Ibid.

[37] Bernard Stancati, "The Future of Canada's Role in Hemispheric Defense," *Parameters* (Autumn 2006), 108.

[38] US Department of Defense, news release "Unified Command Plan," 17 April 2002.

[39] *Proceedings of the Standing Senate Committee on National Security and Defence*, Issue 14, 6 May 2002.

[40] Bi-national Planning Group briefings, October 2003.

[41] See Joel J. Sokolsky, *Guarding the Coasts: United States Maritime Homeland Security and Canada* (Montreal: Institute for Research on Public Policy, 2005), 30.

[42] Chief of the defence staff, "Concept of Operations: CF strategic Command." 18 October 2005.

[43] Chief of the defence staff, CDS Action Team 1 report. Part III. Domestic environment (CANCOM), 2005.

[44] Bi-national Planning Group, *The Final Report on Canada and the United States (CANUS) Enhanced Military Cooperation*, 13 March 2006, 38.

[45] Ibid., 39-40.

[46] "Negotiating Mandate Meeting, 18 February 2005." Files of the office of the assistant deputy minister (policy), Department of National Defence.

[47] The 2006 renewal took an unprecedented form. The text was incorporated into a 28 April 2006 "Agreement ... on the North American Air Defense Command," carrying

the proviso that it would go into effect upon an exchange of diplomatic notes. After the Harper government secured a vote of approval by the House of Commons, the diplomatic notes were exchanged on 12 May.

CONCLUSION

CANADA IN NORAD AT 50

Looming over NORAD's fiftieth anniversary in 2007 was the review it would eventually have to face under the terms of the 2006 renewal. That review seemed bound to be the most thorough, intense, and skeptical bilateral examination of the command ever undertaken. The command's future usefulness was open to question with respect to all three of its core functions Foulkes had identified in 1969, namely warning and assessment, operational control of (air defence) forces and serving as a channel for technical information and planning. It won't hurt to repeat here how Foulkes put it, in its entirety: "NORAD is very efficient for processing of intelligence information regarding the aerospace threat from all sources and operational control of the forces for anti-bomber defence and has also proven a most useful channel for technical information and planning between Canada and the United States."[1]

WARNING AND ASSESSMENT

NORAD's responsibilities included from the start both mounting an active air defence and providing warning so that SAC bombers could get off the ground, even though under the leadership of General Lemay SAC was not particularly interested in waiting to receive the word from Colorado Springs. As the threat shifted from bombers to ballistic missiles (and, it was feared for a while in the 1960s, satellites), NORAD's warning and assessment capabilities were refined, eventually becoming ITW/AA. While ballistic missiles could strike very much faster than bombers, their trajectories, unlike those of bombers, were fixed. That meant their point of impact could be calculated in advance and the nature of the Soviet strike assessed before the warheads reached their targets.

As the US became increasingly vulnerable to destruction at the hands of the Soviets, it sought from the 1960s into the 1980s to shore up deterrence by developing a more sophisticated nuclear strategy based on limited strike options and the ability to fight a protracted conflict. This placed a premium on NORAD's capability to provide timely and accurate assessments of Soviet strikes, so that the US leadership could respond in measured fashion. It also meant that NORAD would need to survive at least the first Soviet strike. When it became clear that Soviet missiles had becomes so accurate and their warheads so powerful that they could destroy even the Cheyenne Mountain complex, the Carter and Reagan administrations moved to equip NORAD with the satellite capability and ground-based terminals that it could rely on after the mountain was gone.

It is not surprising that the US and Canada had different approaches to nuclear strategy. It was only the US that had the strategic nuclear weapons and was faced with reassuring overseas allies that it really was prepared to unleash nuclear war on their behalf, despite the increasing vulnerability of the American homeland to destruction. If NATO Europeans worried that the US was not willing enough to resort to the use of nuclear weapons on their behalf and thus deterrence might fail, Canadians tended to worry that Washington might be too willing, and drag them into an intercontinental thermonuclear war in which they would suffer almost as much as the Americans.

In NORAD's early air defence days, Canadian officials generally saw NORAD's role as providing SAC with warning and a measure of active protection, lest it be destroyed on the ground. US officials (at least those outside of SAC) subscribed to those goals, too. But they also placed somewhat more emphasis on the contribution active air defences could make to saving North American lives by shooting down Soviet bombers. It was a matter of nuance, though, and it did not matter much at the time with respect to the practicalities of active air defence operations with the squadrons in place. As Soviet bombers passed into the engagement zone in southern Canada (the "killing area," the Canadian army had called it in 1958), it was impossible to tell whether they were heading towards SAC bases or cities. The RCAF and USAF would attempt to attack as many of them there as possible. To be sure, when it was time to buy new fighters for the RCAF and to equip them with nuclear weapons, the Liberal party flirted in the early 1960s with "bird watching," an eminently sensible approach if the task of the defence was, or should be, just to alert SAC. When the Liberals backed down in 1963, they did so in the name of keeping commitments, not because they had embraced active air defence.

In the 1970s, Canadians mostly ignored how NORAD's warning and assessment responsibilities fit into increasingly sophisticated US deterrence strategies that were at odds with Canadian strategic approaches. Meanwhile, they comforted themselves with talk of "stable mutual deterrence." That proved more difficult to do after the Reagan administration came to power in 1981 and began to talk more bluntly about US nuclear strategy, while NORAD officials, including the CINC, publicly underlined NORAD's place in it, and peace groups sounded the alarm. It was still not impossible to do, though, as the House of Commons committee studying NORAD renewal in 1985 showed when it waived the entire issue away.

Simply ignoring reality had been a pretty standard way for the two governments to deal with NORAD, though, when it came to the renewals. Both the 1968 and 1973 renewals treated NORAD as if it were still just an air defence command, despite its missile and space detection responsibilities. Not until the 1981 did Ottawa and Washington dare to put "aerospace" into its title.

Canadian territory was all but irrelevant for warning of missile attack. This was strikingly unlike air defence where the first warning of a Soviet bomber attack could well have come from the DEW Line in the high Canadian north and later from the North Warning System, or from fighters and AWACS aircraft operating in an emergency even to the north of those radars. No system to detect or track missiles was ever located in Canada.

Despite this Canadian geographical irrelevance, aerospace warning and assessment, which later became ITW/AA, remained a NORAD mission. And so Canadians also remained at the heart of North American aerospace defence. In the mountain, missile warning crews were made of Americans and Canadians, and Canadian air force generals continued to take their turns as "assessors" standing by to confirm whether or not North America was under attack. USAF officers at NORAD trusted and liked the Canadians right from the moment Slemon and the other RCAF officers arrived. This might in small part explain why Canadians were still welcome in the ITW/AA mission. So might the simple fact, as a senior Canadian defence official put it in 2000 while talking about missile defence, that Americans were just in "the habit" of involving Canada in the defence of North America.[2] So might as well the quality of the Canadians deployed to Colorado Springs – and the longevity of their tours of duty. A 1967 study of NORAD undertaken for the chief of the defence staff argued that "Canadian personnel, with their generally longer tour lengths and with the background of knowledge which they have acquired, are clearly recognized as a stabilizing influence in the operation of the system."[3]

Much more fundamentally though, the "I" in "ITW/AA" stood for "integrated." It was not just warning of ballistic missile attack. The potential role of bombers and cruise missiles in a Soviet assault on North America could never be overlooked, even though they had ceased to be the principal threat. At the end of the 1970s the bomber even made a come-back of sorts in the form of a potential precursor or "decapitation" strike. Here Canadian territory, as well as the radars and fighter aircraft located there and operated by the Canadian military, still counted. The "killing area" was to be moved from southern to northern Canada in the wake of the 1985 North American Air Defence Modernization Agreement, although it was to be nowhere as lethal as it once had been. For a long time as well, Canada's Baker-Nunn cameras also contributed to NORAD's space surveillance responsibilities, which had a role to play in the dependability of integrated warning and assessment. Space surveillance helped insure that a satellite falling out of orbit would not be misinterpreted as a missile attack.

In 1992–1993 NORAD officials envisaged building upon ITW/AA a post-Cold War global warning system, linked to a global missile defence. A decade and a half later, their successors were wondering how long NORAD ITW/AA would last, largely as a result of the Martin government's 2005 decision not to participate in missile defence. The complete integration of aerospace warning and assessment within a single command had become less important, too, once Soviet long-range bombers had ceased to be a real threat. No rogue state or terrorist organization could launch an intensive attack on North America involving both many aircraft and ballistic missiles, as the Soviet Union once could. Tactical warning and assessment of air threats could be conducted apart from missile warning. The Canadians would go with the air defence.

Ironically, the future of NORAD's integrated aerospace warning and assessment role, and hence the very future of NORAD, were being called into question just as its warning responsibilities were extended, for the first time, into the maritime realm by the 2006 renewal.

OPERATIONAL CONTROL

Placing all Canadian air defence forces under the operational control of a binational command headed by a USAF general was politically a dramatic development in Canada in 1957, although the two air forces saw it as just another evolutionary step in their transborder cooperation that had been growing steadily during the 1950s. The distinguished historian Desmond Morton wrote in 1985 that "[i]f politicians such as Robert Borden and Mackenzie King had struggled for Canada's right to control its destiny, Diefenbaker had unwittingly signed away his country's control of when it would declare war."[4] At the time of NORAD's creation, this kind of charge greatly irked Foulkes. He wrote Pearkes in 1957 that

> I feel the impression has got abroad that the Commander of NORAD or his Deputy might be able to plunge Canada into war. This is certainly not the case. All the Commanders at NORAD can do is to put into the air their purely defensive interceptor fighters, and if there are not Russian bombers there, all they can do is bring their fighters down again. If the Russian bombers are there, the peace has been broken not by the Commanders of NORAD but by the Russian bombers, who would have penetrated over 2,000 miles through Canadian airspace. So that, by no stretch of the imagination can the Commanders of the air defence forces plunge this country into war unless the Russians have already broken the peace.[5]

While this was undoubtedly so, it was only part of the story. CINCNORAD had the authority to put US and Canadian air defence forces on alert. As Melvin

Conant noted in his classic 1962 work on Canada–US defence relations, "[o]ne risk is that an alert might be interpreted by the Soviet Union as a signal that the United States has chosen that time to strike first with its strategic forces, although the United States alert might be precautionary in purpose."[6]

In other words, an alert might indeed plunge Canada into war. With that possibility in mind, and prompted by NORAD's July 1958 alert, Canadian negotiators sought and obtained in 1959 Washington's formal, although at the time secret, agreement that CINCNORAD's authority be circumscribed to declaring alerts only in the event of an impending or actual attack. This provision, and with it Canadian sovereignty, were respected by General Gerhart when, at the start of the 1962 Cuban missile crisis, he did not place Canadian air defence forces on alert. Instead, he asked the Canadian government to do so and waited until Ottawa responded. In the event, it was Harkness who first acted, surreptitiously, with the formal decision by the cabinet coming later.

The crisis also demonstrated the usefulness, to both Canada and the United States of the "twin" command structure that had been put in place at Colorado Springs and that was maintained throughout NORAD's existence. As CINCONAD, Gerhart placed US forces and US forces alone on alert. His successor in 1973, General Lucius Clay, was able to do exactly the same during the Yom Kippur crisis. Because of the nature and brevity of the later alert, Clay never requested Ottawa to act and Canadian forces never went on higher readiness. In both crises, the twinned command structure left the US free to act alone. The Yom Kippur War was the last time US aerospace defence forces intentionally went on peacetime alert. Thereafter, NORAD went not once, but worryingly and embarrassingly three times on an accidental, although only partial and short-lived, higher state of readiness in the period 1979–1980, as a result of human error or equipment failure. And of course it put air defence forces on alert on 9/11 after the United States had been attacked.

It should be added that "twinning," while a handy term, it still is not a complete description. CINCNORAD often wore a third "hat" as commander of a USAF command and NORAD itself was outfitted with a US Element under his command in 1985.

"Twinning" also served both countries' interests by providing for the command and control by the US at Colorado Springs, and as part of the broader aerospace defence effort, of systems in which there was no direct Canadian participation. The Johnson Island ASAT was assigned to CONAD. The Safeguard missile defence was assigned to CONAD and later ADCOM, while USNORTHCOM was given operational command over the newer US missile defence. In retrospect, it was a good thing that Partridge was reigned in by the US Chiefs and deflected from his original intent simply to replace CONAD with NORAD.

This is not to say that the Colorado Springs command structure never posed any problems for Canadians. Nuclear air defence weapons were in 1957 a CONAD, not a NORAD, responsibility. Partridge and several of his successors solved the problem that this posed for DCINCNORAD by ignoring the structure and breaking the law. Canadian negotiators had to push quite hard in 1964–1965 to get Washington to agree that in both Canada and the United States, not just in Canada, nuclear air defence weapons would be both a NORAD and a CONAD responsibility. The US Chiefs were overruled by President Johnson, who sided with Ottawa. The Cosmos 954 incident showed that there was a "filter" of sorts between ADCOM and NORAD limiting the information that NORAD – and therefore Canadians – received about certain sensitive space-related information. While Canada was being "punished" in the late 1980s for its stance on SDI, NORAD served as a sort of air defence doghouse to keep Canadians in while the US conducted aerospace defence planning on the USSPACECOM side.

The two air forces wanted in the mid-1950s to create a bi-national air defence headquarters primarily to provide for a single commander with operational control over the vast defences with which he could conduct a continent-wide air defence battle, especially in the Canadian engagement zone or "killing area." Partridge seems to have been pretty confident that his command's great air defence capabilities would soon be complemented by a robust missile defence, for which NORAD would also be responsible. Horner was similarly optimistic in the early post Cold War years that NORAD soon would be given national missile defence responsibilities.

Without robust missile defences, maintaining a vigorous North American air defence made little sense. McNamara began to put US air defences on a downward path in 1964; ten years later, Schlesinger, his successor, increased the rate of decline. Ottawa not only did the same but also took advantage of the dismantling of the robust defences to "Canadianize" or "nationalize" the day-to-day air defence efforts that remained to be undertaken in Canadian airspace and on Canadian soil. It gave North Bay responsibility for the air defence control of all of Canada's airspace, bringing an end to the NORAD regions that had straddled the border and that had operationally controlled much of Canadian airspace from several headquarters located in the US. This "Canadianization" of air defence did not mean that the military had acquired increased capability within Canada to intercept and identify civilian aircraft. Discussions between the departments of national defence and transport over a joint civilian-military radar system first got underway in 1966. But they did not get far, largely because transport officials were highly skeptical of any need to rely on the military to enforce civil aviation rules and procedures. In 2007 Ottawa still faced the decision whether to fill in the gaps in primary radar coverage over much of the country.

The turnaround in continental air defence that began at the end of the 1970s and found form in the 1985 North American Air Defence Modernization Agreement might have intensified had Ronald Reagan's Strategic Defence Initiative ever led to a heavy missile defence; the Air Defense Initiative anticipated this. But the end of the Cold War also put an end both to any prospect of extensive missile defences in the immediate future and to a good deal of the 1985 air defence modernization program. There was no longer a military air threat to North America, Horner said in 1994.

In the new struggle against airborne terrorism, while highjacked aircraft might swiftly cross borders, there would be no vast air defence battle conducted out of Colorado Springs by the NORAD commander. 9/11 revealed publicly not just that the North American air defences were still pointing outward, but also how localized much of the immediate command and control of air defence was. It was not Colorado Springs, but the NEADS, that had controlled the fighters that morning. North Bay and the CANR headquarters at Winnipeg had similar responsibilities for Canadian airspace – and would have been just as blindsided had the attacks occurred in Canadian cities, probably more so given the location of the CF-18 fighters at Cold Lake and Bagotville. To be sure, after the 9/11 attacks NORAD itself had overall charge of the air defence efforts that became Operation Noble Eagle. North American air defences, especially those in the US, were reconfigured so that they could look inward as well as outward.

The terrorist threat was primarily to the US. The post-9/11 arrangements for destruction of highjacked aircraft, whereby the Canadian military did not receive the same authority to act in an emergency that the US military had, underlined this. This difference in delegated authority did not itself call NORAD into question. On the contrary, it showed how national sovereignty and air defence cooperation could be reconciled within NORAD. The same can be said about difference in authority the two governments had given CINCNORAD in 1965 to order the engagement with nuclear air defence weapons of single aircraft. Then, too, Ottawa had reserved the authority to itself. In fact, the NORAD arrangements had always involved the two governments giving the CINC different levels and kinds of authority, beginning right with the distinction between operational control and command. "Twinning" of commands was another reflection of this.

Nonetheless, the question was being asked in 2007: was the bi-national command still the best entity to which to entrust air defence? It was being asked more in the US than in Canada and usually by USNORTHCOM. With the missile defence mission having gone to USNORTHCOM and with the ITW/AA role in decline, the loss of the full air defence mission could easily spell the end of NORAD as a full-fledged bi-national command.

A CHANNEL

Foulkes probably had picked his words carefully when he said that the channel NORAD provided between Canada and the US was for "technical information and planning." The diplomats with whom he had struggled in 1957 over the need for a formal accord saw NORAD as the basis for something broader in the Canada–US relationship than just such a relatively narrow military channel. They succeeded in putting into the 1958 agreement the general consultation pledge and went on to complete the negotiation of the second, secret 1958 agreement specifying that in the event either government felt that the need had arisen to put the air defences on alert, it would consult the other. This was followed by still another pledge of consultation in the 1959 agreement on alerts and by refinements to it, negotiated in 1960. The whole package was revamped by the 1965 accord on nuclear weapons and consultation, which stipulated in fairly great detail who in Ottawa was expected to talk to whom in Washington, at six month intervals and under emergency circumstances. The 1965 agreement removed air defence alerts as the trigger for Canada–US consultation; instead, the two governments agreed on the need to consult whenever North America was in danger of being attacked.

In neither the 1962 Cuban missile crisis nor the 1973 Yom Kippur War crisis did Washington consult Ottawa before putting US forces on alert. Did the US break its commitments to Canada? The answer seems clear in the case of the second alert: the US did not violate the 1965 accord. Nixon and Kissinger never believed that the alert could lead to nuclear war; it was intended only as an unmistakable political signal of resolve to the Soviets. They were therefore under no obligation to consult with Ottawa. On the other hand, the Kennedy administration did not respect the provisions of the various NORAD-related agreements obliging it to consult with Ottawa in the event of an alert. The question then becomes whether, given the nature of the Cuban crisis, it could legitimately have been expected to do so. "D.B.D's" memo, written in the Privy Council Office just after the crisis, made the convincing case that it could not.

In short, the various Cold War emergency consultation pledges that were built upon NORAD were never really tested in either the Cuban missile or Yom Kippur crises. To do so, it would have taken the kind of international crisis that was so feared during the Cold War, one resulting from rising tensions, most likely in Europe, threatening or actually leading to a clash between the East and West.

There were hopes in Ottawa that Canadian participation in NORAD could be turned into a significant and enduring channel of influence in Washington. Foulkes expressed some of this thinking himself with his uncharacteristic remark, quoted at the end of Chapter One, to the effect that because of NORAD the US was obliged to consult Ottawa whenever it contemplated using force anywhere in the world. This is not the place to examine the impact NORAD membership had on Canada's influence over US foreign policy except to note that while it probably did not help much, it could not have hurt, either. Peyton V. Lyon got it no doubt just about right when he wrote in 1963 that "what can scarcely be questioned is that Canada has gained more influence over western defence and foreign policies by being inside NORAD and NATO than if she remained on the outside."[7] It can be added that while NORAD was a little-noted entity in much of Washington, one command among many, had Canada ever withdrawn from NORAD that step nonetheless would have drawn American attention.

Despite Canada's NORAD membership, the US continued to call the major shots by itself when it came to the course of North American aerospace defence. A group of experts, empanelled by the parliamentary sub-committee studying the 1991 renewal of the NORAD agreement, commented on this, identifying

> the fundamental dilemma that Canada faces in cooperating with the US in the air defence of the continent. When radical changes of policy are decided in Washington, Canada may react to them, but it has little opportunity to influence policy prior to decisions, even when such decisions have a profound effect upon Canadian security and defence policy. The 1967 decision in Washington to deploy a limited ABM system, the 1983 Star Wars speech by President Reagan, the 1985 decision to invite the allies to formally participate in the research programme, the future course of SDI, all illustrate that crucial decisions in Washington are made prior to bilateral consultation, not after such consultation.[8]

This pattern extended to air defence. Ottawa reacted to the new architecture of continental air defence announced by McNamara in 1968 and the NORAD agreement was renewed for only two years in 1973 so that Washington could decide how extensive those air defences needed to be in the wake of the ABM Treaty. In other words, the major policy decisions Ottawa faced were largely which tasks to undertake itself, which to leave to the Americans, and how to try to divide any financial responsibility, within a broader continental defence posture set by Washington. The shift in the threat during the Cold War from bombers to ballistic missiles lightened Canada's load, given the irrelevance of Canadian territory to defence against ballistic missiles. There is no indication that the US government took Canadian views into much consideration whenever it refined the deterrent nuclear strategy that NORAD would help execute in the event of a war.

This is certainly not to say that there was nothing whatsoever to negotiate between Ottawa and Washington or that Canada's interests were entirely ignored by the US. There were important, if still secondary modalities to address, especially with respect to air defence. To give but two examples: President Johnson sided with Canada in establishing a NORAD/CONAD regime for air defence nuclear weapons throughout North America and the 1985 air defence modernization program was modified to meet Canada's geographic needs. Ottawa was also able from to time to secure its specific wishes for the renewals of the NORAD accord, most notably the insertion into the 1968 text of the foolish "ABM clause."

In the late 1990s it was the Canadian military, taking a leaf from the diplomats' book, that wanted to build NORAD into something broader than just a technical channel. As discussed in Chapter Five, the Department of National Defence hoped in 1998 that Canadian participation in NORAD could be "leveraged" into a "conduit" into US space and at one point a DCINC even envisaged NORAD's eventually becoming a sort of multilateral space-support command, with a special place for Canada. Here, too, NORAD could not hurt as Canada sought access to US space programs and it might even help. But it is not apparent that the Canadian Forces ever had a strategy for turning NORAD into a space conduit, or that the US military was willing to provide greater access to Canada just because it was in NORAD, especially access to US space programs not immediately related to North American defence. This emerging view of NORAD as a space "conduit" was dealt a heavy blow in 2002 by the dissolution of USSPACECOM, the transfer of its assets to USSTRATCOM, and its replacement by USNORTHCOM as the "twin" command.

With the establishment of Canada COM four years after that of USNORTHCOM, NORAD was faced with being seen, within the Canadian military itself, less and less as a valuable channel, and more as a potential interloper between the two national homeland defence commands. NORAD was a "Cold War apparatus," the planners in National Defence Headquarters concluded in 2005. They expected close ties to develop between Canada COM and USNORTHCOM, especially if Canada COM managed to subsume the responsibilities of the Canadian NORAD Region.

USNORTHCOM, for its part, had a special impetus for acquiring a central role for itself in defence planning with Canada. It was the first US unified command ever to be given responsibility specifically for North America as an "area of operational responsibility" as the Pentagon's unified command plan termed it. As with all US unified commands with geographic responsibilities in whatever region of the world, USNORTHCOM was charged with promoting "theater security cooperation" with the countries in its area. Thus it sought to engage both Canada and Mexico across a wide range of defence issues. Its mandate had implications not only for NORAD, but also for the Pentagon agencies that had long had responsibility for the defense department's relations with Canada, and for the work of Canada–US Military Cooperation Committee, whose Ottawa- and Washington-based members had drawn up continental defence plans since 1946.

This is not to conclude that at the hands of the two new national homeland defence commands, NORAD was facing in 2007 inevitable dissolution or downgrading to the status of a joint combined task force. NORAD could make the case that, despite the importance of localized command and control, air defence still belonged in a bi-national command, especially as the two countries geared up to deal with the emerging threat of cheap sea-launched cruise missiles. A future reversal of the Martin government's 2005 missile defence decision could rejuvenate NORAD as an aerospace command, at the least thereby preserving its ITW/AA role and possibly even leading to missile defence being made a NORAD responsibility, as so many of its CINCs had expected for so many years. Ottawa was expecting in 2007 to launch in a couple of years a satellite, dubbed "Sapphire," that would restore Canada's once longstanding direct participation in NORAD's space surveillance mission. Sapphire would be the heart of the "asymmetrical contribution" the Canadian military first proposed in the late 1990s.

Although the US military may have acquired "the habit" of involving Canadians in continental defence, if NORAD were dissolved or downgraded to a task force, it is most unlikely that it could ever be restored. It was created at a time when Canadian territory and airspace, and the RCAF's nine squadrons of air defence fighters, counted in Slemon's "mighty task" of continental air defence. The USAF was more than willing to put its own interceptors under the operational control of Slemon and the other Canadians who took their turns in command at NORAD; Partridge and at least one of his successors as CINCNORAD ignored the rules and broke the law to make sure that Slemon could exercise that control. A year after NORAD's creation the president of the United States, to make sure that the continental defences were as effective as possible, was ready not only to equip the RCAF with nuclear air defence weapons, but also give Ottawa full legal custody over them.

Thereafter, the story of NORAD is in large part about the decline of its active forces and of the diminishing importance of Canadian geography and the Canadian military to continental defence. While Canada and the US grew economically closer and closer during the missile age, militarily the geographic coupling loosened, briefly tightening with the modest revival of air defence in the 1980s and then tightening again somewhat in the post 9/11 age of terror. Applying Foulkes' criteria, it was not hard to come to conclusion that the bi-national command was not indispensable in 2007 for effective Canada–US defence cooperation. Some, in both the US and Canadian military, were beginning to argue that it was becoming a hindrance. The Canadian government, however, would still tend to see NORAD the way the way it had since 1957, as being something broader and of greater importance than just a military command. So Ottawa would be reluctant to let it go. NORAD was the most important symbol of Canada–US defence cooperation. For that reason alone, letting it go could give Washington pause, too.

NOTES

[1] See note 5 in the Introduction.

[2] Daniel Bon, acting assistant deputy minister (policy) in Standing Committee on National Defence and Veterans Affairs, *Minutes and Proceedings*, 24 February 2000, 1025.

[3] R.L. Raymont, "NORAD," 14 September 1967. Department of National Defence, Directorate of History and Heritage, Raymont fonds, 73/1233 series 5, file 2505.

[4] Desmond Morton, *A Military History of Canada* (Edmonton: Hurtig, 1985), 242.

[5] Memo, Foulkes to Pearkes, "Continental Defence," 25 November 1957. Department Directorate of History and Heritage, Raymont fonds, 47/879.

[6] Melvin Conant, *The Long Polar Watch* (New York: Harper and Brothers, 1962), 75.

[7] Peyton V. Lyon, *The Policy Question: A Critical Appraisal of Canada's Role in World Affairs* (Toronto: McClelland and Stewart 1963), 29.

[8] "Report of the Special Panel to the Sub-Committee of the House of Commons Standing Committee on External Affairs and International Trade considering the question of renewing in May 1991 the North American Aerospace Defence Agreement," Canadian Institute for International Peace and Security, Working Paper 33, March 1991, 52.

APPENDIX

MAPS

LIST OF MAPS

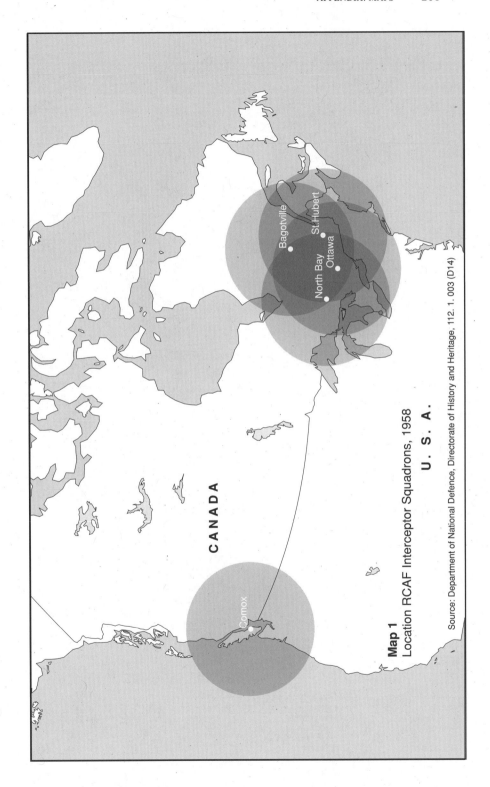

Map 1
Location RCAF Interceptor Squadrons, 1958

CANADA

U. S. A.

Bagotville

St. Hubert

North Bay

Ottawa

Comox

Source: Department of National Defence, Directorate of History and Heritage, 112. 1. 003 (D14)

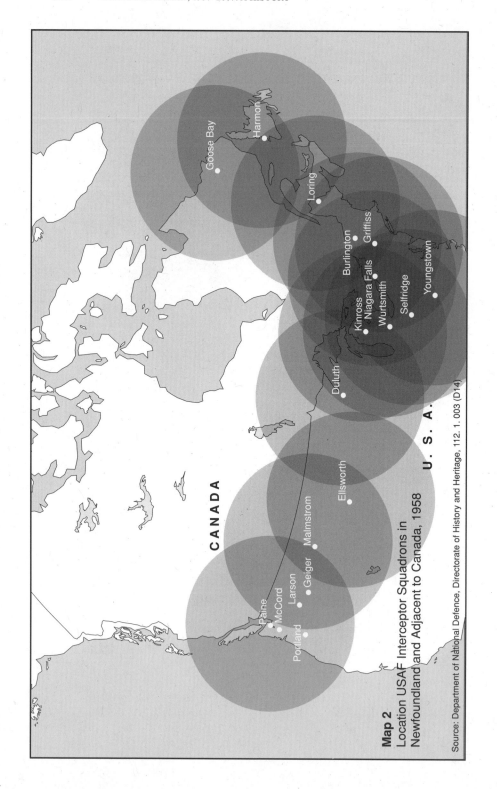

Map 2
Location USAF Interceptor Squadrons in
Newfoundland and Adjacent to Canada, 1958

Source: Department of National Defence, Directorate of History and Heritage, 112. 1. 003 (D14)

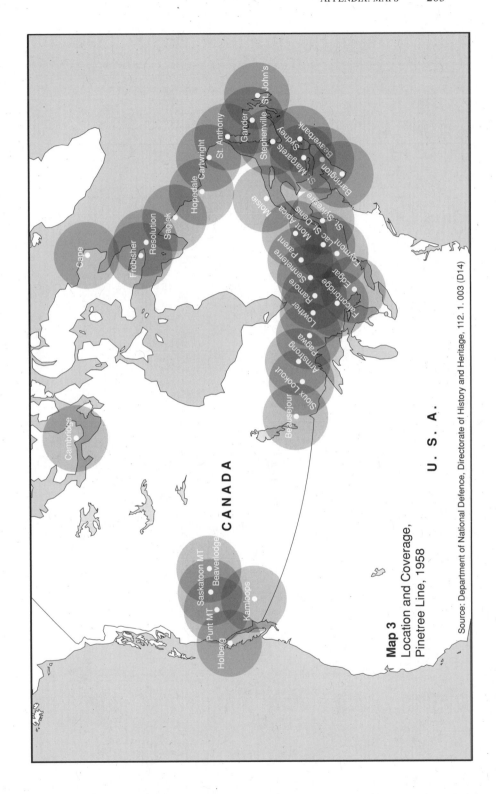

Map 3
Location and Coverage,
Pinetree Line, 1958

Source: Department of National Defence, Directorate of History and Heritage, 112. 1. 003 (D14)

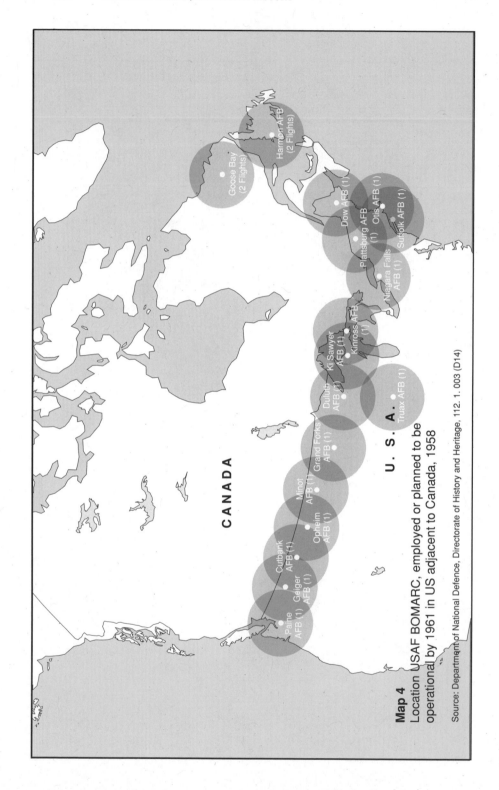

Map 4
Location USAF BOMARC, employed or planned to be operational by 1961 in US adjacent to Canada, 1958

Source: Department of National Defence, Directorate of History and Heritage, 112. 1. 003 (D14)

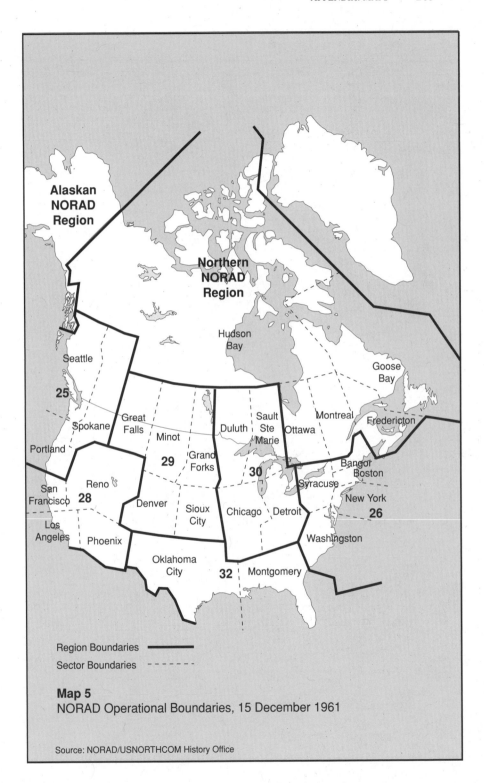

Map 5
NORAD Operational Boundaries, 15 December 1961

Source: NORAD/USNORTHCOM History Office

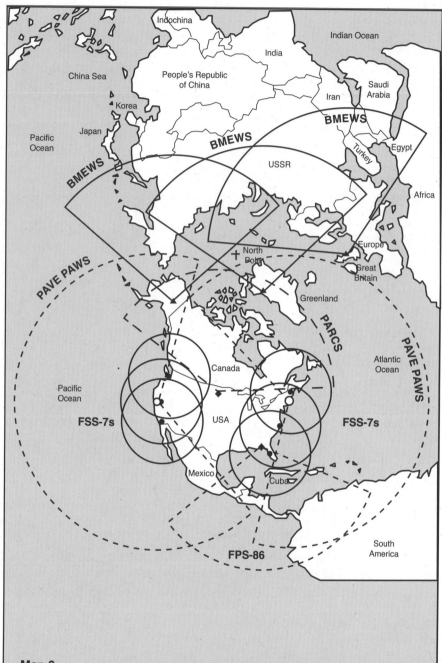

Map 6
Land Based Ballistic Missile Warning Sites and Detection Sweeps, 1981

Source: US Congressional Budget Office, *Strategic Command, Control and Communications:
Alternative Approaches for Modernization* (1981)

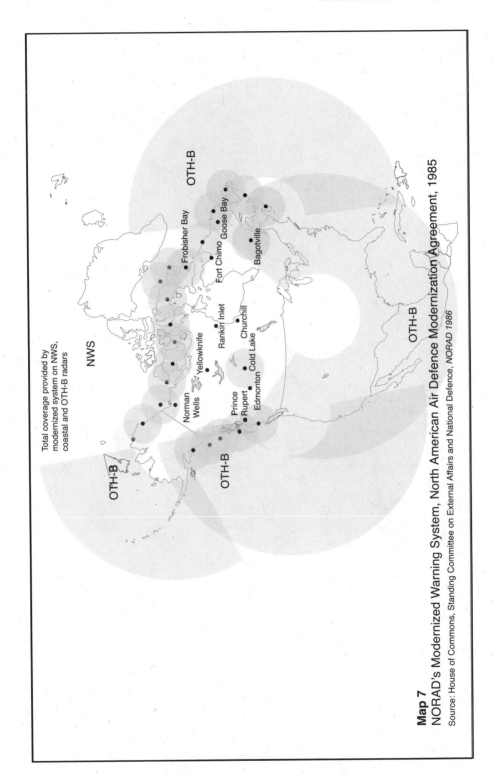

Map 7
NORAD's Modernized Warning System, North American Air Defence Modernization Agreement, 1985

Source: House of Commons, Standing Committee on External Affairs and National Defence, *NORAD 1986*

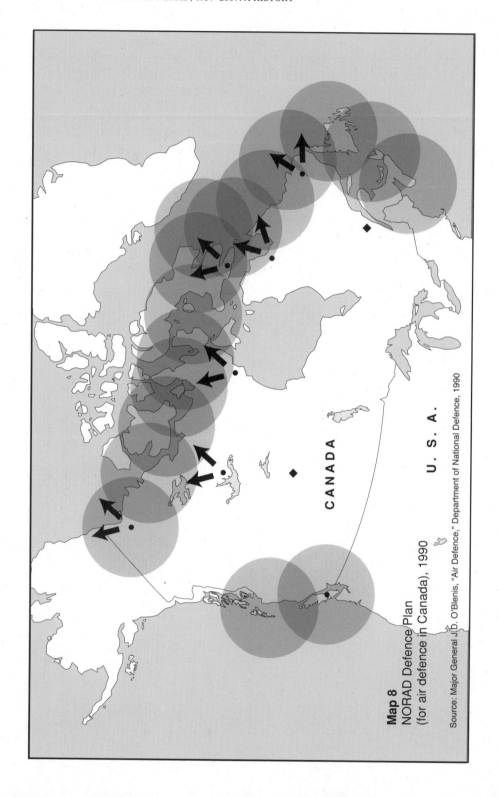

Map 8
NORAD Defence Plan
(for air defence in Canada), 1990

Source: Major General J. D. O'Blenis, "Air Defence," Department of National Defence, 1990

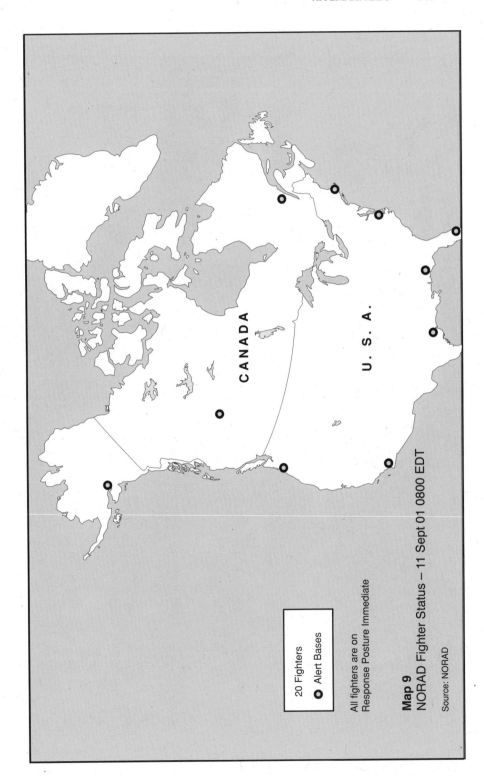

20 Fighters
O Alert Bases

All fighters are on
Response Posture Immediate

Map 9
NORAD Fighter Status – 11 Sept 01 0800 EDT

Source: NORAD

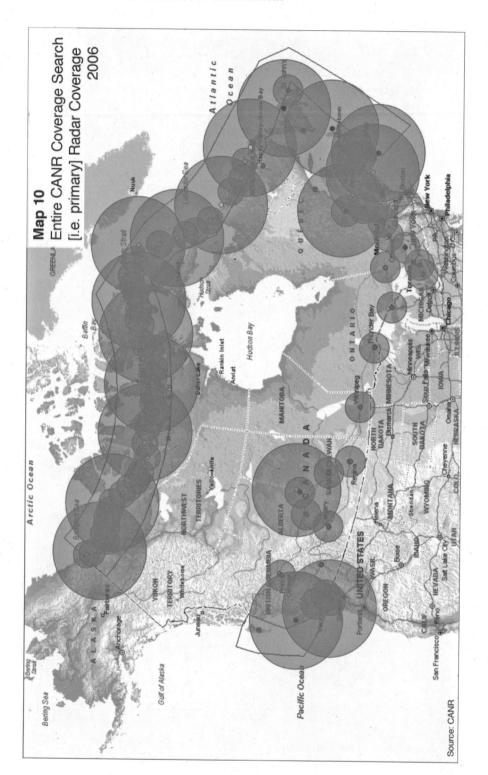

Map 10
Entire CANR Coverage Search
[i.e. primary] Radar Coverage
2006

Source: CANR

INDEX

ABM clause, 89, 91, 98, 108, 110, 132, 133, 195; see NORAD agreements

Advanced Tactical Fighter, USAF, 135

Aerospace Defense Advanced Technologies Working Group (ADATS), ADI, 136; bilateral, 135

Aerospace Defense Command (ADCOM), USAF, 6, 77, 91, 93-94, 102-03, 131; elimination, 104, 129, 178; F-106, 100; information-sharing, 192; NORAD, 94, 136; satellite warning, 107, 191; strategic defence, 102, 192; see CONAD

Air defence modernization, 116, 119, 121; Canadian concerns, 116, 123, 132, 196; end of Cold War, 193; new defence technologies, 134; northern operations, 124; nuclear options, 126; program (1967), 90; see North American Air Defence Modernization Agreement

Air Defense Initiative (ADI, 1986), 193; BM/C3, 135; Canadian involvement, 136; research, 136; surveillance, 134-35; USAF, 134

Air Defense Master Plan, 116, 123; see USAF

Air-launched cruise missiles (ALCMs), testing, 118-19

Airborne warning and control system (AWACS), 67-68, 93, 99, 103, 124, 189; availability of aircraft, 146; Canadian Forces, 101, 124; cruise missiles, 171; expansion, 116, radar, 135; randomness, 125; see McNamara

Aird, John, 94-95, 96

Alaska, 9, 18

Albright, Madeleine, 161

Anderson, John, 99, 100, 116

Anderson, Martin, 109

Annis, Air Vice Marshal Clare, 57

Anti-Ballistic Missile Treaty (ABM), 89, 90, 93, 95; Canadian concerns, 157; Canadian interpretation, 137, 138; limited deployment, 171, 195; missile defence, 108, 126, 127; negotiations with Russians, 171; possible joint statement, 133, 134; renegotiation, 159; strict compliance, 159; US, 119, 171

Anti-satellite capability, 116, 128; US, 5

Anti-satellite (ASAT) system, 72, 128, 191; NORAD, 74, 77; US plans, 132

Argentia, NFLD, 52

Arms control, Canadian objective, 88; joint statement, 133, 134; missile defences, 85, 126; talks (1967), 69; Trudeau, 119; US, 119-20, 171

Arms race, 96, 134; Canada, 70; post-9/11, 172

AVRO Arrow interceptor (CF-105), 5, 15; development, 43-44; role, 45; roll out ceremony, 43; squadrons, 45; see Diefenbaker government

Axworthy, Lloyd, 161

Bagotville, PQ, 122; air defence operations, 146, 193; CF-101, 66; interceptor base, 86

Baker, James, 152

Ballistic missile defence, 2, 5, 6, 18, 133; accord, 153, 154; Canadian defence, 44; Canadian participation, 149, 151, 155, 174; GPALS, 148, 149; layered defence, 171-72, 176; missile deployment, 157, 158, 159; new technology, 137, 156, 158, 171; NORAD renewal, 77, 183; sensors, 160; space-based defence, 155, 156; threat change, 187; US, 66, 69; USNORTHCOM, 179; warnings, 152, 153, 187, 189; see Pearson and Martin governments

Queen's Policy Studies
Recent Publications

The Queen's Policy Studies Series is dedicated to the exploration of major public policy issues that confront governments and society in Canada and other nations.

Our books are available from good bookstores everywhere, including the Queen's University bookstore (http://www.campusbookstore.com/). McGill-Queen's University Press is the exclusive world representative and distributor of books in the series. A full catalogue and ordering information may be found on their web site (http://mqup.mcgill.ca/).

School of Policy Studies

Canadian Public-Sector Financial Management, Andrew Graham, 2007
Paper ISBN 978-1-55339-120-3 Cloth ISBN 978-1-55339-121-0

Emerging Approaches to Chronic Disease Management in Primary Health Care,
John Dorland and Mary Ann McColl (eds.), 2007
Paper ISBN 978-1-55339-130-2 Cloth ISBN 978-1-55339-131-9

Fulfilling Potential, Creating Success: Perspectives on Human Capital Development,
Garnett Picot, Ron Saunders and Arthur Sweetman (eds.), 2007
Paper ISBN 978-1-55339-127-2 Cloth ISBN 978-1-55339-128-9

Reinventing Canadian Defence Procurement: A View from the Inside, Alan S. Williams, 2006
Paper ISBN 0-9781693-0-1 (Published in association with Breakout Educational Network)

SARS in Context: Memory, History, Policy, Jacalyn Duffin and Arthur Sweetman (eds.), 2006
Paper ISBN 978-0-7735-3194-9 Cloth ISBN 978-0-7735-3193-2
(Published in association with McGill-Queen's University Press)

Dreamland: How Canada's Pretend Foreign Policy has Undermined Sovereignty, Roy Rempel, 2006
Paper ISBN 1-55339-118-7 Cloth ISBN 1-55339-119-5
(Published in association with Breakout Educational Network)

Canadian and Mexican Security in the New North America: Challenges and Prospects,
Jordi Díez (ed.), 2006 Paper ISBN 978-1-55339-123-4 Cloth ISBN 978-1-55339-122-7

Global Networks and Local Linkages: The Paradox of Cluster Development in an Open Economy, David A. Wolfe and Matthew Lucas (eds.), 2005
Paper ISBN 1-55339-047-4 Cloth ISBN 1-55339-048-2

Choice of Force: Special Operations for Canada, David Last and Bernd Horn (eds.), 2005
Paper ISBN 1-55339-044-X Cloth ISBN 1-55339-045-8

Force of Choice: Perspectives on Special Operations, Bernd Horn, J. Paul de B. Taillon, and
David Last (eds.), 2004 Paper ISBN 1-55339-042-3 Cloth 1-55339-043-1

New Missions, Old Problems, Douglas L. Bland, David Last, Franklin Pinch, and Alan Okros
(eds.), 2004 Paper ISBN 1-55339-034-2 Cloth 1-55339-035-0

The North American Democratic Peace: Absence of War and Security Institution-Building in Canada-US Relations, 1867-1958, Stéphane Roussel, 2004
Paper ISBN 0-88911-937-6 Cloth 0-88911-932-2

Implementing Primary Care Reform: Barriers and Facilitators, Ruth Wilson, S.E.D. Shortt and John Dorland (eds.), 2004   Paper ISBN 1-55339-040-7 Cloth 1-55339-041-5

Social and Cultural Change, David Last, Franklin Pinch, Douglas L. Bland, and Alan Okros (eds.), 2004   Paper ISBN 1-55339-032-6 Cloth 1-55339-033-4

Clusters in a Cold Climate: Innovation Dynamics in a Diverse Economy, David A. Wolfe and Matthew Lucas (eds.), 2004   Paper ISBN 1-55339-038-5 Cloth 1-55339-039-3

Canada Without Armed Forces? Douglas L. Bland (ed.), 2004
Paper ISBN 1-55339-036-9 Cloth 1-55339-037-7

Campaigns for International Security: Canada's Defence Policy at the Turn of the Century, Douglas L. Bland and Sean M. Maloney, 2004
Paper ISBN 0-88911-962-7 Cloth 0-88911-964-3

Understanding Innovation in Canadian Industry, Fred Gault (ed.), 2003
Paper ISBN 1-55339-030-X Cloth 1-55339-031-8

Delicate Dances: Public Policy and the Nonprofit Sector, Kathy L. Brock (ed.), 2003
Paper ISBN 0-88911-953-8 Cloth 0-88911-955-4

Beyond the National Divide: Regional Dimensions of Industrial Relations, Mark Thompson, Joseph B. Rose and Anthony E. Smith (eds.), 2003
Paper ISBN 0-88911-963-5 Cloth 0-88911-965-1

The Nonprofit Sector in Interesting Times: Case Studies in a Changing Sector, Kathy L. Brock and Keith G. Banting (eds.), 2003
Paper ISBN 0-88911-941-4 Cloth 0-88911-943-0

Clusters Old and New: The Transition to a Knowledge Economy in Canada's Regions, David A. Wolfe (ed.), 2003   Paper ISBN 0-88911-959-7 Cloth 0-88911-961-9

The e-Connected World: Risks and Opportunities, Stephen Coleman (ed.), 2003
Paper ISBN 0-88911-945-7 Cloth 0-88911-947-3

Knowledge Clusters and Regional Innovation: Economic Development in Canada, J. Adam Holbrook and David A. Wolfe (eds.), 2002
Paper ISBN 0-88911-919-8 Cloth 0-88911-917-1

Lessons of Everyday Law/Le droit du quotidien, Roderick Alexander Macdonald, 2002
Paper ISBN 0-88911-915-5 Cloth 0-88911-913-9

Improving Connections Between Governments and Nonprofit and Voluntary Organizations: Public Policy and the Third Sector, Kathy L. Brock (ed.), 2002
Paper ISBN 0-88911-899-X Cloth 0-88911-907-4

Governing Food: Science, Safety and Trade, Peter W.B. Phillips and Robert Wolfe (eds.), 2001
Paper ISBN 0-88911-897-3 Cloth 0-88911-903-1

The Nonprofit Sector and Government in a New Century, Kathy L. Brock and Keith G. Banting (eds.), 2001   Paper ISBN 0-88911-901-5 Cloth 0-88911-905-8

The Dynamics of Decentralization: Canadian Federalism and British Devolution, Trevor C. Salmon and Michael Keating (eds.), 2001   ISBN 0-88911-895-7

Institute of Intergovernmental Relations

Canada: The State of the Federation 2005: Quebec and Canada in the New Century – New Dynamics, New Opportunities, vol. 19, Michael Murphy (ed.), 2007
Paper ISBN 978-1-55339-018-3 Cloth ISBN 978-1-55339-017-6

Spheres of Governance: Comparative Studies of Cities in Multilevel Governance Systems,
Harvey Lazar and Christian Leuprecht (eds.), 2007
Paper ISBN 978-1-55339-019-0 Cloth ISBN 978-1-55339-129-6

Canada: The State of the Federation 2004, vol. 18, *Municipal-Federal-Provincial Relations in Canada,* Robert Young and Christian Leuprecht (eds.), 2006
Paper ISBN 1-55339-015-6 Cloth ISBN 1-55339-016-4

Canadian Fiscal Arrangements: What Works, What Might Work Better, Harvey Lazar (ed.), 2005
Paper ISBN 1-55339-012-1 Cloth ISBN 1-55339-013-X

Canada: The State of the Federation 2003, vol. 17, *Reconfiguring Aboriginal-State Relations,*
Michael Murphy (ed.), 2005   Paper ISBN 1-55339-010-5 Cloth ISBN 1-55339-011-3

Canada: The State of the Federation 2002, vol. 16, *Reconsidering the Institutions of Canadian Federalism,* J. Peter Meekison, Hamish Telford and Harvey Lazar (eds.), 2004
Paper ISBN 1-55339-009-1 Cloth ISBN 1-55339-008-3

Federalism and Labour Market Policy: Comparing Different Governance and Employment Strategies, Alain Noël (ed.), 2004   Paper ISBN 1-55339-006-7 Cloth ISBN 1-55339-007-5

The Impact of Global and Regional Integration on Federal Systems: A Comparative Analysis,
Harvey Lazar, Hamish Telford and Ronald L. Watts (eds.), 2003
Paper ISBN 1-55339-002-4 Cloth ISBN 1-55339-003-2

Canada: The State of the Federation 2001, vol. 15, *Canadian Political Culture(s) in Transition,*
Hamish Telford and Harvey Lazar (eds.), 2002
Paper ISBN 0-88911-863-9 Cloth ISBN 0-88911-851-5

Federalism, Democracy and Disability Policy in Canada, Alan Puttee (ed.), 2002
Paper ISBN 0-88911-855-8 Cloth ISBN 1-55339-001-6, ISBN 0-88911-845-0 (set)

Comparaison des régimes fédéraux, 2ᵉ éd., Ronald L. Watts, 2002   ISBN 1-55339-005-9

Health Policy and Federalism: A Comparative Perspective on Multi-Level Governance,
Keith G. Banting and Stan Corbett (eds.), 2001
Paper ISBN 0-88911-859-0 Cloth ISBN 1-55339-000-8, ISBN 0-88911-845-0 (set)

Disability and Federalism: Comparing Different Approaches to Full Participation,
David Cameron and Fraser Valentine (eds.), 2001
Paper ISBN 0-88911-857-4 Cloth ISBN 0-88911-867-1, ISBN 0-88911-845-0 (set)

Federalism, Democracy and Health Policy in Canada, Duane Adams (ed.), 2001
Paper ISBN 0-88911-853-1 Cloth ISBN 0-88911-865-5, ISBN 0-88911-845-0 (set)

John Deutsch Institute for the Study of Economic Policy

The 2006 Federal Budget: Rethinking Fiscal Priorities, Charles M. Beach, Michael Smart and Thomas A. Wilson (eds.), 2007
Paper ISBN 978-1-55339-125-8 Cloth ISBN 978-1-55339-126-6

Health Services Restructuring in Canada: New Evidence and New Directions,
Charles M. Beach, Richard P. Chaykowksi, Sam Shortt, France St-Hilaire and Arthur Sweetman (eds.), 2006   Paper ISBN 978-1-55339-076-3 Cloth ISBN 978-1-55339-075-6

A Challenge for Higher Education in Ontario, Charles M. Beach (ed.), 2005
Paper ISBN 1-55339-074-1 Cloth ISBN 1-55339-073-3

Current Directions in Financial Regulation, Frank Milne and Edwin H. Neave (eds.),
Policy Forum Series no. 40, 2005   Paper ISBN 1-55339-072-5 Cloth ISBN 1-55339-071-7

Higher Education in Canada, Charles M. Beach, Robin W. Boadway and R. Marvin McInnis (eds.), 2005   Paper ISBN 1-55339-070-9 Cloth ISBN 1-55339-069-5

Financial Services and Public Policy, Christopher Waddell (ed.), 2004
Paper ISBN 1-55339-068-7 Cloth ISBN 1-55339-067-9

The 2003 Federal Budget: Conflicting Tensions, Charles M. Beach and Thomas A. Wilson (eds.), Policy Forum Series no. 39, 2004
Paper ISBN 0-88911-958-9 Cloth ISBN 0-88911-956-2

Canadian Immigration Policy for the 21st Century, Charles M. Beach, Alan G. Green and Jeffrey G. Reitz (eds.), 2003   Paper ISBN 0-88911-954-6 Cloth ISBN 0-88911-952-X

Framing Financial Structure in an Information Environment, Thomas J. Courchene and Edwin H. Neave (eds.), Policy Forum Series no. 38, 2003
Paper ISBN 0-88911-950-3 Cloth ISBN 0-88911-948-1

Towards Evidence-Based Policy for Canadian Education/Vers des politiques canadiennes d'éducation fondées sur la recherche, Patrice de Broucker and/et Arthur Sweetman (eds./ dirs.), 2002   Paper ISBN 0-88911-946-5 Cloth ISBN 0-88911-944-9

Money, Markets and Mobility: Celebrating the Ideas of Robert A. Mundell, Nobel Laureate in Economic Sciences, Thomas J. Courchene (ed.), 2002
Paper ISBN 0-88911-820-5 Cloth ISBN 0-88911-818-3

The State of Economics in Canada: Festschrift in Honour of David Slater, Patrick Grady and Andrew Sharpe (eds.), 2001   Paper ISBN 0-88911-942-2 Cloth ISBN 0-88911-940-6

The 2000 Federal Budget: Retrospect and Prospect, Paul A.R. Hobson and Thomas A. Wilson (eds.), 2001   Policy Forum Series no. 37, 2001
Paper ISBN 0-88911-816-7 Cloth ISBN 0-88911-814-0

Our publications may be purchased at leading bookstores, including the Queen's University Bookstore
(http://www.campusbookstore.com/), or can be ordered online from: McGill-Queen's University Press, at
http://mqup.mcgill.ca/ordering.php

For more information about new and backlist titles from Queen's Policy Studies, visit the McGill-Queen's
University Press web site at:
http://mqup.mcgill.ca/